ALL THE WAY TO GLORY

ALL THE WAY TO GLORY

by
David Petterson

John Ritchie Publishing

40 Beansburn, Kilmarnock, Scotland

ISBN-13: 978 1 914273 50 6

Copyright © 2024 by John Ritchie Ltd.
40 Beansburn, Kilmarnock, Scotland

www.ritchiechristianmedia.co.uk

Personal pronouns referring to Deity have been capitalised.

Quotations are from the King James Version (KJV) except where indicated as follows:
CSB – Christian Standard Bible (Scripture quotations marked CSB have been taken from the Christian Standard Bible®, Copyright © 2017 by Holman Bible Publishers. Used by permission. Christian Standard Bible® and CSB® are federally registered trademarks of Holman Bible Publishers).
ESV – English Standard Version (Copyright: 2001 by Crossway, a publishing ministry of Good News Publishers ©. Used by permission. All rights reserved).
ISV – International Standard Version (Copyright © 1996-2012 by The ISV Foundation. All rights reserved internationally. Used by permission).
JND – Darby Translation.
LEB – Lexham English Bible (Copyright 2012 Logos Bible Software. Lexham is a registered trademark of Logos Bible Software).
NET – New English Translation (The Scriptures quoted are from the NET Bible® https://netbible.com copyright ©1996, 2019 used with permission from Biblical Studies Press, L.L.C. All rights reserved).

Typeset by John Ritchie Ltd. Kilmarnock
Printed by Bell & Bain Ltd., Glasgow

CONTENTS

Preface

He had come from so far, stooping from unimaginable heights. The Son of God, whose "greatness is unsearchable" (Psa. 145:3), left His throne and entered into something so very small—a virgin's womb. It marked the beginning of a journey, the most important mission in the universe, when God invaded our world, not now with judgment for sin, but with a remedy for it, for inside the womb of Mary was the One Who would "save His people from their sins" (Matt. 1:21). But the incarnation was only the beginning. For Christ to achieve this rescue mission, He had to go all the way to Calvary and offer Himself as a sacrifice for our sins. That path involved rejection, betrayal, sorrow, injustice, abuse, vitriol, false accusations, God-forsakenness, and ultimately death on a cross. And on that cross, He "suffered for sins, the Just for the unjust, that He might bring us to God" (1 Pet. 3:18). It was a journey of a little over three decades but was in many ways the longest trek ever travelled and had been planned from a past eternity.

However, if His story ended at the cross, or at His tomb, Paul rightly tells us we would still be in our sins (1 Cor. 15:17). Thank God that Christ "was raised again for our justification" (Rom. 4:25). But emerging alive from His tomb on the morning of that third day was still not the end. Luke summarises the events immediately after His resurrection: "He shewed Himself alive after His passion by many infallible proofs, being seen of them forty days" (Acts 1:3). And after promising His followers the coming of the Holy Spirit, "He was taken up; and a cloud received Him out of their sight" (v9), Mark adding that He "sat on the right hand of God" (16:19). As there had been many steps downward to the shame of the cross, so would there be many steps upward until He sat down enthroned in heaven above. "He that descended is the same also that ascended up far above all..." (Eph. 4:10).

The present book is a follow-up to the title *All the Way to Calvary* by the same author and emphasises those precious events in between the Lord's death and that glorious moment when He was "received up into glory" (1 Tim. 3:16). The One Who was on a *tree* for us is now on a *throne* for us. Praise God! May these short meditations evoke worship from our hearts and make us more like the One Who for us has gone *All the Way to Glory*.

Chapter 1

"HE WAS BURIED"

I've never heard anyone say it. "My husband died *and they buried him.*" "My mother passed away *and was buried.*" We don't usually spend time wondering what happened to the body of someone who has died. But when Paul refers to the death of Christ in 1 Corinthians 15, he includes the detail "He was buried" (v4).[1] His burial is important. Why?

Proof

The burial of the Lord Jesus Christ is significant because it both proves His death and affirms His glorious resurrection, events which would later be doubted. Scripture makes it clear that the Lord Jesus was unmistakably dead. Even though the Gospel writers avoid the use of the word "dead" at the moment when Christ yielded up His spirit (thus demonstrating His sovereign control), all of them use the word afterward (Matt. 27:64; 28:7; Mark 15:44; Luke 24:20,46; John 19:33; 20:9; 21:14). Also, the authorities would never allow crucifixion victims to be removed from their crosses unless they were certain of death, a detail Pilate confirmed with the Roman centurion before granting Joseph of Arimathaea permission

---

[1]All Scripture quotations in this book are from the KJV unless otherwise noted.

to secure Jesus' body (Mark 15:44). So, the swoon theory that Jesus was merely unconscious when they buried Him and subsequently resuscitated in the cool tomb, won't hold. Jesus really died.

And there were witnesses, plenty of them. We've already mentioned the centurion but could add the soldiers under his command. They were probably physically closer to Jesus than anyone else when He gave up His life. And one of them pierced the Lord's side with a spear and watched His blood flow. The Apostle John also saw and recorded it (John 19:34-35). They knew that Jesus was dead. As did the many women who were following the Lord and were present at His cross. Particular names are given by Matthew of women who could later be questioned. "Among them were Mary Magdalene, Mary the mother of James and Joseph, and the mother of the sons of Zebedee" (27:56; see also Mark 15:40-41; Luke 23:49). Luke notes that not only did these women see Christ die, but some of them "saw the tomb and how His body was laid in it" (23:55). Therefore, the "wrong tomb" theory won't wash either. The women knew exactly where the Lord's body was, and they knew He was dead. The fact that they came to His tomb later with spices to anoint his body (Mark 16:1) confirms it.

But two more witnesses could be consulted in the days following Christ's death—Joseph of Arimathaea and Nicodemus. They handled His precious body and knew that He was dead. Why would Nicodemus bring "a mixture of myrrh and aloes, about an hundred pound weight" (John 19:39) for someone who wasn't dead? Why would they wrap His body in linen and place Him in Joseph's new tomb if He were still alive? Also, John notes that this tomb was one "wherein was never man yet laid" (John 19:41). Only one person was ever in this tomb, and therefore, that same person was the only one who could have risen. The burial of the Lord Jesus is proof of His actual death and subsequent resurrection. He alone was buried in the tomb, and He alone burst forth from it in glorious life on the third day. As Paul says, this is gospel truth—"I declare unto you the gospel... how that Christ died for our sins according to the scriptures; And that *He was buried*, and that He rose again the third day according to the scriptures" (1 Cor. 15:1-4).

Prophecy

John mentions two specific prophecies that were fulfilled immediately following Christ's death (see John 19:36-37). The fact that the soldiers didn't break His legs fulfilled Psalm 34:20—"He keepeth all His bones: not one of them is broken". The piercing of His side fulfilled Zechariah 12:10—"they shall look upon Me whom they have pierced".

But in relation to Christ's burial, another Scripture found fulfilment. Isaiah says, "They intended to bury Him with criminals" *(NET)*. Remarkably, Isaiah foretold that Christ would die a criminal's death,[2] which is exactly what death by crucifixion was. Note the word "bury". The Romans left the bodies of crucifixion victims to the vultures, which served as a harsh public warning, but the Jews practiced burial even for such criminals. They didn't allow the bodies of the condemned to be placed in tombs with other corpses (which would desecrate them), but had a separate burial site for them just outside the city.[3] However, such a site

---

[2] See also Isa. 53:12—"He was numbered with the transgressors..."

[3] Andreas J. Köstenberger, *John: Baker Exegetical Commentary on the New Testament* (Grand Rapids, MI: Baker Academic, 2004), 554.

wouldn't be needed for the Lord Jesus, for the next part of Isaiah's prophecy mentions "a rich man in [Christ's] death" *(ESV)*. Enter Joseph of Arimathaea. Although Mark and Luke note that Joseph was a *ruler*, and that he was *righteous*, Matthew points out that he was *rich* (27:57), drawing attention to Isaiah's words. As if right on cue, Joseph, a man of sufficient means to have purchased a new rock-hewn tomb,[4] came to take the body of Jesus. Although the Jews' intention would've been to bury Christ where condemned criminals were buried, Joseph's arrival kept that from happening and fulfilled Isaiah's ancient prophecy.

We must also consider the Lord Jesus' own prophecy in Matthew 12:40, which has given rise to different views about which day He died. The Saviour indicated He would be "three days and three nights in the heart of the earth". On more than one occasion Christ told His disciples He would die and that He would rise again, but here He clearly indicates He would be buried "in the heart of the earth". Some infer from this Scripture that Christ may have been crucified on a Thursday (or even a Wednesday) since "three nights" are mentioned. If He died on a Friday, there would only be two nights in which the Saviour was in the tomb. However, it may be preferable to view the words "three days and three nights" as a Jewish colloquial expression for any part of a day. Thus, "it is probably a mistake to read this [Matt. 12:40] as giving precision beyond what is rhetorically intended".[5] Note that the Jewish authorities quoted the Lord as saying, "*After* three days I will

---

[4] Craig S. Keener, *A Commentary on the Gospel of Matthew* (Grand Rapids, MI: William B. Eerdmans, 1999), 694 [footnote 271].

[5] Darrell L. Bock, *Luke: Baker Exegetical Commentary on the New Testament* (Grand Rapids, MI: Baker Academic, 1996), 2:1894.

rise again" (Matt. 27:63). Did they believe that He was claiming He would therefore rise again on the fourth day? No. They gave instructions to make the tomb secure *"until* the third day" (v64). Note also that when Jesus prophesied His resurrection, He referred to its timing as both "after three days" (Mark 8:31) and on "the third day" (Mark 9:31; 10:34). Neither Christ nor His enemies saw a discrepancy in their own remarks, nor should we. Luke's timeline (see Luke 23:53-54) makes it clear that Jesus was buried on the day before the Sabbath, which would mean a Friday crucifixion. Christ's resurrection is repeatedly said to have occurred on "the third day",[6] not "the fourth day" (or "the fifth day") as a Thursday (or Wednesday) crucifixion would imply. Regardless of the day, the Lord's burial involved a fulfilment of prophecy.

Providence

Sundown was fast approaching, and with it, the Sabbath. This "Sabbath was an especially important one" (John 19:31 *NET*), since it was Passover. The Jewish leaders were facing a significant challenge to have the bodies[7] removed from the crosses and buried before 6pm (at which time the Sabbath began).[8] As it was 3pm when the supernatural darkness lifted and Jesus cried out, "My God, my God, why hast Thou forsaken Me?" (see Matt. 27:45,46), this means the Jews had less than three hours to accomplish the burial task. They couldn't depend upon the Lord's disciples since

---

[6] Matt. 16:21; 17:23; 20:19; 27:64; Mark 9:31; 10:34; Luke 9:22; 18:33; 24:7,21,46; Acts 10:40; 1 Cor. 15:4.

[7] The plural "bodies" implies that the thieves crucified with Christ were also Jews.

[8] Bodies of criminals were to be buried before sunset according to Deut. 21:22-23, so as not to defile the land. As this was on the eve of the Sabbath, a hasty burial was even more important.

they had abandoned Him.[9] No family member stepped forward to claim His body. The women who were present were from Galilee, so what would they be able to do with His body? Again, it is likely that the rulers would've taken the bodies to an outside burial plot for condemned criminals. But just before they were able to act, note the beautiful providence of God, who was working in the heart of two men, to carry out a swift but respectful burial for the Lord Jesus Christ. The 'twelve' may have fled, but two secret disciples suddenly arrived. It seems that God has His servants everywhere!

Joseph and Nicodemus were both members of the Jewish Sanhedrin.[10] Pilate could easily have become irritated by the actions of this ruling body throughout the day. They challenged his loyalty to Caesar. They forced him to act against his own conscience by condemning an innocent man. The whole ordeal troubled his wife with nightmares. Then they tried to pressure him to change the title above Christ's cross. The last person Pilate wanted to see was yet another member of the Sanhedrin coming to him with more demands. Yet Joseph went to ask for Jesus' body. He obviously couldn't claim any rights to the body as a family member, and Pilate might wonder why the rulers who wanted Jesus' death would also want His body. But amazingly, Pilate gave him permission. Again, we see the wonderful providence of God.

So, two Sanhedrin members oversaw the dignified burial of the Man their council had put to a shameful death. Luke informs us that Joseph "had not consented to their plan and action" (23:51

---

[9] John had returned to the cross, but nothing more is said about him until the resurrection narratives.

[10] See Mark 15:43; Luke 23:50,51; John 3:1; 7:45-52.

NET), which was likely also true of Nicodemus. The fact that they worked together to give the Lord Jesus an honourable burial implies they knew of each other's belief in Jesus as the Messiah. To this point, both of them had been relatively low-key about their convictions in relation to Christ. But now everything was out in the open. Their commitment would cost them, as any commitment to the Lord Jesus will. They would lose their positions, their reputations, perhaps even their wealth. But they believed that title on the Saviour's cross, that He was indeed the King of the Jews. Therefore, they sought to give Him a royal burial, evident by the large amount of spices Nicodemus brought.[11] They believed Christ was worthy, regardless of the personal loss to themselves. "Then took they the body of Jesus, and wound it in linen clothes with the spices, as the manner of the Jews is to bury" (John 19:40).

And note how near the tomb just happened to be. "Now in the place where He was crucified there was a garden; and in the garden a new sepulchre, wherein was never man yet laid. There laid they Jesus... for the sepulchre was nigh at hand" (John 19:41,42). So, Joseph had the *sepulchre* and Nicodemus had the *spices*. And the body of the Lord Jesus was in the tomb before sundown. Everything was in place according to God's providential plan. Christ was not only dead but buried. And God wants us to remember that His burial was not an insignificant detail.

---

[11] Note the spices at King Asa's funeral (2 Chron. 16:14). Also, Herod the Great reportedly had 500 servants carrying spices at his burial.

Chapter 2

VAINLY THEY SEAL
THE DEAD

Although the burial of the Lord Jesus was complete and noted by all the Gospel writers, it is Matthew who strongly emphasises the security of the Saviour's tomb (see Matt. 27:60-66). It is likely that disputes about the Lord's resurrection were surfacing (a real threat to gospel preaching) and Matthew wanted to set the record straight. Let's look at this section in a bit more detail.

The Stone

"And he [Joseph] rolled a great stone to the door of the sepulchre, and departed" (v60). The stone was likely four to six feet in diameter and extremely heavy, intentionally so as to ensure the remains would be undisturbed. Joseph may have had assistance in rolling the stone along the groove until it settled into the carved channel just in front of the tomb's opening.[12] It was probably easier to set the stone in place than it would have been to remove it afterwards. Note that the women who later arrived at the tomb

---

[12] Grant R. Osborne, *Mark: Teach the Text Commentary Series* (Grand Rapids, MI: Baker Academic, 2014), 313.

knew they would not be able to move the stone themselves (Mark 16:3). Removing it from inside the tomb was certainly not feasible.

The Spectators

As noted in the previous chapter, there were witnesses to Jesus' burial. "And there was Mary Magdalene, and the other Mary, sitting over against the sepulchre" (v61). The "other Mary" must be "the mother of James and Joses" mentioned in verse 56. Since the text notes that Joseph "departed" (v60) after he set the stone in place, the two Marys are the last named individuals present at the tomb (see also Mark 15:47). As they returned later with spices to anoint the Lord's body (Mark 16:1), it is clear that they knew nothing about the official sealing and guarding of the tomb described by Matthew (27:66). Their only concern was how they would roll the stone away, not how they would overpower the guards and break the seal. Interestingly, the two Marys would not only be the last to leave the tomb, but the first to find it empty!

The Sabbath

After noting the two Marys, Matthew refers to "the next day, that followed the day of the preparation" (27:62). The "day of the preparation" was not the preparation for the Passover, but for the Sabbath, and therefore a Friday as Mark makes clear (15:42). Thus, the day following was a Saturday (the Sabbath). But Matthew seems to purposefully avoid using the word "Sabbath". It may be that the day of Christ's death (which occurred on "the day of the preparation") now holds far more importance than the Sabbath, and so Matthew prefers this terminology (at least here).

It is noteworthy, then, to see the work performed on the Sabbath by the Jewish rulers in the following verses (Matt. 27:62b-66).

The Pharisees in particular were known for their strict Sabbath observance (as well as chastising those who were not so strict). But compliance in this case was not as important as their hatred of the Lord Jesus. Months before this, the Pharisees deliberated as to how they might destroy Christ who had done good on the Sabbath (12:9-14). Here they do not hesitate to perform evil on the Sabbath. And they not only labour themselves but set other people to work also.

The Sanhedrin

Although the entire official body of the Sanhedrin is not mentioned (no reference to "the elders" is made), the two rival groups of the ruling body are named—"the chief priests and Pharisees came together unto Pilate" (27:62). The chief priests were Sadducees. Often divided, these "two opposing wings of the Sanhedrin are still united in their fear of Jesus' influence, to the extent of contravening their own Sabbath regulations."[13] This is also the last time we read about the Pharisees in the Gospels. In their first appearance (3:7), John the Baptist characterised them as a "generation of vipers". In their last appearance, they prove John's description to be true.

Pilate must have been exasperated to see members of the Sanhedrin at his doorstep once more. Perhaps to ingratiate themselves, the rulers begin their request to Pilate with the dignified title "Sir" (27:63). The Greek word is *kurios* (often translated "Lord") and is used in Matthew almost exclusively for the Lord Jesus. It is apparent that the Jewish leaders have rejected their true Lord. They gave Pilate a title of respect, but only after disrespecting and

---

[13] R. T. France, *Matthew: Tyndale New Testament Commentaries* (Grand Rapids, MI: Inter-Varsity Press, 1985), 404.

crucifying "the Lord of glory" (1 Cor. 2:8), whom they now refer to as "that deceiver" (see also John 7:12,47).[14]

We must admire, however, the leaders' ability to recall the words Jesus spoke, which could not be said of His disciples. They began their official request with these words: "Sir, we remember that that deceiver said… After three days I will rise again" (Matt. 27:63). It should be pointed out that some of the scribes and Pharisees were present (12:38) when the Lord said, "For as Jonas was three days and three nights in the whale's belly; so shall the Son of man be three days and three nights in the heart of the earth" (12:40). But since Jesus gave multiple predictions to the disciples about His resurrection (e.g., Mark 8:31; 9:31; 10:34), it is also possible that Judas shared this information with the authorities in his betrayal. I love the fact that these rulers refer to Christ's claim made "while He was yet alive" (Matt. 27:63). They knew that the Saviour was clearly dead and would have rejected the swoon theory.

Their real concern is expressed in verse 64—"So give orders to secure the tomb until the third day. Otherwise his disciples may come and steal his body and say to the people, 'He has been raised from the dead,' and the last deception will be worse than the first" (NET). They feared the Lord's disciples would come to the tomb to steal His body when they weren't even at the cross to take it down. They overestimated the disciples' passion and underestimated the Saviour's power. None of the remaining 11 came to the tomb until it was empty, and Christ would come through on His promise to rise again on the third day.

---

[14] Although they proceed to quote the Lord Jesus' words, they do not even use His name, only this shameful title "deceiver."

But the fear of these leaders was real. They reference both a "first" and a "last deception". The "first" deception (in their thinking) would be the claim that Jesus was the Messiah. The "last" would be a fake resurrection supporting the "first". Essentially, they were informing Pilate that if he thought Jesus' triumphal entry into Jerusalem as Messiah caused an uproar, the fallout of this "deception" would be far more intense. The fear of the leaders was now shared by Pilate. No ruler wants a riot in his territory. So, Pilate consented again to their wishes.

The Soldiers

"Pilate said to them, 'Take a guard of soldiers. Go and make it as secure as you can'" (v65 NET). The Greek word translated "guard of soldiers" is koustodia, of Latin origin suggesting Roman soldiers were dispatched, not officers of the Jewish Temple police. Indeed, it would have been strange for members of the Jewish Sanhedrin to ask Pilate permission for their own soldiers to be moved from one location to another. Matthew 28:14 suggests that these soldiers were ultimately answerable to Pilate. A typical Roman guard consisted of four soldiers (a quaternion, see Acts 12:4), with two on watch while two rested. They were heavily armed with swords, shields, spears, daggers and armour. Thus, the Jews are requesting maximum security.

The Seal

It was not enough that the tomb be secured with a stone and with soldiers. The final security measure was the Roman seal. "So they went, and made the sepulchre sure, sealing the stone, and setting a watch" (Matt. 27:66). The seal consisted of clay or wax pressed into the crack between the rolling stone and the tomb's entrance and stamped with the imperial emblem of Rome's authority.[15] Moving the rock would therefore break the Roman seal, an illegal punishable offense. But in all their earnestness to seal the tomb of the Saviour, His enemies only underscored the reality of His resurrection. The seal was likely the most temporary one ever placed on a tomb by any authority.

But we are getting ahead of ourselves. It was Saturday and it looked like Rome and Israel's leaders had won. Two heavily armed guards were stationed at the tomb, with two resting nearby. If anyone tried to steal the body of Jesus of Nazareth, their efforts would be useless. But...

Vainly they watch His bed,

Jesus my Saviour,

Vainly they seal the dead,

Jesus my Lord![16]

---

[15] David L. Turner, *Matthew: Baker Exegetical Commentary on the New Testament* (Grand Rapids, MI: Baker Academic, 2008), 677.

[16] Robert Lowry (1826-1899).

Chapter 3

THEN CAME THE MORNING

It was still a bit dark, but it was time to go. After the Sabbath's sunset, they had purchased what they needed to anoint the body of the Lord Jesus and now the sun was just about to rise on the first day of the week.[17] The disciples, who promised undying loyalty to the Saviour (Matt. 26:35), were still in hiding, but these women were not. There were at least five of them, for Luke names three and states there were others (Luke 24:10). Putting the Gospel accounts together, we know the names of four in particular—Mary Magdalene, Joanna, Salome and Mary the mother of James and Joses.[18]

As they made the trip, they began to wonder how they would be able to roll away the sepulchre's heavy stone. Too bad none of the twelve were with them. A little muscle would have been appreciated. Apparently, the women were unaware of the presence

---

[17] All four Gospels mention "the first day of the week" (Matt. 28:1; Mark 16:2; Luke 24:1; John 20:1).

[18] See Matt.28:1 (cf. 27:56); Mark 16:1; Luke 24:10; John 20:1-18.

of the guards or the official seal, both implemented after they accompanied the Saviour's body on the day of His burial. Bigger than the problem as to how they would roll away the stone would be how to overpower Roman soldiers. But they would have to do neither. And hopefully, they kept their receipts. For it was soon evident that their purchased spices were not going to be necessary.

A Delightful Disappointment

As the sun rose, it revealed an initially troubling detail, but one which would turn out to be history's best disappointment. "And they found the stone rolled away from the sepulchre. And they entered in, and found not the body of the Lord Jesus" (Luke 24:2-3). They assume the worst. His body must have been stolen. Mary Magdalene's words likely reflected all their thoughts, "they have taken away the Lord ... and we know not where they have laid Him" (John 20:2).

But soon they would learn the truth from a heavenly source. Who could possibly have moved the stone? Who dared to break the Roman seal? Who could overpower the Roman guards? It was the angel of the Lord. "And, behold, there was a great earthquake: for the angel of the Lord descended from heaven, and came and rolled back the stone" (Matt. 28:2).[19] And the earth was not the only thing that shook. "And for fear of him the keepers did shake, and became as dead men" (v4). The angel's presence also terrified the

---

[19] Mark mentions "a young man sitting on the right side, clothed in a long white garment" (16:5), presumably the angel of the Lord Matthew describes. Luke (24:4) and John (20:12) refer to "two men"/"two angels" present. The discrepancy about the number of angels could be explained in that each author may focus on the presence of one or two angels for literary purposes, whatever those might be.

women, who then found themselves "bowed down [with] their faces to the earth" (Luke 24:5). And then the angel spoke.[20]

The Gospel in the Graveyard

"Fear not ... for I know that ye seek Jesus, which was crucified. He is not here: for He is risen"[21] (Matt. 28:5-6). And thus was shared the best news the world has ever heard. Graveyards are generally not places where exciting announcements are made. But from the empty tomb of the Lord Jesus Christ the most thrilling news release in human history was sent forth. But it was news Christ had already told the women, for the angel added, "He is risen, *as He said*." Luke supplements this account with the words, "remember how *He spake unto you* when He was yet in Galilee, Saying, The Son of man must be delivered into the hands of sinful men, and be crucified, and the third day rise again. And they remembered His words" (24:6-8). The Sanhedrin remembered His words (Matt. 27:63), but the women and Jesus' disciples had forgotten. Yet what these women lacked in their minds, they made up for in their hearts. They were here to anoint the One they loved and who loved them in return. And if they had not come, they would have been as miserable as the disciples for a little longer.

The angel then gave the women an invitation, not just the breaking news: "Come, see the place where the Lord lay" (28:6). They had seen the place before and watched with their own eyes the body of the Saviour being tenderly placed in the tomb (Luke

---

[20] Matthew begins and ends his Gospel with the angel of the Lord, who announces both the birth (1:20) and resurrection (28:5-6) of Christ.

[21] Mark records this as a divine passive, reflected by the NET, "He has been raised!" (16:6). God had raised His Son from the dead.

23:55). Now with pounding hearts, they cautiously entered the tomb to discover that indeed, He was no longer there. They were given the facts and an invitation. Would it be enough?

The gospel from the graveyard is still sounding out today. Christ died for our sins and was buried. He rose again the third day, just as He said He would. And the Lord's invitation to you is, "Come." It was enough for these women. Is it enough for you?

The First Great Commission

The angel had yet more to say. "And go quickly, and tell his disciples that He is risen from the dead; and, behold, He goeth before you into Galilee; there shall ye see Him; lo, I have told you" (Matt. 28:7). Mark adds that the disciples would see Him in Galilee "as He said unto [them]" (16:7). When did the Lord Jesus tell them? After they left the upper room on the night of His betrayal: "But after I am risen again, I will go before you into Galilee" (Matt. 26:32). Galilee was the place where light dawned (4:16) and where hope would dawn for the disciples.

Receiving this commission from the angel, the women "departed quickly from the sepulchre with fear and great joy; and did run to bring His disciples word" (28:8). We will need to reconcile this account with Mark's, which says, "And they went out quickly, and fled from the sepulchre; for they trembled and were amazed: neither said they any thing to any man; for they were afraid" (16:8). So there was a period of paralysis. Luke helps us reconcile the two. It was after the women "remembered His [Christ's] words" that they "returned from the sepulchre, and told all these things unto the eleven, and to all the rest" (24:8-9). It was the word of God brought home to their minds that gave them confidence to share the good news with joy.

And so, before the disciples ever received the Great Commission (Matt. 28:18-20), these devoted women were given a commission of their own, one which they were at first reluctant to carry out, but then did so with urgency and great joy. They got to be the first to hear the news of Christ's resurrection as well as the first to share it. Perhaps you are one of the last to hear the news. You can believe it, and you must if you want to be saved from your sins. "Because if you confess with your mouth that Jesus is Lord and believe in your heart that God raised Him from the dead, you will be saved" (Rom. 10:9 *NET*).

What a morning it turned out to be for these women, one initially filled with despair and confusion. But as the sun began to rise, their hopes would rise higher still. And for a world long lost in darkness and death, morning had finally come.

Then came the morning,
Night turned into day;
The stone was rolled away,
Hope rose with the dawn.
Then came the morning,
Shadows vanished before the sun,
Death had lost and life had won,
For morning had come.[22]

---

[22] Chris Christian, William J. and Gloria Gaithers.

Chapter 4

THE AMAZING RACE

Let's back up just a little. The women are on the move early in the morning. Although it was dark when they set out, there was enough light now to make sense of their surroundings. By the time they approached the tomb, they knew something had happened. It is likely that the first one of their group to notice was Mary Magdalene. She is listed first in each of the Synoptic Gospels (Matt. 28:1; Mark 16:1; Luke 24:10) and John actually credits her with the discovery—"The first day of the week cometh Mary Magdalene early ... and seeth the stone taken away from the sepulchre" (John 20:1). Without bothering to brainstorm with the other women as to what may have occurred, she took off. She just had to tell someone.

Mary Running

"Then she runneth, and cometh to Simon Peter, and to the other disciple, whom Jesus loved" (v2). If she had stayed a little longer to hear what the angel announced to the rest of the women, her report would have been entirely different. Instead, the only thing she had to say was, "They have taken away the Lord out of the sepulchre, and we know not where they have laid him" (v2).

We may wonder why she only went to Peter and John (the disciple whom Jesus loved), but it is possible that they were the only two whose locations she knew since the disciples scattered.[23] Also, the repeated preposition "to" ("and cometh *to* Simon Peter, and *to* the other disciple") suggests Peter and John were in separate locations. The order of their mention might indicate Peter was told first. If so, it didn't prove to be an advantage, as we'll see in a moment.

The Women Running

We don't know how far behind Mary the other women were, but they surely had more of a spring in their step than she did, for the news they carried was more accurate and far more significant. No one had taken the Lord out of the tomb; He came out Himself for He had risen from the dead. It's no wonder why the women ran also—"And they departed quickly from the sepulchre with fear and great joy; and did run to bring His disciples word" (Matt. 28:8). But it was not only women running on this monumental day.

Peter and John Running

They wasted no time. All they knew was what Mary Magdalene had told them, but they had to get there and see for themselves.[24] At some point, they must have spotted each other, perhaps coming from different directions, or taking different courses to the destination. Luke suggests something else happened along

---

[23] After Mary's report to Peter and John, it is possible that the other disciples got wind of the news and quickly came together in the upper room, where the other women would find them later.

[24] John 20:11 suggests that Mary Magdalene followed Peter and John back to the tomb and remained after their departure (v10).

the way. As Peter[25] and John ran to the tomb, they were met by the other women who had recently left the tomb and now gave their fuller report.[26] With this additional news, the race was on! "Peter therefore went forth, and that other disciple, and came to the sepulchre. So they ran both together: and the other disciple did outrun Peter, and came first to the sepulchre" (John 20:3-4).

Apparently, the Roman guards not only had been seized by fear at the appearance of the angel of the Lord (Matt. 28:4), but by this time had fled (v11) since no mention is made of them once Peter and John arrive. But John arrived first. "And he stooping down, and looking in, saw the linen clothes lying; yet went he not in" (John 20:5). Was Mary Magdalene right? Had someone indeed taken the Lord's body from the tomb? Or were the rest of the women right? Was it actually possible that Christ had risen from the dead? He didn't have long to ponder the possibilities before John heard Peter panting behind him. And in typical brash fashion, Peter dared to go farther than John.

Not interested in observing from the outside, Peter barged in. "Then cometh Simon Peter following him, and went into the

---

[25] Luke only mentions Peter (24:12), presumably as a representative disciple.

[26] A possible harmonisation of the succeeding events is as follows. Well before the women reached their destination, Peter and John (with Mary trailing) arrived at the tomb. After Peter and John departed to their homes (John 20:10), Mary remained behind and became the first to see the risen Christ (vv11-18; Mark 16:9). In close succession, the Lord appeared to the returning women (Matt. 28:9-10) as they ran to bring the news to the rest of the disciples. Then the Lord appeared to Peter alone on his way home (Luke 24:34; 1 Cor. 15:5), to the two travellers to Emmaus (Luke 24:13ff.), and finally to the assembled disciples (without Thomas) in the upper room. These all occurred on "the first day of the week." For a complete possible order of events between the Lord's death and ascension, see the Appendix.

sepulchre" (v6). What he saw was nothing short of amazing. He saw "the linen clothes lie, And the napkin, that was about His head, not lying with the linen clothes, but wrapped together in a place by itself" (vv6-7). The word translated "wrapped together" (Greek *entulisso*) could be better rendered "rolled up" *(NET, ISV)*. Clearly, the body of Christ was gone, but what thief would take the time to unwrap a corpse, and not only leave the wrappings behind (which in this case, were quite expensive), but roll them back together? Mary wasn't right; the Lord's body wasn't removed by grave robbers.

Incidentally, the wrapping around the Lord Jesus' head said to be "in a place by itself" does not indicate that it was moved by the Lord after He rose. Jesus rose *through* the graveclothes, not *with* them still on His body. There is no indication that Christ removed His own graveclothes, but that one moment He was in them and the next moment He was not. The usual practice of wrapping a body was not one continuous wrapping from head to foot, but two wrappings, one for the head and one for the remainder of the body. Thus, when the Saviour rose, there would be a visible gap between the two wrappings with the headpiece being "in a place by itself".

The presence of the graveclothes in the tomb suggests something else to us. John records that when Lazarus was raised and came out of his tomb he was still wrapped in his graveclothes, including the headpiece (11:44). Lazarus would need them again because he would die again. But Christ would never need them again, for He had risen never to die again (Rev. 1:18).

Luke tells us what was going on in Peter's mind as he left the Saviour's tomb. He "departed, wondering in himself at that which was come to pass" (24:12). John's reaction was not mere wonder. "Then went in also that other disciple, which came first to the sepulchre, and he saw, and believed" (John 20:8). John doesn't use the word "believe" lightly in his Gospel. I think he means by this that he believed that Christ was risen, even though John had not seen Him, thus making him the first of the disciples to do so. "Blessed are they that have not seen, and yet have believed" (v29). Yet John is careful to add, "For as yet they knew not the scripture, that He must rise again from the dead" (v9). So even though John believed, it was eyewitness testimony combined with evidence, not Scripture, that led to his proper conclusion. "He had faith but no understanding or knowledge; the knowledge would come later and affirm the faith."[27] This knowledge would come to the disciples as Christ expounded from the Old Testament Scriptures "the things concerning Himself" (Luke 24:27, 44-46).

A wondering Peter and a believing John departed. "So the disciples went back to their homes" (John 20:10 NET). The amazing race was over. John had gained a precious prize, not for arriving at the tomb first, but for believing what he heard and saw once he got there. And in all probability, John brought the good news of the Lord Jesus' resurrection to His mother, whom he had taken "into his own home" (19:27).

We close the chapter by noting how the Lord prizes our faith. He could have appeared to all His own immediately after His resurrection. They would have seen and believed. Instead, He chose to commission angels to report the news and for those who

---

[27] Philip W. Comfort and Wendell C. Hawley, *Opening John's Gospel and Epistles* (Wheaton, IL: Tyndale House Publishers, 2007), 251.

heard it to spread it further, so that Christ's followers could each experience the blessing of believing without seeing. And such a blessing is still available today.

We stood not by the empty tomb
Where late Thy sacred body lay,
Nor sat within that upper room,
Nor met Thee in the open way;
But we believe the angel said,
Why seek the living with the dead?[28]

---

[28] Anne R. Richter (died 1857), altered by John Hampden Gurney (1802-1862).

Chapter 5

MARY MAGDALENE

Mary was alone. She must have followed Peter and John back to the Saviour's tomb after giving them the news that it was empty. But now they were gone. Overwhelmed by grief, she decided to stay a little longer. Memories likely came flooding back of that transformational moment when she met this Man from Galilee Who with incomparable authority rid her of the demons in her life and instantly gave her peace. And she wondered how anyone could wish such a Man dead. Tears filled her eyes as she pondered the apparent fact that it wasn't enough for Jesus' enemies to cruelly execute Him; now they have desecrated His grave and stolen His precious body. She decided to take a closer look.

"And as she wept, she stooped down, and looked into the sepulchre" (John 20:11). The sight she beheld earlier was merely the rolled away stone (v1), but now Mary got her first look inside the tomb. Apparently, she could see what John saw (the careful arrangement of Christ's graveclothes), but did not believe what John believed (that rather than His body being stolen, the Lord Jesus had risen). Suddenly she was allowed to see something John did not.

Mary "seeth two angels in white" (v12). It was not merely their *presence*, but their *position* that was significant, for they were "sitting, the one at the head, and the other at the feet, where the body of Jesus had lain" (v12). Their location was meant to convey to Mary that God had done something, that a divine invasion of power was responsible for the absence of Jesus' body. Mary was given a little more light (or rather, a lot more) to bring her to faith in the resurrection of Christ. But it still was not enough. And her grief was so heavy that not even angels dressed in white could shake Mary from it. So they asked her, "Woman, why weepest thou? She saith unto them, Because they have taken away my Lord, and I know not where they have laid Him" (v13). To her, she simply would not accept any other possibility than that Christ's body had been stolen. Why should she not weep? Mary had now seen and spoken to angels yet remained fixed in her faulty assessment. But that all was about to dramatically change.

First to See Him

"And when she had thus said, she turned herself back, and saw Jesus standing, and knew not that it was Jesus" (v14). Some explain that Mary did not recognise the Lord because tears filled her eyes. That might be true. But there were other occasions when Christ was not recognised by His followers after His resurrection (Luke 24:15-16,36-37; John 20:4). In any case, we must not be too hard on Mary. As followers of Christ, we often fail to recognise the presence of the Lord. We have certain expectations about how He will work or what He will do, and because He does not conform to our expectations, we fail to see where He *is* working and what He *is* doing. There is admittedly a bit of Mary Magdalene in us all.

And yet she was the first to see the risen Saviour,[29] even though she was unaware of it at the time. But she was not only the first to see Him, but the...

First to Hear Him

"Jesus saith unto her, Woman, why weepest thou?" (v15). The first words spoken by the risen Christ were a repetition of what the angels earlier asked. The question may contain a gentle reproof. There was enough evidence for Mary to believe He had risen. But the Lord also asked Mary, "whom seekest thou?" This second question directed Mary's attention away from herself to the Lord Jesus. And it may have contained an invitation for Mary to reflect on the kind of Messiah she was expecting.[30] John may want readers of his Gospel to reflect on this question also, lest our estimate of Him fall far short.

Notice that Mary was being given a little more light at a time. First, she saw the stone rolled away. Second, she saw the angels and heard them speak. Third, she saw Jesus Himself and heard His voice. How gracious the Lord is with His people, working to encourage our faith.

But Mary's faith was still forthcoming. She thought the man asking her these questions was the gardener. John has already told us that the tomb was in a garden (19:41), and who would be present this early in the morning in the garden but the person

---

[29] See Mark 16:9.

[30] D. A. Carson, *The Gospel According to John* (Grand Rapids, MI: William B. Eerdmans, 1991), 641.

charged with the responsibility of caring for it?[31] Therefore, Mary, "supposing Him to be the gardener, saith unto Him, Sir, if Thou have borne Him hence, tell me where Thou hast laid Him, and I will take Him away" (20:15).[32] And as if the Saviour could bear Mary's grief and misunderstanding no longer, He spoke her name. "Jesus saith unto her, Mary" (v16). It was enough. She knew His voice. "He calleth His own sheep by name...they know His voice" (10:3-4). "She turned herself, and saith unto Him, Rabboni; which is to say, Master" (20:16). "Rabboni" is Aramaic and contains more affection than "Rabbi". John translates it for his Greek-speaking readers as *didaskalos*. Its meaning in English might be something like "My dear Master".

At that moment, Mary may have done what the women would later do in Matthew 28:9, holding Him by the feet, but in her case, doing so as if to keep Him from leaving. Perhaps Mary thought His promise in John 14:3 was about to be fulfilled. Christ had "come again" and was about to "receive [her] unto Himself". But this was not His promised return in which He would take believers with Him. The ascension and sending of the Holy Spirit must come first. Therefore, Jesus instructed her, "Touch me not" (20:17). A better rendering, which reflects the present imperative of the verb, is "Stop clinging to Me" *(NASB)*. Incidentally, this direction by the Lord to Mary confirms His was an actual physical resurrection, not a vision or hallucination. She was clinging to the body of the

---

[31] Leon Morris, *Expository Reflections on the Gospel of John* (Grand Rapids, MI: Baker Book House, 1988), 700.

[32] D. A. Carson notes "that she should offer to make the arrangements to fetch the body and give it a proper burial suggests she was a woman of some wealth and standing (as Luke 8:2-3 attests)".

glorified Lord. But she must not, Jesus adds, "for I am not yet ascended to My Father" (v17).

Then the Lord gave Mary a mission: "but go to my brethren, and say unto them, I ascend…" (v17). The instruction was not to send the news to His brothers in the flesh (i.e., His siblings). There is no indication that Mary went to members of Jesus' family with this report. Rather, Christ's resurrection created a new relationship wherein now He referred to His disciples as "brothers" (see also Matt. 28:10; Heb. 2:11-14). Notice also that the Lord's instruction to Mary was not to tell his brothers about His resurrection, but His ascension. His resurrection was but a necessary step in Him going all the way to glory.

The final bit of news she was to share with them included the words, "I ascend unto My Father, and your Father; and to My God, and your God" (John 20:17). This particular wording unites the Lord Jesus with His followers, yet at the same time emphasising a substantial difference, for He does not refer to "Our Father and Our God". As Augustine wrote, "He saith not, Our Father: in one sense, therefore, is He mine, in another sense, yours; by nature mine, by grace yours…my God, under whom I also am as man; your God, between whom and you I am mediator."[33]

First to Tell About Him

Mary wasted no time. She "came and told the disciples that she had seen the Lord, and that He had spoken these things unto her" (v18). This is consistent with Mark's report: "And she went and

---

[33] Quoted in Leon Morris, 703.

told them that had been with Him, as they mourned and wept" (16:10). We should not conclude that the disciples were all in one place at this moment, although they would be together in the upper room later in the day (without Thomas). Nearly bursting with excitement, Mary likely made visits to a few different homes sharing this news. But when she did, she was not believed. "And they, when they had heard that He was alive, and had been seen of her, believed not" (v11).[34] Because her report included news of His ascension, it may have sounded to them as fabricated. They would never see Him again if His ascension was about to occur (or already had). In other words, they may have interpreted Mary's news as, "The Lord appeared to me, but it's not likely He'll appear to you, for He is ascending." Yet His words earlier to them in the upper room assured them they would see Him again (16:16-22).

At this point, there were few believers in the Lord's resurrection. John was the first to believe, but Mary Magdalene was the first to hear His voice, see His face, and share the wonderful news He instructed her to give. And even the world's first evangelist was met by disbelief, so don't be discouraged if people reject the news you bring of a risen, glorified and coming Saviour.

---

[34] The fact that they did not believe tells us John was likely not among those she visited (for John 20:8 indicates he did believe).

Chapter 6

TWO REACTIONS TO THE RESURRECTION

A woman, Mary of Magdala, was the first to see the risen Saviour. Matthew tells us a group of women were the next to see Him (28:9-10),[35] who then rushed to the disciples to share the exciting news. Meanwhile, the religious leaders in Israel received the same report of the Lord Jesus' empty tomb from some of the soldiers who were guarding it. Their response was altogether different from that of the women. Matthew 28:9-15 records two reactions to the resurrection: the women and their worship, the leaders and their lie.

The Women and Their Worship

The angel instructed the women to "go quickly, and tell His disciples that He is risen from the dead; and, behold, He goeth before you

---

[35] Paul makes no mention of these women in his list of witnesses to the resurrection in 1 Corinthians 15, noting Cephas (Peter), the twelve, the 500, James, all the apostles (presumably including the twelve) and Paul himself. It is possible that by the time Paul wrote this letter, belief in Jesus' resurrection was being rejected because women were, reportedly, the primary witnesses and their witness would be considered invalid by many. Paul wants to emphasise that there were many male witnesses also.

into Galilee; there shall ye see Him" (v7). They likely expected no one to see Him until they arrived there. But they obeyed the angel's words, running to tell the others. "And as they went to tell His disciples, behold, Jesus met them" (v9). What a reward for their obedience! And what a surprise, not having to wait until they arrived in Galilee to see their blessed Saviour.

He met them with a greeting—"All hail." The Greek word is *chairō* and can mean "rejoice" *(NKJV, NASB2020)*. If ever there were a reason to rejoice, it was then. It was one thing to hear it from the angel, but quite another to be witnesses to such a dramatic reality. Then Matthew says, "And they came", implying that when the women saw Christ, there was some distance between them, which they in turn quickly eliminated. And when they arrived, they kneeled on the ground before Him and "took hold of His feet".[36] It was an act of homage, confirmed by the next statement that they "worshipped Him". Matthew probably means by this that they regarded Him as divine. How could He not be, having displayed such exceptional power?

After His initial greeting, Christ calmed them with the words, "Be not afraid", a phrase He had used often during His public ministry. The women had just been visited by a spectacular appearance of the angel of the Lord and now a Man they had watched die stood alive before them. It's natural to be somewhat frightened by the supernatural, thus the Saviour's exhortation, "Be not afraid".

Jesus proceeded to reinforce the instructions of the angel—"go tell my brethren that they go into Galilee, and there shall they see

---

[36] This phrase, along with John 20:17 ("stop clinging to Me"), emphasises the physical reality of the risen Lord.

Me" (v10), but He uses a word the angel does not—"brethren". As pointed out in the last chapter of this book from John 20:17, the Lord was not referring to His brothers in the flesh, but to His disciples. And what a beautiful, gracious term it is. "The 'family' metaphor shows much love and patience, since the disciples have just run away from home, as it were, when they deserted Jesus. But Jesus welcomes the prodigals back."[37] His instruction is that His brethren "go into Galilee". There is a notable absence of the mention of Jerusalem since the Lord's lament in Matthew 23:37.[38] But most of Christ's public ministry had taken place in Galilee and it was fitting that His disciples should go there, where they received this promise from their Lord—"there shall they see Me".

With this commission from the risen Saviour, the women departed to inform the disciples. Thus, the first reaction to Christ's resurrection in this section of Matthew is entirely fitting. The women respond with joy, worship, and obedience. Any other response falls far short, which Matthew proceeds to present.

The Leaders and Their Lie

"Now when they [the women] were going, behold, some[39] of the watch came into the city, and shewed unto the chief priests all the things that were done" (v11). While Christ's followers were rejoicing, worshipping Him and sharing the news, His enemies

---

[37] David L. Turner, *Matthew: Baker Exegetical Commentary on the New Testament* (Grand Rapids, MI: Baker Academic, 2008), 682.

[38] Before the Lord's lament, Jerusalem is noted 11 times in Matthew, but not once afterward. In contrast, Luke's Gospel mentions Jerusalem 14 times after the Lord's lament in 13:34, and figures prominently after the resurrection (24:13,18,33,47,49,52).

[39] We might wonder what happened to the other guards.

began to plot a massive lie. The chief priests received troubling information from some of the soldiers charged with guarding the Lord's tomb. We cannot be certain how comprehensive Matthew's use of the word "all" is here (they "shewed unto the chief priests *all* the things that were done"), but at a minimum, their report included the absence of Jesus' body, which presented a serious problem for these Roman guards. The tomb's seal had been broken, the stone was rolled away, and the body of Christ was missing. These facts would combine to make the soldiers guilty of dereliction of duty, an offense punishable by death. But rather than reporting to Pilate or to their superior officers, they shrewdly decided to report to the Jewish chief priests, whom they knew were just as anxious to cover up the resurrection story as the guards themselves. Thus, the big lie was concocted.

"And when they were assembled with the elders, and had taken counsel, they gave large money unto the soldiers, Saying, Say ye, His disciples came by night, and stole Him away while we slept" (vv12-13). Interestingly, the proposed lie still incriminated the soldiers, who would be admitting to falling asleep on their watch and failing in their duty to guard the tomb. The lie also didn't make sense. How could the soldiers know the disciples stole the body if they were asleep when it happened? But two things made them willing to cooperate. The first was money, and plenty of it, with the *KJV* capturing the meaning of the phrase well—"large money" (or a large amount of money). This was not the first payoff by the religious leaders over the past few days, but was likely a considerably larger sum than paid to the traitor Judas.

The other factor that persuaded the guards to lie was a word of assurance from the Jewish leaders—"And if this come to the governor's ears, we will persuade him, and secure you" (v14). If they could pay off the soldiers with a bribe, they could probably do the same with the governor Pilate. The irony of it all is that the same men who predicted deceit about the resurrection (27:63-64) ended up committing deceit themselves. The Jewish authorities "had feared that the body might be stolen and resurrection stories circulate on the basis of an empty tomb. They were now ensuring that precisely those stories were circulated, the only difference being that behind the stories was a risen body instead of a stolen body."[40]

The guards complied and received their pay. "So they took the money, and did as they were taught: and this saying is commonly reported among the Jews until this day" (v15). Matthew wants his readers to know that this story was not invented some time later. It was a common report, circulated among the Jewish people when it occurred.[41]

These two reactions to Christ's resurrection could not be more opposite. A group of women believed and worshipped, experiencing joy and purpose. A group of men refused to believe the obvious truth and slipped further into their darkness, deceit and eternal danger. One's response to the resurrection of Christ has eternal consequences. How have you responded?

---

[40] Leon Morris, *The Gospel According to Matthew* (Grand Rapids, MI: William B. Eerdmans, 1992), 741-2.

[41] Such stories were still being disseminated in the days of Justin Martyr (ca. 150 AD). See his *Dialogue with Trypho* 108.2.

Chapter 7

AN UNEXPECTED ROUNDTRIP

Apart from the Lord's appearance to the disciples in Galilee (John 21), the Emmaus journey (Luke 24:13-35) is the longest post-resurrection narrative. There is something sweet about the fact that Christ revealed Himself to these lesser known followers of His in such dramatic fashion. The Saviour's loving concern for all His own was impartial. And it still is.

We only know the name of one of these travellers, identified in Luke 24:18 as Cleopas. Although some seek to identify him as the same person named in John 19:25 ("Mary the wife of Cleophas [or Clopas]"), the names are slightly different. Attempts to identify the wayfaring couple as Cleophas and his wife, Mary, the earthly uncle and aunt of the Lord Jesus, are not very persuasive. Luke's aim is to shine the spotlight on the unrecognised traveller not the unnamed one.

Back to Emmaus

The two are headed "to a village called Emmaus" (Luke 24:13). The fact that they later *return* to Jerusalem (v33) indicates that their journey *began* from Jerusalem. As they make their way back to Emmaus, about a seven-mile trek, they have no idea just how quickly they are about to retrace their own steps.

It is still the first day of the week, Easter Sunday, since Luke mentions the "same day" (v13, c.f. v1). With heads hung low, the companions were dejectedly rehearsing all the events of the last few days. They could not believe how wrong they were about Jesus of Nazareth. Then suddenly "Jesus Himself drew near, and went with them" (v15). But they had no idea who their fellow traveller was. Luke informs us that "their eyes were kept from recognising Him" (v16 *NET*). The verb "kept" is in the passive voice, likely a divine passive, meaning that God kept them from recognising Christ.[42]

At this point, Jesus asked them His first question, "What are these matters you are discussing so intently as you walk along?" (v17 *NET*). It was a question so jarring, it stopped them in their tracks: "And they stood still, looking sad" (v17 *NET*). Cleophas chimes in: "Are you the only visitor to Jerusalem who doesn't know what happened there in the past few days?" (v18 *ISV*). Where has this Man been? How could He be so uninformed? The Saviour's second question, "What things?" (v19) lead His co-travellers to take Him back to the beginning.

Back to the Beginning

"And they said unto Him, Concerning Jesus of Nazareth, which was a prophet mighty in deed and word before God and all the people" (v19). It must have been heartening for the Lord Jesus

---

[42] Such concealing is noted elsewhere by Luke (9:45; 18:34).

to hear their assessment of His ministry and impact, from its inception to the present moment. But their focus then turned to the last few heartbreaking days: "the chief priests and our rulers delivered Him to be condemned to death, and have crucified Him. But we trusted that it had been He which should have redeemed Israel" (vv20-21). The verb "trusted" (or better "hoped") is in the imperfect tense; they were hoping Jesus of Nazareth would be the long-promised Redeemer, Who would grant Israel's political release from Roman oppression. But their hopes were shattered at the cross. The words "death" and "redeemed" did not connect in their Messianic theology.

The travellers add, "and beside all this, to day is the third day since these things were done" (v21). Why do they reference "the third day"? Since they proceed to mention that women in their group told them they had seen and heard from angels at the tomb (vv22-23), and since Luke records earlier that the angels told the women that Christ would rise again on "the third day" (v7), this detail was likely shared with the two travellers. It was now the third day. Where was He? His body was missing from the tomb, but apparently, no one had seen Him. Of course, "the irony of the narrative is that they are in the midst of what they desired and what the others had not experienced [seeing the risen Lord]".[43]

We cannot help but be touched by the followers' disappointment, disillusionment and despair. In the presence of their unknown companion, they let it all out. And their spiritual transparency is about to be rewarded. But first, a rebuke.

---

[43] Darrell L. Bock, *Luke: Baker Exegetical Commentary on the New Testament* (Grand Rapids, MI: Baker Academic, 1996), 2:1915.

Back to the Bible

"Then He said unto them, O fools, and slow of heart to believe all that the prophets have spoken: Ought not Christ to have suffered these things, and to enter into His glory?" (vv25-26). The rebuke centres on the word "all" in Christ's reference to their failure to believe "all that the prophets have spoken". They certainly believed the prophets, but not "all" that the prophets had said about the coming Messiah. They would be happy to assert those Old Testament texts predicting the Messiah's sudden coming to smash the nations and establish His kingdom. But that is not "all" that the prophets had written. They foretold not only a ruling Messiah but a suffering One. There is always the danger of reading the Scriptures selectively or partially.

The Saviour tells them here that Christ's sufferings were a must. "Ought" (v26) is the Greek *dei*, meaning "it is necessary".[44] Before entering into His glory, Christ must suffer the very things these travellers were discussing and that so disheartened them. They needed to get back to the Bible, which is where the Saviour took them. "And beginning at Moses and all the prophets, He expounded unto them in all the scriptures the things concerning Himself" (v27). In all their conversation, they never referred to the Scriptures. The Lord took them there, expounding things they had never understood before. It is more important for Christ's followers to recognise Him in His Word than to recognise Him in the flesh. And learning Christ is more valuable than erasing sorrow. So here we begin to see why they were kept from recognising Him (v16). Their understanding of the resurrection would need to be based on

---

[44] *Dei* is one of Luke's key words (2:49; 4:43; 13:33; 18:1; 19:5; 21:9; 22:7,37; 24:7,44).

Scripture, not experience. So the Lord gave them a firm foundation in this unforgettable Bible study.

We are not told which Scriptures He referenced, but another "all" grabs our attention in verse 27—"all the scriptures". The theme of all Scripture is Christ Himself. Although we cannot be sure, the Saviour may have taken them to the Bible's first prophecy (Gen. 3:15) which indicated some sort of suffering to come for the Promised Seed of the woman. The slaying of the Passover lamb, the upraised bronze serpent in the wilderness, the piercing of Messiah's hands and feet in Psalm 22, the Suffering Servant passages of Isaiah, Zechariah's mention of Him being pierced and smitten, may all have been part of Christ's marvellous explanation as to why He must first suffer.[45] And there is not a saint on earth who would not have loved to have been there to hear it!

As the truth of God's Word about the Messiah sank into their souls, their despair began to melt like snow before the blazing sun. They did not see the full picture until now. Yes! Christ had to suffer. And He did suffer, fulfilling Scripture perfectly. How crucial it is for us to interpret God's Word accurately. "If we find ourselves hurting and despairing and do not find that Scripture speaks to our condition, it is not because the Bible has failed us, but because we do not know it well enough".[46]

---

[45] The sermons in Acts refer to many OT texts which were fulfilled in the Lord Jesus (e.g., Deut. 18:15; Psa. 2:7; 16:8-11; 110; 118; Isa. 53). These passages and others were likely those Christ expounded to these travellers and later to the whole group in the upper room (Luke 24:44-46).

[46] R. Kent Hughes, *Luke Volume 2: That You May Know the Truth* (Wheaton, IL: Crossway, 1998), 410.

Their trip went by much faster than they expected. "And they drew nigh unto the village, whither they went: and He made as though He would have gone further" (v28). Likely testing their desire for His company, Christ continued walking. But having so enjoyed His fellowship, they dared not let Him go. "They constrained Him, saying, Abide with us: for it is toward evening, and the day is far spent. And He went in to tarry with them" (v29). It is always wise to allow Christ's presence to fill our homes.

The meal began, but the guest strangely became the host. "And it came to pass, as He sat at meat with them, He took bread, and blessed it, and brake, and gave to them" (v30).[47] Perhaps the hosts asked the Lord Jesus to give thanks (i.e., the blessing) out of respect for His knowledge of the Scriptures. Whatever the case, it was at this point that they finally recognised their traveling companion. "And their eyes were opened, and they knew Him" (v31). Some suggest that the reason for their recognition of Him was the visibility of the nail prints in His hands as He broke the bread, but the text states the reason—"their eyes were opened". Had they not been kept from realising who He was, they doubtless would have already. But as in verse 16, here we have another divine passive (the verb "opened" is in the passive voice). The God Who conceals is the God Who reveals. God is the Revealer of the risen Christ.

No sooner were their eyes opened but a seat was empty—"and He vanished out of their sight" (v31). Notice the absence of the spectacular here. No trumpet sounded; no heavenly light blinded them; no voice thundered from the skies. He was with them and

---

[47] The language recalls Luke's account of the feeding of the 5,000 (9:16) and of the last supper (22:19).

then He was gone. What fascinated them was not the manner in which He appeared nor the manner in which He vanished. Rather, "they said one to another, Did not our heart burn within us, while He talked with us by the way, and while He opened to us the scriptures?" (v32). It was His exposition of the Word that lit a fire under them, and now they could not wait to tell the others.

Back to Jerusalem

They certainly did not expect to be making another trip that evening, but "they rose up the same hour, and returned to Jerusalem" (v33). Their friends had to know what they now knew, not only that Christ was risen, but that His sufferings were necessary and predicted in their own Scriptures.

Although they had a big surprise to share, they were about to be surprised themselves. Luke tells us they returned "and found the eleven[48] gathered together, and them that were with them, Saying, The Lord is risen indeed, and hath appeared to Simon" (v34). They were not the only ones to see the risen Saviour. The appearance to Simon Peter, although noted here and in 1 Corinthians 15:5, is not detailed anywhere. But it was evident that Christ was seen now by multiple witnesses. Notice also that their report is that "*the Lord* is risen", emphasising His authority. Not only is He alive but bears authority.

At last, it was their turn to share their news—"And they told what things were done in the way, and how He was known of

---

[48] Note that these two are distinguished from "the eleven." The unnamed traveller could not, therefore, have been one of the eleven.

them in breaking of bread" (v35). No doubt, their hearts were not the only ones now burning within them. What they did not realise was that everyone in the room was about to become an eyewitness to the glorious fact that "the Lord is risen indeed"!

Chapter 8

THE LORD'S EASTER GIFTS

When our Saviour was born, valuable gifts were brought by those who were looking for Him. When our Lord rose again, far more valuable gifts were presented to those who were not looking for Him. They thought He was dead and gone, and rather than searching for Him, they remained behind locked doors.

The group in the upper room included more than "the eleven" for Luke refers to "them that were with them" (24:33). John tells us that the doors were locked "for fear of the Jews" (20:19). The Jewish authorities might think His followers had stolen the body of Jesus and would come looking for them to acquire it.

He Gave Them His Presence

It was into this atmosphere of fear that the Saviour unexpectedly appeared. The Emmaus travellers were just wrapping up their report when "Jesus Himself stood in the midst of them" (Luke 24:36), appearing as suddenly as He had disappeared before (see v31). There was no knock at the door, nor was there a voice calling to them from the outside to let Him in. This was one of those pleasant invasions of the Lord into the lives of His people; indeed, the most pleasant of all. A shut tomb could not keep Him in nor could these shut doors keep Him out.

It is sweet to think about the fact that our Lord might have gone anywhere and done anything after He arose, but what He desired above all was to be with His people, whether they were grieving in a graveyard, discouraged while traveling on a road or gripped by fear behind closed doors. What a precious gift this was and still is. We have our Saviour's presence with us in our grief, despair, and fear. "For He hath said, I will never leave thee, nor forsake thee" (Heb. 13:5).

He Gave Them Peace

There was no moment of silence allowing them to absorb the reality of His presence. No sooner did the Lord Jesus appear but that the most welcome words came from His lips—"Peace be unto you." He had just made peace by the blood of His cross (Col. 1:20), and therefore, dealt with their sins. But now He deals with their fears. John records that He spoke these words twice (John 20:19,21). We have to remember that among this group of Christ's followers were those who had forsaken Him when He was arrested, and Peter, who had denied even knowing Him. This repeated greeting of "Peace be unto you" would certainly put them all at ease and calm their fears. What a beautiful gift to those who were anxious and ashamed.

Our blessed Lord still offers the gift of peace. Anyone who receives Christ as Saviour receives peace with God and can say with the Apostle Paul, "Therefore being justified by faith, we have peace with God through our Lord Jesus Christ" (Rom. 5:1). As believers, we not only been given peace *with* God, but the peace of God. "And the peace *of* God, which passeth all understanding, shall keep your hearts and minds through Christ Jesus" (Phil. 4:7).

But even though the Lord Jesus said, "Peace be unto you", those gathered in the upper room "were terrified and affrighted, and supposed that they had seen a spirit" (Luke 24:37). And so, He gave them something else.

He Gave Them Proof

Notice the honesty of Scripture. The Lord's followers are not portrayed as perfect models of faith to imitate. They were just like us, faults and all, and disappointedly slow to accept the reality of Christ's resurrection. And so, He asks them two questions: "Why are you frightened, and why do doubts arise in your hearts?" (v38, *NET*). The first question addresses their mood, the second concerns their lack of perception.[49] There was no reason for their fear and no justification for their doubts. Yet Jesus still gave them proof that it was really Him. "'Look at My hands and My feet; it's Me! Touch Me and see; a ghost does not have flesh and bones like you see I have.' When He had said this, He showed them His hands and His feet" (vv39-40, *NET*). He tells them to "look" with their eyes and invites them to "touch" with their hands. "They must be convinced *that* Jesus rose, but they must also be convinced that the *same* Jesus arose as was crucified, and so He told them to look at His hands and feet...indeed, He made a point to show them."[50]

---

[49] Darrell L. Bock, *Luke: Baker Exegetical Commentary on the New Testament* (Grand Rapids, MI: Baker Academic, 1996), 2:1932.
[50] Dale Ralph Davis, *Luke 14-24* (Scotland, UK: Christian Focus Publications, 2021), 234.

ALL THE WAY TO GLORY
ALL THE WAY TO GLORY

They don't deny that it was the Lord Jesus. He must have been physically recognisable. Their eyes (unlike the two on the road to Emmaus) were not kept from recognising Him. It may have just taken awhile for the shock factor of His resurrection to wear off. John says that after showing them His hands and His side,[51] they were glad when they saw the Lord (20:20). Luke notes their gladness also by recording their reaction as "believing not for joy" (24:41). This does not mean they were necessarily unbelieving. They had joy, and there can be no joy where there is unbelief. Luke seems to be saying that it was hard to believe this was all actually happening and that they were witnessing it with their own eyes. It was just too good to be true. But it was true. And amazingly, the Saviour predicted their joyful response. Before His death, He said to them in the upper room, "A little while, and ye shall not see Me: and again, a little while, and ye shall see Me...ye shall weep and lament, but the world shall rejoice: and ye shall be sorrowful, but your sorrow shall be turned into joy" (John 16:16,20).

But He not only gave them proof it was Him by what *they* would do ("look" and "touch"), but by what *He* would do. "He said unto them, Have ye here any meat? And they gave Him a piece of a broiled fish, and of an honeycomb. And He took it, and did eat before them" (Luke 24:41-43).[52] Apparitions don't eat. Ghosts don't gulp down dinner. Christ's resurrection was actual and physical. With the evidence before them, it became crystal clear. They had all the proof they needed. It really was the Lord Jesus among them, risen from the dead. What a gift these proofs turned out to be.

---

[51] John is the only one to mention the Lord's "side".

[52] When Peter was preaching in the house of Cornelius, he included this detail of Christ eating and drinking as proof of His physical resurrection (Acts 10:41).

We also have been given proof of the Lord's resurrection. There is still an empty tomb. No one has ever produced His body. We have the written record of Jesus' death, burial, and resurrection. The biblical witnesses are not in short supply, and they gave their lives for the One they know is living and seated on His throne in glory. You may know also that Christ is alive because you can see Him in His people, a little more day by day as they are being conformed to His image.

But John recalls two more Easter gifts the Lord gave to His own.

He Gave Them a Pledge

After His second "Peace be unto you", John notes, "And when He had said this, He breathed on them, and saith unto them, Receive ye the Holy Ghost" (20:22). The KJV rightly emphasises the preposition "on" in the phrase, "He breathed on them". This was not a "breathing into", but a "breathing on". It is possible to interpret this action as the Lord giving to His disciples what would sustain them in their present need prior to His ascension. However, it might make better sense to view this as a pledge of what was to come. To refer to this gift as a pledge (or earnest) rather than the full reception of the Holy Spirit is further supported by what the Lord said in Luke 24:49—"And, behold, I send the promise of My Father upon you: but tarry ye in the city of Jerusalem, until ye be endued with power from on high". That enduement with power would occur in Acts 2. The John 20 breathing is not the Acts 2 filling. And yet there is a connection. The light breathing in John 20 would eventually give way to the rushing mighty wind of Acts 2. But notice that the rushing mighty wind was not *felt* but *heard* as a "sound from heaven" (v2). It came from heaven because that was where the Lord is now seated, sending forth the promised Holy Spirit He had pledged to them earlier. Another reason to view this as a pledge is by noticing the behaviour of Christ's followers immediately afterward. Their boldness is not evident until after the early verses of Acts 2. They locked the doors to the room again in John 20:26 and Peter decided to go fishing in John 21, recruiting a handful of others to join him. One would expect more of a transformation if they had indeed received the Holy Spirit in John 20.

He Gave Them Power

Maybe we should more accurately say, he gave them *a message* with power. After the Lord breathed on them, He added, "If you forgive the sins of any, they are forgiven them. If you retain the sins of any, they are retained" (John 20:23, *LEB*). This does not mean that the apostles had authority to forgive anyone of their sins nor is there any record in the New Testament of them understanding the Lord's words in this way. Only God can forgive sins (Isa. 43:25; Mark 2:7). We need to interpret Christ's words here in the context of the gospel mission He just gave them—"as My Father hath sent Me, even so send I you" (John 20:21). They were sent forth to proclaim the good news. And there is inherent power in the gospel message entrusted to them (and us) that offers forgiveness of sins through the person and work of our Lord Jesus Christ. When Peter later preached the gospel, he noted that the authority to receive forgiveness of sins was only in the name of Jesus Christ (Acts 2:38; 10:43), not any supposed power he had personally received. Remember also that Peter and the apostles were not the only individuals in the upper room to whom the Lord spoke these words. This gift was given to believers as a whole, so we should not read any ecclesiastical authority into this passage. All who have received Christ by faith have the privilege to take the gospel to everyone with the promise that all who believe in Him will experience the power of sins forgiven. Refusal of the message means that their sins "are retained", that is, they remain on those who have committed them; they bear the guilt and face the coming judgment of God.

A risen Saviour is still offering the best gifts. Not only did He bless His followers with these Easter gifts, but to lost sinners, He offers forgiveness of sins, peace with God, eternal life, the guarantee of heaven in your future and fulfilling purpose in the present. These will all be yours the moment you receive the greatest Gift of all—Christ Himself. "For God so loved the world, that He gave His only begotten Son, that whosoever believeth in Him should not perish, but have everlasting life" (John 3:16).

Chapter 9

"MY LORD AND MY GOD"

You missed a really good meeting on Sunday. Many of us have heard these words before. But never were they more true than when spoken to Thomas just after our Lord's resurrection. John tells us that "Thomas, one of the twelve, called Didymus[53], was not with them when Jesus came" (John 20:24) on the first day of the week. There was one of the twelve absent that does not surprise us—Judas. He had betrayed the Lord, taken his life, and gone "to his own place" (Acts 1:25). There was one of the twelve present that does surprise us—Peter. He had denied the Lord three times, his public restoration not recorded until the next chapter. But there was one of the twelve absent that does surprise us—Thomas. He had spoken to the other disciples earlier about dying with Jesus (John 11:16), but as they glanced around the upper room, Thomas was notably missing. And what a day to be missing! The Lord Jesus had suddenly appeared to them, giving them peace, power and purpose, but Thomas missed it all. And for at least a week, Thomas was likely the most miserable man in Jerusalem.

---

[53] The Greek *Didymus* means "twin." We are not told who his twin was, but we have all played the role of his twin in our doubts.

The Stipulation

We are not told why Thomas was elsewhere, nor did the Lord rebuke him later for his absence. But the disciples informed him that "we have seen the Lord", yet he refused to believe. And they told him more than once. The verb tense for "said" (20:25) is imperfect, meaning, "they kept telling him". "But he said unto them, Except I shall see in His hands the print of the nails, and put my finger into the print of the nails, and thrust my hand into His side, I will not believe." Thomas claimed to need visual and tangible evidence. He stipulated that he must be able to both see and feel before he would believe. Words, no matter how often repeated, would not be enough for him. Thus, the disciples' first witnessing experience was a bust. The Lord commissioned them to tell the world about Him; they told one in their own group, and he did not believe. Just remember that the next time someone rejects your testimony about the Lord Jesus.

The Invitation

A week went by. The disciples met again, apparently in the same place, with the same locked doors. The Lord would appear the same way and with the same greeting. But this time, something was different. "And after eight days[54] again His disciples were within, and Thomas with them" (v26). This time, the doubter was there. Yet as strong as Thomas' doubts were, he did not let them keep him away from the Lord's people.

And then it happened. "Then came Jesus, the doors being shut, and stood in the midst, and said, Peace be unto you." It was an

---

[54] John is likely using an inclusive method of counting meaning "seven days later".

exact repeat of the week before. Everything was the same, just as his fellow disciples had told him. Clearly, they *had* seen the Lord, and now Thomas had also. There was no doubt about it. Christ was risen.

Once inside the room with His own, the Saviour immediately addressed the neediest man among them with an invitation. Rather than scolding him for refusing to believe the other disciples' testimony, the Lord graciously said to Thomas, "Reach hither thy finger, and behold My hands; and reach hither thy hand, and thrust it into My side: and be not faithless, but believing" (v27). Notice that the Lord used Thomas' own words about having to see and feel the marks on His body in order for him to believe Christ was risen. How could Jesus have known he said this if He were still dead? Not only did it become clear to Thomas that the Lord was risen right then, but that He was risen a week before. He heard everything Thomas had said, although He was not physically present. We too can find comfort in the fact that our living Lord always hears what His people say, even though He is not here in the flesh.

The Declaration

Thomas thought he would need to see and feel. And the Lord Jesus invited him to do both. But Thomas was not as big a doubter as he thought, nor as some allege. There is no indication that he actually touched Jesus' wounds, since the Lord replied, "Because thou hast seen Me [not touched Me], thou hast believed?" (v29). He did not need anything more than the presence and words of the Saviour. Based on what Thomas just witnessed, it was obvious that Jesus hears everything, sees everything, and knows everything. The only logical conclusion was the declaration Thomas made, "And Thomas answered and said unto Him, My Lord and My God"[55] (v28). Ironically, one of the strongest affirmations of Jesus' deity in the Gospels[56] comes from a man often labelled as "doubting Thomas". John and his early readers were familiar with slogans of emperor worship such as, "Caesar is Lord, Caesar is God!" But Thomas got it right. Jesus is Lord! Jesus is God! And there is no other!

Notice that Jesus did not refuse to accept Thomas' declaration. He did not inform Thomas that he was mistaken, and that his words were spoken in error. Rather, He commends him for what he expressed. Thomas' confession is what John hopes for his readers, and what Jesus Christ wants from us all. Do you believe He is risen? Have you acknowledged that He is Lord, your Lord? Have you recognised He is God, your God? The consequences will change your eternity. For the apostle Paul wrote, "If you confess with your mouth that Jesus is Lord and believe in your heart that God raised Him from the dead, you will be saved" (Rom. 10:9 *NET*).

The Benediction

Next comes the last of two benedictions in John's Gospel (see 13:17). Jesus said, "Thomas, because thou hast seen Me, thou hast believed: blessed are they that have not seen, and yet have

---

[55] Note the double personal pronoun ("my"), emphasising the personal nature of Thomas' declaration.

[56] John bookends his Gospel with these strong affirmations of the deity of Jesus (1:1,18; 20:28; see also 8:58; 10:30-33).

[57] Forms of the word "believe" dominate this section, appearing seven times in eight verses (vv24-31).

believed"[57] (20:29). This does not mean Thomas was not blessed. You would have a hard time convincing him that he was not, as he looked upon his risen Lord. But "Jesus here foresees a time when He will not provide the kind of tangible evidence afforded the beloved disciple and Thomas; in short, He will ascend to His Father permanently, and all those who believe will do so without the benefit of having seen their resurrected Lord."[58] As believers, we obviously come into the good of this benediction, having never seen the Saviour with our physical eyes. But we heartily agree with Peter, "You have not seen Him, but you love Him. You do not see Him now but you believe in Him, and so you rejoice with an indescribable and glorious joy, because you are attaining the goal of your faith—the salvation of your souls" (1Pet. 1:8-9 NET).

Have you believed in Him? Have you received God's salvation? Do you have "eternal life through Jesus Christ our Lord" (Rom. 6:23)? John recorded this sign along with a handful of others "that ye might believe that Jesus is the Christ, the Son of God; and that believing ye might have life through His name" (John 20:31). Why not believe Him now?

---

[58] D. A. Carson, *The Gospel According to John* (Grand Rapids, MI: William B. Eerdmans, 1991), 659.

Chapter 10

AN UNCHANGED CALLING

Now what? The disciple of action just had to have something to do. Peter and the others had been told to wait in Galilee until they were clothed with power from on high (Luke 24:49). But it wasn't happening, and Peter likely wondered what to do next.

Filling the Time

The old way of life may have been tugging hard at him. Or perhaps a fishing excursion was simply a way to fill the time. Either way, Peter made up his mind that he was not going to simply sit around and do nothing. "Simon Peter saith unto them [the disciples], I go a fishing. They say unto him, We also go with thee. They went forth, and entered into a ship immediately" (John 21:3). Apparently, it didn't take too much arm twisting to convince some of the others to go along. After all, at least two of the others were fishermen—James and John.[59]

---

[59] John names those on the expedition as Simon Peter, Thomas, Nathanael and the sons of Zebedee (21:2). Two others accompanied them, but are unnamed, something not unusual for John (cf. 1:35-39; 18:15-16; 20:2-8).

We must not be overly critical of the disciples here. After all, the Lord wasn't. We should try to appreciate their difficult position in the interim between the Lord's resurrection and His ascension. Forty days is a long time. What were they to do? Where were they to go? At least a fishing expedition would both give them something to do and put food on their tables. Remember also that the disciples had been obedient to the Saviour's message forwarded to them by the women—"go tell My brethren that they go into Galilee, and there shall they see Me" (Matt. 28:10; cf. 26:32). They had seen the Lord in Jerusalem and had obediently travelled to Galilee. But they had not yet seen the Saviour there. Thus, this fishing trip to the Sea of Galilee.[60]

It would be after a long frustrating and fishless night that Jesus would appear to them. There are likely many reasons why He chose this moment and this place for His appearance, but one might simply be that the Lord revealed Himself on this occasion to save them from the pull of the old life. It was Peter's passion, as well as that of the sons of Zebedee, and Jesus knew it. He made sure the old pull wasn't too strong—"that night they caught nothing" (John 21:3). The Lord knows how to keep fish out of nets as well as how to bring them in. The incident would take them back in their minds to empty nets in these same waters, the instruction of Christ to cast those nets on the other side of the boat, the miraculous catch which occurred at His direction, His call to make them "fishers of men", and their decision to forsake all and follow Him (Luke 5:1-11). After this miracle, which was so incredibly similar to the earlier one, the disciples could conclude that their calling remained unchanged. But we are getting ahead of ourselves.

---

[60] John refers to it as both the Sea of Tiberias and the Sea of Galilee (see John 6:1).

Filling Their Nets

After a disappointing night, "when the morning was now come, Jesus stood on the shore: but the disciples knew not that it was Jesus" (John 21:4). There are probably at least two reasons why they failed to recognise Him. First, note that the Greek word for "morning" indicates the time before sunrise while it is still dark. John used this word in 20:1, adding this description—"when it was yet dark". Second, 21:8 indicates that the distance from the ship to the shore was approximately 200 cubits (or nearly 100 metres). The distance combined with the darkness made it difficult to recognise the Saviour.

But notice also that "Jesus stood on the shore". He did not appear on the boat with them, nor did He come out to them walking on the water. He remained a good distance away and in the darkness. Is the Lord giving them another lesson in trust here? He will soon be physically absent, but they will need to learn how to recognise His presence, His voice and His ways after His ascension.

Eventually, the disciples heard the "stranger's" voice—"Then Jesus saith unto them, Children, have ye any meat? They answered Him, No" (21:5). The Greek construction of the sentence expects a negative answer, translated nicely by the NET—"Children, you don't have any fish, do you?" Perhaps they wondered, how does this stranger know about our failed mission? How does He know our nets have been empty? And so the Saviour told them how their net could be filled. "Cast the net on the right side of the ship, and ye shall find" (v6). Did some of them roll their eyes or shake their heads? After all, experienced fishermen are not likely to take instructions from total strangers, particularly one standing on the shore. To their credit, they obeyed without an argument. "They cast therefore, and now they were not able to draw it for the multitude of fishes" (v6). As the great fish which swallowed Jonah, so did these fish obey their Master, swimming into the disciples' net. And John records this as the final "sign" in his Gospel, showing that the Lord Jesus is indeed sovereign over all, "the Christ, the Son of God" (20:31) Who must be believed to receive eternal life.

John's reaction to this sign is recorded in 21:7—"Therefore that disciple whom Jesus loved saith unto Peter, It is the Lord." As John was the first of the disciples to believe in the resurrection (20:8), so was he the first to recognise the Saviour on the shore. But unsurprisingly, Peter was the first to take action yet again. "Now when Simon Peter heard that it was the Lord, he girt his fisher's coat unto him, (for he was naked,) and did cast himself into the sea" (v7). Peter's actions imply that he was hurrying to where Christ was. If only he could have walked on water again, he would certainly have beat all the disciples to the shore! His reaction to the Lord's miracle is altogether different from his response in Luke 5. There he had asked the Lord to depart *from* him. Here, he hurries *to* Him.[61] Meanwhile, the other disciples were doing all they could to drag the net which the Saviour had filled to the shore.

Filling Their Stomachs

It had been a long night and they were hungry. Normally, it would take hours to clean the fish and cook them before they could have their stomachs filled. But ever the servant, Christ had already

---

[61] His eagerness to get to Christ implies that his private restoration had already occurred when the Lord appeared to him personally on resurrection day (see Luke 24:34; 1 Cor. 15:5).

thought of their need and worked to meet it. "As soon then as they were come to land, they saw a fire of coals there, and fish laid thereon, and bread" (v9). Not only was Christ Himself a welcome sight, but what He had prepared! He cared about their physical needs, and He cares about ours also.

Amazingly, He then gives them credit for the catch—"Jesus saith unto them, Bring of the fish which *ye* have now caught" (v10). How gracious the Lord was with them. Simon Peter volunteered to bring them. He "went up, and drew the net to land full of great fishes, and hundred and fifty and three: and for all there were so many, yet was not the net broken" (v11). Earlier, they were not able to haul in the net (v6), but now Peter does it himself, which tells us something of his strength. No doubt, he was energised by this appearance of the risen Lord.

The number of the fish is noted. Rather than calling for some symbolic interpretation of the number 153, John's recalling of the exact number simply authenticates the eyewitness account. John is simply saying, "I still remember how many fish were in that net. It was 153!"

And so they all sat down to eat after the Lord's call to "Come and dine. And none of the disciples durst ask Him, Who art Thou? Knowing that it was the Lord" (v12). After He filled their stomachs, John notes that this was "the third time that Jesus shewed Himself to His disciples, after that He was risen from the dead" (v14). The first two appearances were recorded in chapter 20 (vv19-25 and vv26-29). But note the word "shewed" (or "manifested") here. It is the same word used twice in 21:1, but there it is found in the active voice, here in the passive voice, meaning literally that Jesus "was manifested". John may be implying something remarkable here. It is possible that the Lord was present with His own for long periods of time after His resurrection, but was not always seen by them. On certain occasions, the veil was lifted for them to see Him. Regardless, John recorded this third manifestation, where lasting lessons were given about the disciples' future work. Their calling remained unchanged as fishers of men (vv1-14). But added to that responsibility was their call to shepherd God's sheep (vv15-17). These are still the highest calls in the world twenty centuries later.

Serviceable Lessons About Service

We end the chapter by noting some valuable lessons left by our Lord about our service for Him. First, note that *effective service requires divine life*. The previous chapter ended with the disciples believing that the Saviour was indeed risen. It is implied that they, too, believed that Jesus is the Christ, the Son of God, and by believing they received life in His name (20:31). To serve the Lord, we too, must receive divine life, which only comes through faith in the Lord Jesus Christ. We need His life, His power to serve Him effectively.

Second, observe that *effective service requires divine direction*. The seven men aboard that vessel in the Sea of Galilee caught nothing without the Saviour's guidance. In fact, the disciples never catch a single fish in the Gospel records without Jesus' instruction. He told them here to "cast the net on the right side of the ship". Unlike what occurred in Luke 5, there was no argument. They received the Lord's direction, obeyed it, and He blessed their actions. Fittingly, Christ told them in the upper room, "without Me ye can do nothing" (15:5). It's not that we can do a little *without* Christ and even more *with* Him, but that we can do nothing without Him! Rather than rushing along in our work for the Lord, how important it is to get His direction for all we do.

Finally, it might be helpful to remember that *effective service requires divine fellowship*. The Lord Jesus commanded them to "Come and dine". And He didn't simply lead them to the fish and bread and disappear from their midst. He stayed with the disciples, spending valuable moments with them, challenging them, and teaching them. They needed time with the Lord to enable effective service for Him. To all who serve our risen Saviour, let us never forget that we must be fed ourselves before we can feed others. We must have our hearts warmed by His presence before we can bring blessing to anyone else. We must see the Lord ourselves if we expect others to see the Lord in us.

We too, have an unchanged calling. It is true of every believer that we "serve the Lord Christ" (Col. 3:24). Don't let the pull of the old life distract you. Don't let the attraction of the present world entice you. Don't let the lies of the Devil discourage you. And don't let the pride of your own flesh deceive you. To effectively serve the Lord Christ, we need Him—His life, His power, His direction. For without Him, we'll always find ourselves on the wrong side of the ship.

Chapter 11

JOHN'S ENLIGHTENING EPILOGUE

All of John 21 comes as a bit of a surprise. The final words of chapter 20 sound like a fitting conclusion to John's Gospel, but John's pen went back into the ink and wrote out what is now considered to be his epilogue. And his final words are enlightening, for they answer a few questions that may have been lingering in the minds of his early readers. First, John shows that Peter's death had been prophesied by the Lord Jesus, including the manner in which he died (vv18-19). This recollection could strengthen the faith of these first-century believers. Second, John provides clarity about his own death by restating what the Saviour said to Peter. Apparently, a rumour was circulating that Christ would return before John died. John sets the record straight in this epilogue (vv22-23). Finally, John identifies himself as "the disciple whom Jesus loved" (v20), a phrase he has used repeatedly throughout his Gospel.

We will take a closer look now at John's concluding words and notice three particular relationships—the Lord and Peter, the Lord and John, and the Lord and us.

The Lord and Peter

They had just finished breakfast after their miraculous catch. The Lord had met His disciples' physical needs and now began to address the spiritual needs of Peter in particular. Jesus began with a question—"Simon, son of Jonas, lovest thou Me more than these?" (21:15). Perhaps the best way to interpret the Lord's question here is to rephrase as, "Do you love Me more than these other disciples love Me?" On the night of the Saviour's arrest, He informed them that they would all fall away because of Him. Peter had boasted, "If they [the disciples] all fall away because of You, I will never fall away!... Even if I must die with You, I will never deny You" (Matt. 26:31-35 *NET*). He was in effect saying, "I love You more than the rest of the disciples!" But Peter did fall away. He did deny his Lord. His bold claim turned out to be a big collapse. Now as he sat by the fire with some of the same men present, would Peter dare to make such a rash declaration again?

Peter answered wisely, "Yea, Lord; Thou knowest that I love Thee" (21:15). He said nothing about the other disciples, but pledged his own love for his Lord. Jesus asked him the same question three times, and Peter affirmed his love three times. This was likely meant to draw a contrast with Peter's three denials of the Lord, which also occurred by a fire (Luke 22:55ff.).

A word should be said about Peter's professed love. Much ink has been spilled on seeing a difference between the Greek words *agapao* and *phileo* here. It seems that John used these words interchangeably throughout his Gospel, so it may be wise to interpret them as being synonymous here.[62] Therefore, Peter is

---

[62] See NET Bible study notes.

not pledging a lower form of love for the Lord (i.e., *phileo* rather than *agapao*). Because the Saviour asked Peter the same question three times in the presence of the other disciples, He was helping Peter declare his love publicly. At the same time, Peter's answers demonstrated that he would not unfairly attempt to assess the love of his fellow disciples for their Lord. We should note, then, that this was **Peter's restoration**, not privately (for that likely occurred when the Saviour appeared to him on resurrection day), but publicly. Jesus was helping to re-establish the others' confidence in Peter, as he would be an early leader among the twelve.

We should also point out **Peter's responsibility**. After Peter answered the Lord's question each time, professing his love, Jesus followed up with the exhortation, "Feed my sheep." Therefore, one of the ways we prove our love for the Saviour is to feed His sheep. Perhaps the Lord Jesus even used His hands to point to the other disciples as He gave Peter this new responsibility to feed His sheep (one which they would also share). Rather than comparing himself with them, or elevating himself above them, Peter would have to put their needs above his own, as do all shepherds. This was a lesson Peter learned well, for he told the readers of his first epistle to care for God's flock, and not to act as lords over them, but to be clothed with humility (1 Pet. 5:2-5).

Notice also that the Lord said something about **Peter's release**, telling him, "'When you were young, you used to dress yourself and walk wherever you wanted, but when you are old, you will stretch out your hands, and another will dress you and carry you where you do not want to go.' (This He said to show by what kind of death he was to glorify God")" (John 21:18-19a ESV). Perhaps this was why Peter was able to sleep in prison in Acts 12. Although Herod's intention was to execute him as he had done with James, Peter was not "old" by anyone's reckoning, so he had nothing to fear.

Peter had likely been dead for nearly thirty years by the time John wrote this. Now it has been almost twenty centuries, and there is still mystery about exactly what the Lord meant by these words. Early Church Fathers like Tertullian and Eusebius state that Peter was crucified in Rome under Nero in the 60's, fulfilling the Lord's words that his hands would be "stretched out". It is difficult to know with absolute certainty. But we do know that this prophecy remained with Peter all his days, for he wrote these words about his coming release: "Knowing that shortly I must put off this my tabernacle, even as our Lord Jesus Christ hath shewed me" (2 Pet. 1:14).

After the Lord's prophecy about his death, notice *Peter's recommissioning*. "And when He had spoken this, He saith unto him, Follow Me" (John 21:19b). The present tense imperative of the verb means, "Keep on following Me". Peter was called, as he had been at the beginning, to once again follow Christ and continue following Him until the end, even if that end meant being martyred for his faith. But it is here that the narrative shifts its focus from Peter to "the disciple whom Jesus loved".

The Lord and John

"Then Peter, turning about, seeth the disciple whom Jesus loved following; which also leaned on His breast at supper, and said, Lord, which is he that betrayeth Thee?" (v20). Here we have *John's identity*. At last, the secret is out. We wondered who it could be when John first used the phrase in the upper room. John was the one who leaned upon Jesus (13:23). John was the one who returned to the scene of Christ's death (19:26). John was the one who ran with Peter to the Lord's tomb (20:2). And John was the one who noticed that it was the Lord on the shore (21:7). And just to make things crystal clear, John writes, "This is the disciple which testifieth of these things, and wrote these things" (v24). John, the author of this Gospel, is "the disciple whom Jesus loved".

But note also *John's mortality*. Peter was curious about John's future, after having his own future spelled out by the Lord. So he asked, "Lord, and what shall this man do? Jesus saith unto him, If I will that he tarry till I come, what is that to thee? Follow thou Me. Then went this saying abroad among the brethren, that that disciple should not die: yet Jesus said not unto him, He shall not die; but, If I will that he tarry till I come, what is that to thee?" (vv21-23). The Lord only meant that John could stay alive until He returned, not that he would stay alive. And quite obviously, John's mortality has been proven. Although many believe he lived into his late 80's, death claimed John, just as it has everyone else.

We also need to appreciate *John's reliability* as a witness. In the epilogue's penultimate verse, John writes, "and we know that his testimony is true" (v24). John's words are dependable because he was an eyewitness of the Saviour's life, ministry, miracles, death and resurrection. We can and should believe all he wrote about the Lord Jesus Christ.

Finally, *John's selectivity* is highlighted. He could have written so much more, but space was limited. "And there are also many other things which Jesus did, the which, if they should be written every one, I[63] suppose that even the world itself could not contain the books that should be written. Amen" (v25). Is John using hyperbole here? I believe he is being quite literal. The Psalmist wrote, "Many, O LORD my God, are Thy wonderful works which Thou hast done, and Thy thoughts which are to us-ward: they cannot be reckoned up in order unto Thee: if I would declare and speak of them, they are more than can be numbered" (Psa. 40:5). If it is impossible to record all that our omnipotent, omniscient, loving God has done for us, is it not equally impossible to count and record all that our infinite Saviour (Who is divine) did while here on earth, not only in deed but in thought? John is aware of his Gospel's limitations. He could have written so much more. But he is also aware of his Gospel's sufficiency. There is enough recorded to believe on the Lord Jesus Christ and receive eternal life through Him.

The Lord and Us

John has packed a lot into his epilogue about Peter and about himself. But as his readers and believers in the Christ about whom he wrote, let us not miss what is critical for us. We might scratch our heads about the 153 fish, about the Greek words for love, and about the Lord's prophecy concerning Peter's death. But in John's closing chapter, there is something so clear it is impossible to miss. The Saviour wants us to love Him, follow Him and take care of His people. And if this is all we learn and all we do, we will not have missed a thing.

---

[63] This is the only use of the first person singular by John in his Gospel.

Chapter 12

THE GREAT COMMISSION

Although Matthew provides us with the most detailed account, all four Gospels record the Great Commission, or at least components of it.[64] For the purposes of this chapter, we will confine our study primarily to what Matthew reports.

The People the Lord Sends

"Then the eleven disciples went away into Galilee, into a mountain where Jesus had appointed them" (Matt. 28:16). Apparently, the seven disciples who met the Lord by the Sea of Tiberias reunited with the others and arrived at the designated mountain[65] where the Saviour told them to go. Although there were others present in the Upper Room in Jerusalem when Christ appeared (Luke 24:33), Matthew mentions only "the eleven" (the original twelve minus Judas) when the Great Commission was given. But we must not restrict what the Lord said to them as if there were no application

---

[63] See Matt. 28:16-20; Mark 16:14-18; Luke 24:44-49 (esp. v47); John 20:21.

[64] Note these previous mountain experiences in Matthew (4:8; 5:1; 14:23; 15:29; 17:1; 24:3; 26:30).

for us. The Lord Jesus is still sending His people to carry out His mission.

Notice how Scripture describes those whom the Saviour sent—"And when they saw Him, they worshipped Him: but some doubted" (Matt. 28:17). The Greek word for "doubt" here *(distazo)* means a state of uncertainty or hesitation. It was not that the disciples failed to believe in the resurrection, but only that some took longer to realise it was Christ, as was the case in His previously recorded appearance (see John 21, esp. v4). Again, we can appreciate the honesty of Scripture, not portraying the Lord's followers as perfect, but recording their flaws and failures without covering up anything. These are the people the Lord sends. And if He only sent perfect people, He would not have any candidates to carry out the Great Commission.

Charles Spurgeon said, "Who is to go out of that first band of disciples? It is Peter, the rash and the headstrong. It is John, who sometimes wishes to call fire from heaven to destroy men. It is Philip, with whom the Saviour has been so long, and yet he has not known Him. It is Thomas, who must put his finger into the print of the nails, or he will not believe Him. Yet the Master says to them, 'Go... You are as good for My purpose as anybody else would be.'" As we are about to notice, it is not our supposed strengths which determine the Great Commission's success, nor will our weaknesses hinder it; therefore, the Lord sends people just like these eleven, and just like us!

------

[66] His authority is seen in Matthew 1, where He is presented as the heir to David's throne and Emmanuel, meaning "God with us." In chapter 2, He is called "King of the Jews." In chapter 3, John announces the coming of His kingdom (v2). For other examples of His authority in Matthew, see 7:28-29; 8:27; 9:6; 10:1; 11:27; 16:18-19; 21:23.

The Power the Lord Possesses

To these imperfect followers, who saw Him approaching, the Lord Jesus said, "All power is given unto Me in heaven and in earth" (Matt. 28:18). This, and this alone, would be the secret of the Great Commission's effectiveness. The Saviour has been given "all power". The word for "power" here (Greek *exousia*) means "authority", and it is not surprising to find this word in Matthew, where Christ is presented as King. Notice that the Lord says this authority was "given" unto Him. Although we see Christ's authority during His earthly ministry emphasised throughout Matthew's Gospel, it appears that the Saviour is making a larger claim here. He is claiming to have been given universal authority, "all authority", that which is "in heaven and in earth". It is precisely because He had suffered and died, completing the work His Father sent Him to do, that He has received this authority now as the risen, glorified, and soon to be enthroned Saviour (see Phil. 2:8-9; Heb. 2:9; 1 Pet. 1:21; Rev. 1:5). It would not be long before His followers would see this authority demonstrated in their midst when Christ would send the Holy Spirit and give gifts to the Church (John 16:7; Acts 2:33; Eph. 4:8-12), empowering them to carry out the Great Commission. With His universal authority as the basis for the Great Commission, He instructs them (and us) to "Go" (Matt. 28:19). We go in His power, not our own. Therefore, we can have confidence to carry out His program, even if it means meeting hostility and opposition.

The Program the Lord Announces

"Go ye therefore, and teach all nations, baptising them in the name of the Father, and of the Son, and of the Holy Ghost: Teaching them to observe all things whatsoever I have commanded you" (vv19-20a). The word for "teach" here (Greek *matheteuo*) means "to make disciples". Disciples are learners, students. And notice that disciples are made, they are not spontaneously created. It takes time and involves the work of other believers to make disciples. But foundational to the making of disciples is the preaching of the gospel, which Mark highlights in his account, recording Jesus as saying, "Go ye into all the world, and preach the gospel to every creature" (16:15). Disciples cannot be made without the message that will make them, the gospel, which Paul summarises as "Christ died for our sins... He was buried, and... He rose again the third day" (1 Cor. 15:3-4).

The Lord's program involves not only the making of these disciples, but their baptism. We should both teach what baptism means and encourage new believers to take this obedient step. And we are to baptise these new followers "in the name of the Father, and of the Son, and of the Holy Ghost". The singular noun "name" (rather than "names") underlines the unity of the three Persons in the Godhead.

Notice also that the Lord's program includes teaching these new converts "to observe all things whatsoever I [Jesus] have commanded you". It is not enough to preach the gospel to individuals and baptise them, we must teach them the whole counsel of God. Are we leaving anything out of the Great Commission? How easy it is to focus our attention on a few teachings we deem most important, while excluding vast portions of Scripture, ignoring even the fundamentals of the faith.

But we must not miss another part of the Lord's program and it involves its intended audience. The Saviour said the Great

Commission is for "all nations". The word for "nations" here (Greek *ethnos*) is the regular term for "Gentiles" in the New Testament. But to send the disciples to the Gentiles was simply to *extend* the range of their mission, not *exclude* the Jewish people from it. It is clear from Acts that the Lord's followers continued their mission to the Jews. In short, the Lord Jesus was sending out the disciples to everyone everywhere. And we can be confident still today that everyone everywhere is within the scope of the Great Commission. We can boldly go "into all the world and proclaim the gospel to the whole creation" (Mark 16:15 *ESV*).

The Presence the Lord Promises

If we obey, we are not on our own. Jesus said, "and, lo, I am with you always, even unto the end of the world" (Matt. 28:20). These words contain the fourth "all" in the Great Commission. Christ has been given *"all* authority". He wants us to make disciples of *"all* nations". He instructs us to teach them *"all* things" He has commanded. And now He promises His presence to be with us *"always"*. "Always" (Greek *pas hemera*) means literally "the whole of every day". The Lord is with us every moment of every day, not just those particular seasons when we feel close to Him. Because He is with us "always", we need not fear any opposition as we seek to carry out the Great Commission. And as He is with us, we can rejoice that we work not only *for* the Lord, but *with* Him (1 Cor. 3:9)! Therefore, let us "Go!"

> *See o'er the world wide open doors inviting:*
> *Soldiers of Christ, arise and enter in;*
> *Christians, awake! Your forces all uniting,*

Send forth the gospel, break the chains of sin.

All power is given unto Me;

All power is given unto Me;

Go ye into all the world and preach the gospel;

And lo, I am with you alway.[67]

---

[67] James McGranahan (1840-1907).

Chapter 13

THE ASCENSION

Forty days had passed since their sorrow was expelled by His appearance to them on resurrection day. In addition to "many infallible proofs" that He was indeed alive, Christ's followers received teaching about the kingdom of God. But the Lord was on a timetable. Pentecost was approaching. The time for Him to be "taken up" into heaven had arrived.

His teaching about the kingdom was certainly on the disciples' minds on the day of His ascension. They asked Him, "Lord, wilt Thou at this time restore again the kingdom to Israel?" (Acts 1:6). Maybe they reasoned that the time had finally come. Christ, the prophesied Son of Man, was about to "sit on His glorious throne" (Matt. 19:28) and establish the Messianic Kingdom on earth. They were right about the throne, but wrong about its location. The fulfilment of Psalm 110:1 was mere moments away, when the Father would address His Son upon His arrival into heaven, "Sit Thou at my right hand."[68]

---

[68] Ten days later, Peter stated in his sermon that Psalm 110:1 had now found its fulfilment in the ascension of the Lord Jesus Christ (Acts 2:34-36).

The Vicinity of His Ascension

Luke tells us that the ascension took place from *the Mount of Olives* in the vicinity of Bethany, just outside Jerusalem (see Luke 24:50 *CSB*; Acts 1:12). This location would have future significance. The disciples were told after Christ ascended, "This same Jesus, which is taken up from you into heaven, shall so come in like manner as ye have seen Him go into heaven" (Acts 1:11). That coming will occur when the Lord sets up His Messianic kingdom on earth. "And His feet shall stand in that day upon *the mount of Olives*, which is before Jerusalem" (Zech. 14:4).

The Validity of His Ascension

Although Luke is the only Gospel writer to record the ascension narrative in any detail, He is not the only writer to mention it. Mark's longer ending reports the ascension (16:19). Peter refers to it in his sermon on the Day of Pentecost (Acts 2:34-36) as well as in his first epistle (1 Pet. 3:22). John includes a reference to it in his Gospel when the Lord appeared to Mary Magdalene (20:17). Additionally, both Paul (e.g., Eph. 1:20-23; 4:8-10; 1 Tim. 3:16) and the writer to the Hebrews (e.g., 9:24: 10:12) acknowledge the reality and significance of the ascension. Of course, all eleven disciples were also eyewitnesses to the Lord's ascension and could be consulted in the days which followed. Just as there were many who saw the risen and glorified Lord, so were there witnesses to His glorious ascension.

The Visibility of His Ascension

Christ's followers were not all receiving some simultaneous vision or having an ecstatic experience. They watched the Lord Jesus ascend with their own eyes. Luke notes that they *"beheld"* the event and that "a cloud received Him out of their *sight*" (Acts 1:9). They "*looked* stedfastly toward heaven as He went up" (v10) and were "*gazing* up into heaven" (v11). They saw with clear vision the ascension of the Saviour. Notice also that He did not suddenly vanish, leaving the world one moment and arriving in heaven the next. It appears that some of His post-resurrection occurrences ended with Him vanishing (see, e.g., Luke 24:31), but this was radically different. And the ascension is the only thing that explains the sudden end of His post-resurrection appearances.

So, the disciples watched as He left them. They not only saw Him, they saw a cloud—"while they beheld, He was taken up; and a cloud received Him out of their sight" (Acts 1:9). Perhaps it was the *Shekinah*, the visible representation of the pleasure and presence of God, the cloud Moses encountered on Sinai, the cloud which guided Israel in the wilderness, the cloud that lay over the tabernacle and filled the temple, the cloud which Ezekiel saw departing over the east gate, the cloud that overshadowed Moses and Elijah at Christ's transfiguration and out of which could be heard the Father's voice, "This is my beloved Son."[69] Now the cloud receives Him approvingly and the disciples could see Him no longer. But His ascension was visible. They saw it all.

The Vindication of His Ascension

The ascension validates the claims of Christ. We have already pointed out that the cloud received Him, yet another indication of heaven's approval of His finished work. But note Luke's use

---

[69] R. Kent Hughes, *Luke Volume 2: That You May Know the Truth* (Wheaton, IL: Crossway, 1998), 423.

of the passive voice in the two verbs translated "was taken up" (Acts 1:2,9). This seems to imply the action of the Father, Who took Him up, thus vindicating Christ's claims. Remember also that the ascension fulfils the Lord's words spoken to the members of the Jewish council, "Hereafter shall the Son of man sit on the right hand of the power of God" (Luke 22:69). As He took His seat on His heavenly throne, His claim to be the Son of God (see v70) was confirmed once more. And we must not rush past the significance of where the risen Lord is presently seated. His ascension was not just a departure but an arrival, an arrival to the most exalted position in the universe—Christ has "gone into heaven, and is on the right hand of God; angels and authorities and powers being made subject unto Him" (1 Pet. 3:22). Paul agreed with Peter— God "raised Him from the dead, and set Him at His own right hand in the heavenly places, Far above all principality, and power, and might, and dominion, and every name that is named, not only in this world, but also in that which is to come: And hath put all things under His feet, and gave Him to be the Head over all things to the church, Which is His body, the fullness of Him that filleth all in all" (Eph. 1:20-23).

The One Who was dishonoured on earth, being spit upon, scourged, stripped, struck and spiked to a tree, has been greatly honoured in heaven, completing the journey which took Him *All the Way to Glory*. "God has given the highest place to the Man to whom earth gave the lowest place. He is not just exalted but highly exalted, not only above all but far above all. God could not honour His Son in any higher measure."[70]

---

[70] A. J. Higgins, *The Ascension of Our Lord Jesus Christ* (Truth & Tidings, January 2023, Vol 74, No 1).

To Him whom men despise and slight,
To Him be glory given;
The crown is His, and His by right
The highest place in heaven.[71]

Fitting Responses to the Ascension

When our Saviour ascended, it is helpful to notice that His followers responded in at least four ways. *First*, Luke says "they worshipped Him" (24:52). And so should we. Anyone elevated to such a high place is worthy (and alone worthy) of our worship.

Second, Luke tells us that the disciples "returned to Jerusalem with great joy" (v52).[72] When He told them He was leaving them before He died, they were filled with sorrow. But now that the Lord had died, was risen, and ascended, they rejoiced once He departed! One of the reasons for their joy was not only what the ascension meant for Christ, but what it would mean for them. He had told them that the Holy Spirit could not come until He had departed (John 16:7). Now that He had departed, they would know that very shortly they would be "endued with power from on high" (Luke 24:49).

A *third* response by the Lord's disciples was their arrival "in the temple, praising and blessing God" (v53). Note that the disciples are "blessing" God. This is the third use of the word in four verses. Christ "blessed" them first (24:50,51), thus guaranteeing the success

---

[71] Thomas Kelly (1769-1855).

[72] Both Christ's birth and ascension produce joy in the Gospel of Luke (2:10; 24:52).

of their mission. Now they bless God, being witnesses of the Lord's ascension. Thus, Luke ends his Gospel in the same place where it began—in Jerusalem in the temple (1:9); and he began with a man in the temple who could not bless (1:22) but ends with a group of men in the temple who could bless. And they had great reasons to do so!

Luke's account in Acts gives us one more response to the ascension. *Fourth,* and quite obviously, the *eye*witnesses became effective witnesses. At first, the disciples' attention needed some refocusing. Two men in white apparel (angels) appeared to them as they stared into the skies with this message: "Ye men of Galilee, why stand ye gazing up into heaven?" (Acts 1:11). The implication is that they needed to get to work. They had seen the ascension, but it was over now. The Lord did not need stargazers, but witnesses. And they did get to work. Shortly thereafter, on the Day of Pentecost, they received the Holy Spirit and became "witnesses unto [Christ] both in Jerusalem, and in all Judaea, and in Samaria, and unto the uttermost parts of the earth" (Acts 1:8). How thankful we ought to be that this was one of their responses to the reality of the ascended Lord, or we would never have heard the gospel ourselves.

Worship, joy, praise, witnessing—all appropriate responses to the Lord's ascension. He is worthy. How are we responding?

Chapter 14

WHAT THE LORD'S ASCENSION MEANS FOR HIS PEOPLE

Before His death, the Saviour said to His own in the Upper Room, "it is to your advantage that I am going away" (John 16:7 *NET*). It made no sense to them at the time and even caused them sorrow to think that He would leave them. Why could He not remain with them here on earth, even after His death and resurrection? How could His departure be advantageous to them? In this closing chapter, we will explore why that was indeed the cas—what the Lord's ascension means for His people.

He Took Humanity Through the Heavens

The writer to the Hebrews says that "Jesus, the Son of God" "has passed through the heavens" (4:14 *ESV, JND*). In this particular text, "the heavens" (Greek *ouranos*) were the veil which He passed through. Note that His humanity is being emphasised ("Jesus"). Jesus, the Son of God, has taken humanity through the heavens. Elsewhere, the similar word "heavenlies" (Greek *epouranios*) is used to refer to Satan's realm (Eph. 6:12 *JND*). Indeed, he is the "prince of the power of the air" (2:2). Christ took humanity into enemy territory as He ascended, passing through Satan's headquarters without being hindered or harmed. By His victorious death, He had already "disarmed the rulers and authorities and put them to open shame" (Col. 2:15 *ESV*). And so He ascended in His glorious humanity, unscathed through the heavens.

This was the first time a human being passed through this realm.[73] But it will not be the last. "For the Lord Himself shall descend from heaven…the dead in Christ shall rise first: Then we which are alive and remain shall be caught up together with them in the clouds, to meet the Lord in the air" (1 Thess. 4:16-17). We will be raptured into "the air", enemy territory. The Lord will bring us through the same realm through which He has passed, and we will be unharmed also!

He Took Humanity Into Heaven

Christ not only took humanity *through* the heavens but *into* heaven. Peter tells us that He has "gone into heaven" (1 Pet. 3:22). There is a real Man living in heaven still today, our Lord Jesus Christ. In this way too, He is our forerunner. His presence there in a glorified body ensures our presence there in glorified bodies also. Where the Risen Head is (heaven), so will the members of His body be (Eph. 1:20-23).

He Sent the Holy Spirit From Heaven

If He had remained physically on earth after His resurrection, He could not have been with every follower. But the sending of the

---

[73] It does not appear that this was the case for Enoch and Elijah.

Holy Spirit would enable all His followers to enjoy His presence. And so the Saviour ascended to His heavenly throne to send the Holy Spirit, thus fulfilling His promise, "if I depart, I will send Him unto you" (John 16:7). Peter tells us that it was from His exalted position in heaven that He sent the Spirit. "Therefore being by the right hand of God exalted, and having received of the Father the promise of the Holy Ghost, He hath shed forth [i.e., poured out] this, which ye now see and hear" (Acts 2:33). And the ascended Lord has given us power to witness (1:8) by His Spirit and power to serve, being equipped with gifts of the Spirit (Eph. 4:8-12). Thank God that Christ ascended *into* heaven and sent the Holy Spirit *from* heaven.

He Became Our Advocate in Heaven

John writes, "My little children, these things write I unto you, that ye sin not. And if any man sin, we have an Advocate with the Father, Jesus Christ the Righteous" (1 Jn. 2:1). First, notice that God's desire for His people is that we "sin not". But what happens when we do sin? Do we lose our salvation? Absolutely not! John notes that God is still our "Father". And he does not say, "if any man sin, we have a Saviour". He is writing to people already saved. When believers sin, we need (and have) an Advocate. The word "Advocate" (Greek *parakletos*) means "one called to another's side". The implication is that, when we sin, we need someone to come to our side, to represent us, and to plead our cause. That is exactly what the Lord Jesus does for His people as He is in heaven.

Christ is able to represent us because He knows the subject—sin! Although He is the sinless One, He knows more than anyone the seriousness of sin, the damage it causes, the rebellion it demonstrates, and the pain He Himself endured because of it. There is no one Who understands the subject better, not because He sinned Himself (an impossibility), but because He "bore our sins in His body on the tree" (1 Pet. 2:24 *ESV*).

Our Advocate is not only fit to represent us because of what He knows, but because of Who He is. He is fit to stand for us because of His humanity (John uses His human name "Jesus" here). He is fit to stand before the Father because He is without sin (John also calls Him "the Righteous"). When we sin, our Advocate stands for us in heaven before the Father and pleads the merits of His own sacrifice for sin on our behalf. We have an *accuser*, Satan, who can say, "Sin was committed!" But we thankfully have an *Advocate*, Jesus Christ, who can say, "My blood was shed!"

He Became Our High Priest in Heaven

Christ's work as our Advocate is part of His high priestly ministry in heaven. The writer to the Hebrews said, "We have such an High Priest, Who is set on the right hand of the throne of the Majesty in the heavens; A minister of the sanctuary, and of the true tabernacle, which the Lord pitched, and not man" (Heb. 8:1,2). If Christ had remained on earth, He could not be a priest here (v4), since He was not from the line of the Levites, but Judah. But the Psalmist already prophesied that the Levitical priesthood would come to an end. Indeed, it must! After the order of Melchizedek, a priest would arrive, David's Lord, and inaugurate that priesthood when He sat at God's right hand. That Priest was none other than our ascended Lord Jesus Christ. The first hint that the Levitical priesthood had terminated was the tearing of the temple veil when the Lord Jesus died (Matt. 27:51). Now risen and ascended as our Great High

Priest, "He always lives to make intercession" (Heb. 7:25 *ESV*) for us. Because Christ ascended, He became our High Priest in heaven. "Seeing then that we have a great High Priest, that is passed into the heavens, Jesus the Son of God, let us hold fast our profession. For we have not an High Priest which cannot be touched with the feeling of our infirmities; but was in all points tempted like as we are, yet without sin. Let us therefore come boldly unto the throne of grace, that we may obtain mercy, and find grace to help in time of need" (Heb. 4:14-16).

He Has Prepared Our Home in Heaven

The Saviour said in John 14, "There are many rooms in My Father's house… I am going away to prepare a place for you" (vv2,3 *ISV*). The Carpenter from Nazareth, Who likely built homes on earth, has prepared a heavenly home for you and me. This does not mean that every time a soul is saved, Christ adds another dwelling place to the Father's house. When the Lord Jesus told His disciples He was going away, He spoke of His departure as including His death, resurrection and ascension. Thus, the way He prepared our home in heaven was by His death, resurrection and ascension. And now exalted in glory, He is there doing so much for His people. His "going away" (John 16:7) has indeed been to our advantage! Thank God for our ascended Saviour and Lord!

> *Lamb of God! Thou now art seated*
> *High upon Thy Father's throne;*
> *All Thy gracious work completed,*
> *All Thy mighty vict'ry won.*
> *Every knee in heaven is bending*

To the Lamb for sinners slain;
Every voice and harp is swelling,
"Worthy is the Lamb to reign."

Lord, in all Thy pow'r and glory,
Still Thy thoughts and eyes are here,
Watching o'er Thy ransomed people
To Thy gracious heart so dear.
Thou for us art interceding,
Everlasting is Thy love;
And a blessed rest preparing
In the Father's house above.[74]

---

[74] James G. Deck (1802-1884).

Appendix

Possible Order of Events Between the Lord's Death & Resurrection[75]	Matthew	Mark	Luke	John
Lord's Burial	27:57-61	15:42-47	23:50-56	19:38-42
Roman Guard and Seal	27:62-66			
Women Arrive at the Tomb (with Mary Magdalene Leading)	28:1	16:1-2	24:1	20:1
Mary Magdalene Departs with Inaccurate Report Given to Peter and John				20:2

---

[75] Not included in this chart are two additional events which are difficult to pinpoint in their timing—the Lord's appearance to the 500 and James (see 1 Cor. 15:6-7).

Remaining Women Receive Angelic Report of Christ's Resurrection	28:2-7	16:3-7	24:2-7	
Remaining Women Depart to Report the News	28:8	16:8	24:8-11	
Peter and John Arrive at the Tomb (with Mary Magdalene Trailing)			24:12a	20:3-9
Peter and John Depart the Tomb			24:12b	20:10
Lord's Appearance to Mary Magdalene		16:9-11		20:11-18
Lord's Appearance to the Women Leaving the Tomb	28:9-10			
Report of the Guard	28:11-15			

Lord's Appearance to Peter on His Way Home (see also 1 Cor. 15:5)			24:34	
Lord's Appearance to the Two Emmaus Travellers		16:12-13	24:13-32	
Lord's Appearance in the Upper Room to the Disciples (without Thomas)			24:33-49	20:19-25
Lord's Appearance in the Upper Room to the Disciples (with Thomas)				20:26-29
Lord's Appearance in Galilee to Seven Disciples				21:1-25
Great Commission	28:16-20	16:14-18		
Lord's Ascension (see also Acts 1:1-11)		16:19-20	24:50-53	

MORE FROM THE AUTHOR

ALL THE WAY TO CALVARY
MEDITATIONS ON THE CROSS

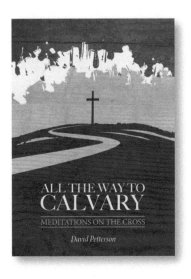

Calvary. The word is found only once in Scripture. But, in our meditations, Calvary is the most frequented place on earth. This book traces Jesus' pathway, from the predictions He made of His passion to the yielding up of His life while hanging on the tree. It is the author's prayer that this book will prompt deeper worship and greater devotion. Any book written about Christ's cross will have its limitations, and this brief work is certainly no exception. But it is the author's prayer that these twenty short chapters will prompt us to deeper worship and greater devotion to the One who went all the way to Calvary for us.

9781914273261 • RRP: £8.99

Find out more online: www.ritchiechristianmedia.co.uk

Chapter 1

PASSION PREDICTIONS

Calvary. The word is found only once in Scripture,[1] and most of us have never visited the actual site. But it is undoubtedly the most frequented place on earth in our meditations. Hardly a day passes without thinking about our Saviour and "the place, which is called Calvary," where "they crucified Him" (Luke 23:33).

No matter how many times we read the Gospel narratives describing the final days of our Lord Jesus Christ, His willingness to go all the way to Calvary astounds us again. That Calvary and His approaching death there were constantly on His mind is evident from the many predictions He made. Some of these were clearly stated, others given in pictures, and one expressed in the form of a heartbreaking parable.

Plain Predictions

Our Saviour plainly foretold *the place of His death*. He informed His disciples, "Behold, we go up to Jerusalem; and the Son of man shall be betrayed unto the chief priests and unto the scribes, and they shall condemn Him to death" (Matt. 20:18).[2] He told them Jerusalem

---

[1]"Calvary" is from the late Latin *calvaria* ("skull") translation of the Greek *Kranion*. "*Golgotha*" is the Aramaic name ("place of a skull").

[2]All Scripture quotations in this book are from the KJV unless otherwise noted.

would be the place of His death, the very location where decades previously His parents had presented Him to the Lord with the proper accompanying sacrifice (Luke 2:22-24). In Jerusalem again, He would present Himself to the Lord, not with an accompanying sacrifice, but as a sacrifice, offered up to take our sins away.

He also spoke about *the perpetrators of His death*. The Jewish leaders had been plotting His death for some time, and our Lord named them in His predictions (elders, chief priests, scribes). But not having power themselves to carry out the death penalty, they were forced to take their case against Jesus to the Roman authorities. Pontius Pilate, the governor of the Roman province of Judaea, eventually granted them permission to crucify Him (John 19:16). Our Saviour predicted Gentile involvement in His death – "He shall be delivered unto the Gentiles … and they shall scourge Him, and put Him to death" (Luke 18:32-33). Note the accuracy of Christ's words. The Jewish authorities *condemned* Him to death. The Roman authorities *put* Him to death. But there was another perpetrator. The Lord stated that the Son of Man would be "betrayed into the hands of men" (Matt. 17:22), an early hint (see also John 6:70-71) that one of the Twelve would be involved in a treacherous plot against Him.

Unsurprisingly, the omniscient Lord foretold *the mode of His death*. "And they shall condemn Him to death, and shall deliver Him to the Gentiles to mock, and to scourge, and to crucify Him" (Matt. 20:18-19). Given the horrific nature of suffering and death by crucifixion, one wonders if there was a perceptible trembling in His voice as He spoke those words, "to crucify Him."

But Christ also predicted *His own role in His death*. Describing Himself as "the good shepherd" that gives His life for the sheep, our Lord added, "I lay down My life, that I might take it again. No man taketh it from

Me, but I lay it down of Myself. I have power to lay it down, and I have power to take it again" (John 10:11,17-18). The Lord Jesus was the only person who had the authority to lay down His life. Rather than simply recording passively, "And Jesus died," all four Gospel writers are careful to describe the actual death of Christ as something He Himself accomplished (Matt. 27:50; Mark 15:37; Luke 23:46; John 19:30).

The disciples failed to comprehend the many plain predictions Christ had given in relation to His death (e.g., Mark 9:32). His clear announcements would not make sense until after His resurrection.

Pictorial Predictions

The Lord Jesus not only foretold His death with carefully worded sentences, but also with memorable metaphors. For one, He spoke of His death as *an exodus*. On the Mount of Transfiguration, "there talked with Him two men, who were Moses and Elias [i.e., Elijah]: who appeared in glory, and spake of His decease which He should accomplish at Jerusalem" (Luke 9:30-31). The word "decease" is a translation of the Greek word *exodus*, meaning "departure." As Peter, James and John listened in wonder, perhaps their thoughts led them to consider another exodus. Moses had guided their nation in an exodus from bondage to Pharaoh in Egypt. Elijah led an exodus of sorts in bringing the nation out of bondage to false gods. Soon it would become clear to them that the Messiah they had embraced would lead the greatest exodus of all from the heaviest bondage of all for the greatest number of all. Christ came to deliver a world in bondage to sin, Satan and death.

Our Saviour also spoke of His death *as a ransom* in a response to James and John's request for honour in His coming kingdom. "The Son of man came not to be ministered unto, but to minister, and to give His life a ransom for many" (Matt. 20:28). His death as an exodus focuses on a release from bondage. His death as a ransom focuses on how that release would be effected. Christ would give His precious life as a ransom payment necessary to free us from bondage to sin. James and John (and their mother) had it all wrong. Self-sacrifice characterises those who will be great in His coming kingdom.

His death *as a planting* is yet another of Christ's memorable metaphoric predictions. Just days before His lifeless body would be placed in a tomb, bringing bewilderment and immeasurable grief to His followers, the Lord said, "Unless a kernel of wheat falls into the ground and dies, it remains by itself alone. But if it dies, it produces much grain" (John 12:24 *NET*). Ironically, the Pharisees had just said that "the world is gone after Him" (v19). Even the Greeks wanted to see Him (vv20-21). But Christ spoke of Himself as being buried in the earth, out of sight, like a kernel of wheat. Yet such a planting was most necessary if there was to be a harvest to follow. How many grains have come from that one seed! Thank God we are a part of such a bountiful harvest.

In striking contrast to His being planted in the ground, the Lord spoke on the same occasion of His death *as a lifting up*. "And I, when I am lifted up from the earth, will draw all people to Myself. (Now He said this to indicate clearly what kind of death He was going to die")　(John 12:32-33 *NET*). This is the third time in John's Gospel that we find this metaphor, a clear indication of His death on a cross. In John 8:28, He foretold that His lifting up would lead some to recognize Him ("When ye have lifted up the Son of man, then shall ye know that I am He"). Here in John 12, His lifting up would lead the world not just to recognize Him, but to come to Him, as if drawn by a spiritual magnet ("I … will draw all people to Myself"). In John 3, the result of coming to Him is described to Nicodemus and all those who have placed their faith in Christ – "even so must the Son of Man be lifted up: That whosoever believeth in Him should not perish, but have eternal life" (vv14-15).

Chronologically, the last of the Lord's metaphoric predictions of His death came when He sat down at the table with His disciples and instituted the Lord's Supper. Taking bread, He said, "This is My body which is given for you ... Likewise also the cup after supper, saying, This cup is the new testament in My blood, which is shed for you" (Luke 22:19-20). Quite evidently, He spoke of His death *as a sacrifice*. He was just hours away from giving His all for us. Don't overlook those precious words stated twice – "for you."

Parabolic Prediction

In Matthew 21, the Lord gave two vineyard parables, the first (vv28-32) foretelling the rejection of the Father by Israel's leaders. In the second (vv33-41), He predicts their rejection and killing of the Son, "the heir" (v38), who had been sent to receive the fruit that the vineyard owner expected. Rather than receiving and honouring the son, the tenants of the vineyard cast him out and kill him (v39) in the hope that the inheritance might become theirs. But rather than the tenants receiving the inheritance, the owner sends judgment for their wicked actions. The Lord then quoted Psalm 118:22-23, explaining that He was the rejected Son and the religious leaders of Israel were the tenants. Interestingly, although the Lord's disciples often failed to comprehend His passion predictions, Israel's leaders didn't miss it here – "And when the chief priests and Pharisees had heard His parables, they perceived that He spake of them" (Matt. 21:45).

We have only scratched the surface of our Saviour's passion predictions. Remarkably, the Apostle John tells us, "Jesus therefore, knowing all things that should come upon Him, went forth" (John 18:4).

In the pages to follow, we will attempt with great reverence to study Christ's sacred path to the cross, moving from prediction to fulfillment. As we do, may we pause often to marvel and worship the One whose steps took Him all the way to Calvary.

> *To Calvary, Lord, in spirit now*
> *Our weary souls repair,*
> *To dwell upon Thy dying love,*
> *And taste its sweetness there.*[3]

---

[3]Sir Edward Denny (1796-1889)

Clancy Goes To France

The Travel Memoirs of a Single Mum's 3,000 Mile Road Trip with her Young Daughter in a Classic Car

All profits from this book are to be donated to the MS Society UK in support of their research and awareness of the disease.

A CIP catalogue record of this book is available from the British Library.

ISBN 978-0-9932865-0-6

www.livinglavidalola.com

To Dad

This book would not have been possible without your support and
the inspiration you continue to share.

Thank You

Emma-Kate and Lolly

A Note From The Author

Firstly, before you start reading this book I would like to thank you for your purchase – you have just helped support the fight to beat Multiple Sclerosis (MS).

For most of my life my father has suffered with MS – when I was six years of age, things changed at home when he was first diagnosed. Despite this, he has enjoyed many trips to France in his beloved Peugeots – that is, until recently as his health no longer allows it.

The journey that this book takes you on – the initial challenge of the road trip in our old Peugeot and now writing the book – is a way for me to support the MS Society and it allows my father to see the trip through my eyes.

I am pleased to be able to promote awareness of MS through donations from the sales of the book and other fundraising activities on an ongoing basis.

About MS

- Multiple sclerosis (MS) is a neurological condition which affects around 100,000 people in the UK.
- Most people are diagnosed between the ages of 20-40, but it can affect younger and older people too.
- Roughly three times as many women have MS as men.
- MS is complex, and has many symptoms. Most people won't experience them all, certainly not at the same time.
- Symptoms might include fatigue, vision problems and difficulties with walking, but MS is different for everyone.
- There are lots of options for treating and managing MS. These include drug treatments, exercise and physiotherapy, diet and alternative therapies.
- We currently don't know what causes MS and there is no known cure.

About the MS Society

- The MS Society is the UK's leading MS charity. Since 1953, it has been providing information and support, funding research and fighting for change.
- It is a democratic organisation: one member, one vote.
- The Society funds research, gives grants, campaigns for change, provides information and support, invests in MS specialists and lends a listening ear to those who need it.

Approximately 300 local voluntary branches provide support and information for people who need it.

Every branch is different, but services they offer include:

- emotional and practical support
- financial help
- information
- events

- social events
- MS support groups

They also raise millions of pounds every year to help people affected by MS.

Above all, they bring people affected by MS together in communities around the UK.

www.mssociety.org.uk : Helpline 0808 800 8000

Registered charity nos 1139257 / SC041990. Registered as a limited company in England and Wales 07451571

Acknowledgements

Many thanks to Peugeot UK, Al Fresco Holidays, Siblu and Michelin for your support in this challenge to cover 3,000 miles in our old Peugeot 504, Clancy.

Thank you to Annette at Casa Annette in Cortelazor, Spain. We didn't quite make it to you but appreciate your kind offer and support throughout the challenge.

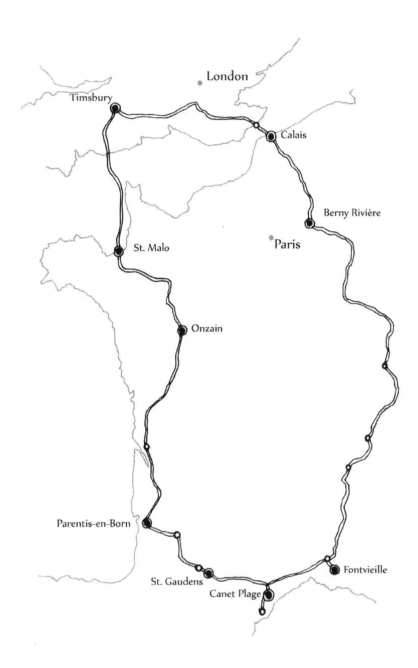

London

Timsbury

Calais

Berny Rivière

St. Malo

Paris

Onzain

Parentis-en-Born

St. Gaudens

Fontvieille

Canet Plage

Contents

Appendices

Wakey Wakey Mummy!

The delicate melody of dawn birdsong floats through the window on a gentle summer breeze, breaking the silence and stirring my senses from a dream filled sleep. All remains peaceful until –

"MUMMY, we're going to Francey in Clancy today!"

Lola bounces on the bed before she launches into her rendition of our little song:

"We're going to Francey,
We're going in Clancy,
We're going to Francey in Clancy!"

At three years old, Lola is a bundle of innocence and excitement all wrapped up in a happy little package. She is turning four while we are away and my plan is to make sure she has a wonderful time. She will have been on the road with me for twenty-five days when the day comes around and well deserving of a special day.

Lying here I ponder how today has come around so quickly. It has been six months since I originally came up with the idea of a long road trip for charity in one of my dad's cars and time has flown past. All of the careful planning is just about to be tested. I know that the trip is unlikely to go past without a hitch or changes to the itinerary but that is the whole point – I want to make the most of the time with Lola, to roll with the punches and to embrace any obstacles that challenge me. Am I scared? Well yes, I am a little, but I'm on autopilot. Today I have to be in Portsmouth at six o'clock in the evening, ready to head off on our adventure, and I have no time to think about being scared. The only thing left to do is get on with it.

Over the course of the next month we are taking on a challenge with Clancy, a forty-year-old Peugeot which has become part of our family. As much as I would love it to be a holiday, there is no getting away from the fact that it is far from it – my commitment to the MS Society and my father means that there will be little time to relax. With a goal to cover 3,000 miles on the lesser known roads of continental Europe, I have to be switched on at all times, and the responsibility of travelling safely with my three-year-old daughter will never be far from my mind.

Excitement is not at the forefront of my emotions. I am certainly not jumping out of bed with joy or enthusiasm – I have a head full of concerns which are holding me back from doing so. The anxiety manifests itself in a queasy feeling. How can this have come around so quickly?

Lola comes back into my room and jolts me out of my train of thought, bouncing around excitedly.

"Come on, mummy. We have to go to see Grampy!"

Well, Lola, not until midday but yes, I should probably get out of bed.

We're heading over to dad's for lunch before departing this afternoon. My paperwork is all up together, with copies of everything to be left with dad. As well as life and travel insurance, there are permission letters translated into multiple languages from the Multiple Sclerosis (MS) Society which explain why I am travelling alone with a child. Security measures are high these days and I will get stopped and questioned at the ports, but I don't mind because I understand the need to protect children.

All that is left to do is fix the toll tag from Sanef to the windscreen. It is not my plan to take the *autoroute* during my time away but I am aware that circumstances may be such that there is no choice. Having this tag means that we can go through the toll booths without having to stop to pay, and since I get billed in the month following, this helps with my budgeting too. I don't have a GPS or SatNav, so I'm driving on my wits and using traditional maps with my own route cards – it's all part of the experience for me and I don't want the fun removed by modern technology.

Clancy is outside, full service complete, new Michelin tyres fitted ready to be worn in and a boot which not only will contain our luggage but also a toolkit and spares just in case; it's one of the great things about taking an old car on a road trip, any mechanic worth their salt will be able to fix an old diesel engine, even in rural France! I'm not concerned about the car one bit. Clancy's history precedes him at 1 million km and counting, and I have no reason to think he's going to stumble now.

Lola is still bouncing. She's been to France together with Clancy and me earlier this year when we took a little tester trip to Brittany and she loved it. I think she has visions of being on the ferry forever, something which would make her very happy because she loves being on the water. She has inherited my love of travel, cars and a natural curiosity to learn about everything around her, and I think that makes me a lucky mum.

On that last trip we were introduced to the best hot chocolate we have ever had in Carantec, just a few minutes from the port of Roscoff. We had arrived early in the morning and driven down through St Pol de Leon to our campsite, and upon arrival it was fairly obvious we were too early. It was around nine in the morning, so we gave the representative our phone number to let us know when our cabin would be ready, before setting off to explore. It was a perfect example of a saying my dad has which may sound a little strange –

"You know you're in France as soon as you get off the ferry."

Here we were, fifteen minutes from the port, the ferry still visible from our vantage point on Carantec beach, yet we were unmistakably in France. A few locals were walking their children to school and fishermen were bobbing up and down in their little boats. Despite it being an overcast morning, I immediately felt the stress drain from my body and felt a few pounds lighter. The motion of the waves captivated me, and the houses perched high above on the cliffs overlooking the bay stirred an element of envy in me. I felt I would never tire of the view. Lola played happily in the damp sand which had yet to shake the coolness of the night. With the first batch of French sand successfully transferred from between her toes to Clancy's floor, we made our second attempt to find something open in the village square. My goodness, I'm glad we did.

Ask me what my idea of heaven is and I may well tell you fresh bread and good coffee – so you see, in Carantec I found a little piece

3

of heaven.

The village square was small but perfectly formed, with a church, a small shop and an eye-catching *Salon du Thé* with a red and gold sign. It was only when we entered and I was greeted by a display of hand-made chocolates that I understood the true beauty of this place. I turned to my right to see a wall of bread and patisserie before I spotted the coffee machine. Somewhat overwhelmed, I chose a simple croissant and Lola a *pain au raisin*. Coffee and hot chocolate were our drinks of choice. We sat at the end of the counter on soft red velvet seats and awaited our breakfast. It came in just a couple of moments and was placed on the dark solid wooden table in front of us.

"But mummy, it's milk – there's no chocolate!"

I looked at her cup, almost the size of her head and yes, it looked like steamed milk. I decided to investigate further before asking our host. Surely my French was not that bad – *chocolate chaud* was the simplest and most descriptive way I could think to make our request. As I stirred the milk, I felt a foreign body in the bottom of the cup. My mission now was to rescue it from its milky grave. I pulled it to safety only to find that it was a large chunk of the chocolate that I had seen on our arrival, and with that I apologised to it and sent it to milky heaven, allowing it to dissolve until all that was left was a rich, luscious hot chocolate.

My coffee now seemed insignificant and was soon a distant memory. Lola's small belly only able to accommodate half of her drink and even less of her *pain au raisin* meant I had a croissant and her delightful pastry to dunk in the hot chocolate of the century.

It is with the pleasant memory of our morning arrival in Brittany last May that I finally agree to Lola's persistent begging me to get out of bed. Perhaps I'm feeling a little better about things now having recounted that morning – it's time to get ready.

These thoughts flow into other memories of that short trip as I pack the car and check our paperwork one last time. I'm starting to get a little more excited. I can picture Lola marching off in front of me on the ferry in search of snacks and shops but not before she has tested the lifts and surveyed the children's area. She is very confident and authoritative and I have to smile as I remember her leading the way, long brown hair swinging behind her with a glance over the shoulder, saying "come on, mum." Yes, I'm starting to feel better about things now. This is the reason for the whole trip, enjoying the simple things in life and appreciating our loved ones.

2

Dad

The preparation is almost complete. Lola is strapped in, I'm wondering if I've forgotten anything and it's time to go. Driving to dad's gives me the opportunity to consider my surroundings. The views across to the Mendip Hills today are clear and beautiful and as I descend to my childhood home I take a moment to appreciate where we are. We are only a few miles from the much-visited City of Bath but whilst many make the trip to see the stunning Roman Baths and architecture that we take for granted, few make the trip further south and go past the comfort of the guided tour.

Here we are blessed with the rich history of the Somerset Coalfields and whilst no longer home to working mines, the miners' cottages which could tell a thousand tales remain in their neat rows in villages throughout the region. In stark contrast to the beautiful sandy-toned grandeur of many of Bath's landmarks, our villages offer a glimpse back in time through the traditional stone terraces. We have a local museum in Radstock which harnesses this history beautifully – I have taken Lola there several times as it is part of my family history. One grandparent was a miner and another hauled coal for many years, at first with a wagon and horse and later with a fleet of trucks. Whilst the slag heaps that remain on the horizon may appear as an eyesore to those who don't know, to us it is a reminder of the past.

I refer to this now because although we are heading off to explore the continent, the journey and the belief of making the most of each day start at home.

This home is also the one where at thirty-nine years old my father was diagnosed with Multiple Sclerosis. It was coincidentally around the same time that Clancy was being manufactured in Melbourne, Australia, although he didn't touch his wheels down on British soil until much more recently. I was just six years old but I have memories of life changing somewhat. My father was forced into early retirement but it was also the point where his love affair with Peugeot started to blossom.

Dad's first Peugeot was a 504 estate which was bought when I was born. There was not enough room in the Daimler Sovereign with the existence of my three older siblings but did dad think the Peugeot was a downgrade from the Daimler? Not at all – in fact, quite the opposite.

He had first driven a Peugeot while helping a local Saab dealer move a part-exchange vehicle. When he drove the Peugeot, he felt the smooth gear change and comfort so outshone the Daimler that he decided that when it came to buying a car for a family of six, it was going to be a 504 estate. This was the start of what has been a large part of my life and the reason for my trip.

My father loves his Peugeots and owns six classic cars to this day. In the days when his health was better, he enjoyed trips over to France, exploring the back roads and getting lost in the scenery. He can no longer do this.

Last year dad broke the news that on top of the MS he had been diagnosed with Prostate Cancer. Of course this was a huge shock but I don't think the reality set in immediately. That reality hit me six months ago and is what started this idea of taking Clancy off on another long road trip.

"I think we are going to have to sell the cars."

In some ways, that statement had a greater impact on me than the news of his Cancer. You see, I know that it is his cars that have kept him going through thirty-five years of Multiple Sclerosis – being able to potter around, polish the cars and keep his body and mind active have allowed him to live a fairly active life despite being given a diagnosis of imminent paralysis back in the 1970s.

But he had now resigned himself to not being able to go to France just one more time and was now considering selling his Peugeots.

The feeling of helplessness you experience at a moment like this is something that is hard to describe. I wandered the house looking at the countless model cars and pictures that dad has collected over the years and felt incredibly sad. It was a couple of days later that I asked dad if I could take Lola in Clancy to France so that I could record

7

the trip in photos for him. Dad agreed and then shortly afterwards, I realised that this was a great opportunity to raise awareness and tell our story while raising some money for MS. The idea went from a week in Brittany to a 3,000 mile challenge very quickly and I set about planning almost straight away

This idea for this trip was first conceived through a feeling of overwhelm, being unable to help my father with his fatigue and quality of life related to suffering with both Multiple Sclerosis and Prostate Cancer. Knowing that his two great passions, cars and France, were now beyond his reach was unimaginably difficult to comprehend. Hearing someone talk of selling his cars, whose life has been devoted to them, is heart breaking. I felt a sense of desperation. I wanted to do something I could share with him to try to help. Having received his blessing and permission to take Clancy, I started planning. But let's not make bones about this – I do have a background in Marketing and a sound business knowledge and I saw an opportunity to leverage the history of Clancy. The story of a car with 1 million km on the clock, which has driven from Australia to the UK, is intriguing and fascinating, and I realised I could possibly use Clancy to raise money for charity. Single mum takes battered old car on continental road trip with a three-year-old! Crazy, right?

Over the past six months I have learned that you need thick skin and determination when putting together any kind of charity event. Emails and phone calls to many organisations and a crowdfunding campaign to help me fund the trip have been very time consuming but it has paid off. I have raised money direct for MS through Just Giving, boosted my fuel fund through Indiegogo and gained relationships with Peugeot, Al Fresco Holidays and Siblu, who have each helped me to bring this crazy idea to life.

Many hours have been spent with maps and spreadsheets, researching where to go and how to get there on the old roads. We plan to cross the English Channel from Portsmouth to St Malo before heading south-east to Onzain in the Loire Valley. After a couple of days we will head south-west past Bordeaux to Parentis-en-Born, which lies near the beautiful Atlantic beaches of the Aquitaine, and from there I have yet to decide the route but we intend to have a short stay at Canet Plage on the Mediterranean coast. From there I have some flexibility depending on how things are going but the aim is to visit Spain before heading east across the South of France to

Provence and Italy, and then heading back up to the Picardie region, which is one of my father's favourites.

With all of this planning in place, I am now in a position to embark upon the challenge with my little girl. Lola, at three years old, has lived in New Zealand, Australia and the UK. She is a great little traveller, and is more excited than me about the trip. She, at her young age, understands her Grampy's affinity with his cars and seems to have adopted his love of France after our trip earlier this year. How she will cope when driving 300 miles a day in a car that will probably average 45-50 mph on the back roads, I don't know, but I do know she won't forget the experience. That's what this comes down to: making the most of the time we have with our loved ones.

On The Road At Last

It's early afternoon and the sun is shining brightly on Clancy. He has his new blinkers on courtesy of insulation tape placed skilfully by dad – he won't be blinding approaching traffic now that his beams have been adjusted, he will be gliding over the miles with us, slow and steady, much like a steam engine.

Comparing Clancy to a steam train is not such a bad analogy. He is heavy and old, but reliable as long as you keep him in tip top condition. Before he made his trek back around the world from Gympie, Queensland, he had an overhaul. Many people would have given up on the old boy after 800,000 km, but instead Graham, his then owner, had a plan to show his wife the way he had travelled to Oz from Ireland forty years prior – on a Vespa, no less. It puts my measly attempt at a road trip to shame, doesn't it! Taking in Tibet and Afghanistan, before driving up from Turkey to the UK, Clancy survived donkey kicks and arms builders (yes, they were building guns) before he met my father and since then he has made trips up to Scandinavia and down to Italy, as well as multiple trips to France. This car just keeps on chugging along – I stoke the fire and add water when necessary and he looks after us and takes us where we want to go.

Right now, it is Portsmouth that we need to get to, so Lola and I say an emotional farewell and start our adventure. The first port of call is a quick stop in Frome for diesel so that Clancy is full to the brim before we go. The fuel is cheaper in France but I don't want to be searching on a Sunday – there is a high probability that the non-automated fuel stations will be closed; add to the mix driving on the old roads and we're left with a very slim chance of success. Clancy when full will have more than enough fuel in his belly to sustain us to Onzain, which will be our first stop in France. We are travelling on the overnight ferry, so once we disembark at St Malo we will have a drive of around 220 miles tomorrow – breaking me in gently!

From Frome the driving is easy, as we coast along happily to Salisbury on the A36 before joining the motorway for the last part of the drive. Driving into Portsmouth on a Saturday afternoon turns out to be a breeze, and we follow the signs and reach the port quickly. The anxiety is shifting, and now we just need to wait for our invitation to board. Lola received a little kids' pack from Brittany Ferries when we checked in, which she is colouring merrily whilst singing a little song.

"Michelin Man, The Michelin Man
He's a funny old Grampy like my Grampy"

The catchy tune has me joining in, and wondering if I am actually as bonkers as many people assume. If the cap fits, Emma!

Boarding starts just as the sun is dipping over the funnel of the ferry into the English Channel beyond. Our early arrival means we have a spot at the front of the deck and in minutes we are in our cabin. Lola is full of excitement at the prospect of going up and down in the lifts all night, and thoughts of sleep appear to exist in my mind only – I need as much as possible before we coast off the ramp of the boat where Clancy's rubber will meet French tarmac.

How silly am I to think that Little Miss Memory wouldn't remember our previous trip to France and the rough whereabouts of the lift. Once we've freshened up, I succumb to a couple of trips to explore all the decks before we find the play area which is fortunately near the café. A pot of mini Oreos and a bottle of milk for Lola, a hot chocolate for me and we're set for a play before we retire.

The shops on Brittany ferries are good, and for us it is all part of the experience to have a little wander around, for Lola to choose a little reminder of her trip and for me to wait patiently while she does so. On this occasion there is a mission though, as my sunglasses have broken and I don't fancy starting this trip under the unprotected glare of the French sunshine. Lola finds me some diamante-studded glasses and my initial reaction is one of horror. I am not a sparkly kind of girl, but on reflection I decide that if it makes her happy and they do the job perhaps some sparkle would make a nice change.

Two minutes later, feeling a little silly and rather glitzy we leave with my shiny new glasses and a Hello Kitty to add to Lola's collection.

By the time we retire to our cabin it is almost ten o'clock. Lola dozes off in my arms on the narrow single bed, and the frantic muddle of thoughts racing through my head slowly fades to a blur until I too drift off, lulled by the slow rise and fall of the waves that surround us.

4

Long Straight Roads and Empty Plains

Six o'clock and the music starts. France is an hour ahead, so I change my watch ready for life on the continent. I managed about five hours' rest and I'm not feeling too special, but there's nothing I can do about it now – quick shower, get Lola organised and in search of coffee we go. A wall of extremely grumpy-looking people greets us, a long queue of bodies craving their caffeine, sending out the "don't even look at me" signal. Knowing that we only have about twenty minutes until we dock, I take the sensible option of the vending machine. It is not roasted perfection but it does the job and allows Lola and me the chance to wander over to the play area where we can get our first glimpse of St Malo. A nervous excitement rumbles in my tummy as I anticipate what is ahead – or is that just the need for a croissant?

If you have never travelled by overnight ferry let me enlighten you. After all, this story is all about slowing down, not jumping on a plane to sunny Spain. The time I would have spent hanging around in an airport is spent sitting having hot chocolate, watching Lola play. Despite having had a lacklustre sleep, I had privacy in my cabin without being disturbed by fellow passengers. Of course, for those travelling with older or no children there is evening entertainment, akin to a mini cruise. Brittany Ferries are very good at what they do and all in all it is an enjoyable experience.

The beds in the small economy cabins serve their purpose: single, firm mattresses with ample pillows. There are more expensive options but this suits us just fine. The shower is good and yes, you do get toiletries as well as towels. This means that you can just go up from the car deck with only a toothbrush and clean underwear if you so choose – well, don't forget to keep your passports and money with you – but the point is that the beauty of travelling on a ferry is freedom with the ability to travel light. You only need exactly what

13

you'll use for the next few hours.

When you wake there is breakfast available but plan well and make sure you have time if you wish to squeeze it in. When you are arriving early in the morning you may not want to be getting up an extra half an hour earlier. The pricing is good but you could also take your own food, and it's certainly a good idea to carry snacks if you have children in tow.

Now that we are docking I start to consider what lies ahead, and let's face it – I have no idea. The tannoy tells us we may return to our vehicles, so we climb down the steep metal stairs to find our boy sitting ready to go. I take a deep breath, strap Lola into her seat and slide into my sheepskin-covered seat. I rest my hands on the large, worn steering wheel that has seen so much and it is with a feeling of excitement, nerves, tiredness and, to be honest, being coiled like a spring that I shift Clancy into gear and start our journey. Seeing sideways glances from my fellow ferry travellers, I wonder whether they are in awe or perhaps thinking "she's mad"?

For those who don't know, these old diesels announce themselves with their deep rumble of a chug as the engine gets warmed up. A cloud of blue smoke engulfs the deck on the ferry but I don't really care what they're thinking and have a smug smile to myself – our car is probably more comfortable than theirs and whilst he may have the odd dent, I would rather be in Clancy than any newfangled car.

Shifting my focus from those immaculate cars and their drivers to the job in hand, I realise that over thinking the task ahead is a bad idea, yet I already doubt my decision to have satellites as a base in each region. The idea was to have pre-booked accommodation and although I know this is an essential element of the planning and safety for us on this trip (being expected at the end of each drive by the accommodation providers, with a red flag system in place), I wish I could just drive off the ferry and only go as far as feels safe, to be able to meander and explore. I feel somewhat pressured, which was not the idea of the trip. I hope that once we get the first day out of the way I'm able to re-frame that and build in time to explore and reach our destination on time. It's all a bit of a learning experience, and I guess that's part of the story.

We disembark to a beautiful sunny morning in the walled city of St

Malo where my expectation of being questioned is not met. We are soon joining the main route out of the port but sadly this time there is no chance to take in the local scenery. The weather is forecast to be in the low thirties today, so it will be interesting to see how warm Clancy gets. He's seen higher temperatures than this in the Outback and has had a few unique modifications to ensure he's as safe as possible but this is my first time with him in the heat. He has a manual temperature gauge and the ignition wiring has been split to ensure the wires don't fuse together but I don't think France is going to deliver temperatures of Ozzy standards today.

Isn't it amazing to think of this old car traversing hundreds of thousands of miles in extreme conditions and now being here with me to tell another tale.

Of course, the story began several months ago and as I sit here, I find it hard to believe that six months of planning is now about to take shape. I know that my plan to drive down to the South of Spain and Italy is unlikely to happen as I now only have twenty seven days as opposed to the seven weeks which was my original estimate. In March I sat in the Peugeot offices in Coventry pitching my cause and I told the guys my plan to cover 5,000 miles in five weeks; they looked at each other, raised their eyebrows and laughed! At that point I realised my pipe dream needed some work! Being someone who tends to go my own way despite what others recommend, part of me thought "just watch me" – I guess that's what brought me to where I am today, sitting in Clancy's comfy, armchair-like seats, staring at the stunning blue sky and taking a breath of the fresh, early morning sea air of Brittany.

Even now, one thousand miles per week seems realistic but I know that having an almost four-year-old in the car means it isn't quite that straightforward. Yes, I could drive non-stop but it would not be fair on either of us and would also defeat the object of what I'm trying to do: to have people understand that time is not indefinite, to make the most of life, to stop and enjoy the journey.

My father said to me that only when you get into your latter years do you start to reflect and realise how fast time has passed, the opportunities you missed and what is really important. I think I'm fortunate to have discovered this in my forties - being able to share my time with Lola and my loved ones is quite simply the most important thing in the world.

So today we're driving to Onzain in the Loire Valley, and we have three days there to explore the area. I'm unsure if we'll manage everything – I'm fairly sure the scenic drive along the river, taking in several châteaux which I excitedly traced with my finger on the map, may be too much for this visit. I had a vision of a day following the river and stopping for picnics along the way but perhaps that is a romanticised idea given my need to hit my targets. We'll see.

In theory, this drive is 216 miles and could be done in five hours but of course it isn't going to be that straightforward; there will be toilet stops required as well as safety and sanity breaks. It's going to be a good test of our endurance and I take comfort from knowing it's a good day to start, as Sunday is a day of rest in the Brittany countryside. Actually, now I come to think of it, last year when we arrived in Roscoff on a Friday morning it was much the same – I struggled to find coffee in Carantec at half past nine in the morning but when I did, it was worth it!

But today we aren't in Carantec and my plan is to head down to Rennes before cutting across country to avoid Angers, coming into Onzain from the north. Leaving St Malo is the first indication I see of exactly what I am trying to avoid. The fast cars and their drivers following me from the ferry seem anxious and angry, and for a moment I am on my high horse.

"What's the point? The sun is out, you're in a beautiful country with lovely roads and you're driving like an idiot – not to mention putting your family and others in danger."

I resign myself to the fact that some people will just never get it, this whole enjoying touring and making the most of time thing that we strive for. We, however, do get it, and I trundle along with Clancy at around 50 mph enjoying the glorious views that surround us. I'm not sure whether it's really sunk in yet, after so much planning and to now be here on the road, feeling an element of relaxation mixed with a good degree of nerves. Today is going to be a baseline to help me understand exactly how much ground we can cover safely and will enable me to get a better idea of what I can achieve.

The first hour of our drive south on the D137 is straightforward but I remain surrounded by idiots; I accept this and drive at a comfortable speed, chatting to Lola and sharing common thoughts about their silliness as they fly past – sunglasses on, foot down, eye on the final destination rather than the journey. It is only when we reach Rennes that I finally get to say goodbye to the last of them as they peel off towards the motorway – poor souls, you're missing out on so much.

Rennes is a hub when it comes to arriving in northern France. The ring road provides access to several routes in all directions, sending you on your way to Brittany, Le Mans, Paris and the coastal regions of western France. I think it's fair to say that the majority of travellers don't take the time to stop here which is a shame as it is a beautiful city. From the Mordelles Gates (Portes Mordelaise), which date back to 1440, to the spacious Parliament Square, you are spoiled with beautiful architecture. Narrow streets with stunning buildings offer plenty of opportunity to simply wander and enjoy all that is on offer.

Today Lola and I are only passing but we do take the chance to drive through and appreciate the town on a quiet Sunday morning. There is of course the toilet search to consider – this is not just an appreciation of a lovely French town! Being Sunday morning at around ten o'clock there is little in the way of movement and there is certainly no sight of the required facilities, but it is a great opportunity for me to get my head around town centre road signs and traffic lights without fear of being attacked by an annoyed local for the act of switching lanes. All joking aside, the French roads are so well signposted that common sense prevails the majority of the time, and it is nice to settle in gently today.

From Rennes it is south-east towards Angers and across country to the famed Loire Valley. I'm excited about this. I have never visited the area and I think it will be a good place to start, not too busy and options for lots of things to explore.

Take note, the small price to pay for taking the beautiful back roads is the lack of facilities en route. Whilst the vast open air roadside laybys (signposted "*Aire de…*") on the main routes are wonderful, you will struggle to find them elsewhere. There is of course the hedge, which isn't really a problem as the roads are quiet outside of the busy summer season but today we found something that you need a strong stomach for!

17

We depart Rennes on the D163 after I accept it is a fruitless exercise and a waste of precious time hunting for a toilet. As we head south-east we come across a nice little layby complete with a concrete box approximately five cubed metres in size. Picture the scene – a lone concrete structure, one door with no obvious handle, pleasantly set off the road and backed by rolling countryside. Sounds like a great toilet, doesn't it?

Wrong! Our first problem is how do we get in? With no other cars around or people to spy upon for clues to entry, I eventually manage to find the secret button which opens the electronic door, phew! Relief turns to horror as we are hit in the face by the stench of what I can only assume is a long drop toilet with a little concrete hut over it and no ventilation! Now let me tell you, I have lived in Thailand where holes in the ground are normal but never have I come across such a bad smell – it was horrible! On reflection, it reminds me of a toilet I came across near a train station in Corsica many years ago except that particular model had a saloon style door, swinging freely in the wind. I'm not sure which is worse – lack of privacy but some ventilation, or something which I can only compare to an unventilated prison cell. Modern technology, my friends, is not always progress!

Next problem is Lola's refusal to go anywhere near the toilet. Now you might think "that's ok, just go in on your own" or "just use the fields behind" but at this point both of us have been in the car for around two hours and sensible thoughts are not at the front of my mind. I can't leave Lola alone in the car, so I have to run back and get a cotton scarf to wrap around her head, mouth and nose so she will at least come in with me, but even with the assistance of my anti-smell creation she still won't entertain using this thing. I agree to take her to the fields behind us instead, and this is when we hit problem number three, getting out!

While hoppity Lola is desperately trying to cover her nose doing her little dance, I finally manage to find the secret switch to let us out. Technology has its place, but my goodness – just give me a door handle! Space age toilets that smell like something from the dark ages are not my thing.

Once all of this drama is over, we return to Clancy, who has been waiting patiently in the heat of the autumn sunshine. We have a little break and play with some of Lola's games. She has Michelin Eye Spy

On The Road books as well as some other wipe clean cards given as a gift from her school teacher before we left; these are great to keep her entertained, so I sit with her for a while in the back of the car. Together, we see if we can spot some road signs we've already seen – it's nice to share a quiet, pleasant moment with her after the toilet incident.

Before we get back on the road, I make use of the dried milk and milkshake powder I brought with us which enables us to make drinks on the road without the need for milk. All it takes is bottled cool water and a couple of spoons of each powder into another bottle, a good shake and you have a palatable drink without the risk of milk going bad. It also stores a long time and is more filling than just water – not to mention the fun shaking it, which entertained Lola for at least thirty seconds!

We both have a milkshake and I notice we have been stopped for forty-five minutes, and we'd probably best get back on the road as there is a long way to go. As I fasten Lola back into her seat, a small convoy of campervans approaches. They pull up, tanned bodies spill out, lighting cigarettes before they have both feet on the ground, and they have a picnic hamper and table cloth laid out with wine and bread in less time than it takes me to belt up and start Clancy. It appears these folks are well practised in the art of enjoying life.

Lola and I had been gasping for fresh air when we left the toilet and here I see these people inhaling their cigarettes with the same urgency. After a moment and a visible change in posture from getting their fix, the silence is broken and the chatter begins followed by wine and more cigarettes. It's only eleven in the morning but I guess if you're on the road and enjoying a country famous for wine, why not! I smile to myself, and we get back on the road with the reality kicking in that there is still a long drive ahead and the sun is getting increasingly hot. Still, the toilet saga gave us something to write about, didn't it!

As we start back on our journey, the scenery is varied but at the same time blends seamlessly. At times, we roll through the miles, surrounded by farmland, with solitary trees silhouetted on the horizon against the clear blue sky. We drive long, straight roads shaded by towering dark green forests, approaching each peak of the undulating hills wondering if the view at the top will bring new landscapes only to find the same lie ahead summit after summit.

Take a moment to imagine a roller coaster ride, except as you decelerate nearing the top in anticipation of the descent, your breath is taken away not through fear or adrenalin, but through the beauty that surrounds you. You exhale a happy sigh and just enjoy the ride – I will definitely remember this feeling and the smile that creeps over my face as the tapestry of the French countryside unfurls in front of me.

Gendarmerie and the Fête du Vélo

The rest of our drive down to the Loire is fairly smooth, continuing through rural landscapes under blue skies and with a surprisingly patient Lola. We stop one more time for a break when I find a road wide enough to do so with tall trees for shade; Clancy hasn't got too hot so far but it's warm out there now, so a break for us all for a few minutes is a sensible idea. I am starting to feel the inevitable neck ache and the makings of a headache, so a couple of pain killers and something to eat and drink is necessary. While we are stopped, I discover that the French do not share the same coyness when it comes to toilets. A car pulls in a couple of metres in front of us and the chap proceeds to relieve himself next to the car. Clancy, despite big orange stickers on the doors which were provided by the MS Society, must be invisible!

As I mentioned earlier, we will cut across country rather than follow the E60 *autoroute* from Angers to Tours before heading across to Onzain. Part of the fun for me is tracing my finger over the paper of my maps and creating my own route cards, which I find therapeutic. We take the D41 then the D94 before joining the D775. I drive across slightly north of Angers taking in a number of small villages before joining the D766 for the final part of the drive. I am a very visual person, so from my hours of studying the maps I know that once I hit that road I am on the final straight.

The undulating forest green of the rolling, wooded hills gives way to vast plains. We drive for miles without seeing a soul, only the odd house sitting lonely on the horizon and the occasional level crossing with grasses waving their willowy heads between the railway tracks. My tiredness at this point is getting quite significant as is my headache but I feel that we are in touching distance, so I decide not to stop. I know that I need to turn right at some point to head down to Onzain, and when I pass a tiny lane I realise very quickly that the village of Herbault where I was going to turn off is little more than a few houses. I turn around and take the lane with no signpost, and it's got to be worth a punt – I need to go south and the sun tells me this road goes south, easy!

Driving down this twisty lane into the unknown, I feel quite confident that we are in the right place and sure enough after about five minutes we arrive in Onzain - only to be greeted by local *gendarmerie* (police). Isn't it funny how even when you haven't done anything wrong, an officer of the law can make you feel like you have.

I have no cause for worry, it is simply the Fête du Vélo and the town is filled with cyclists and spectators. On any other day I may have thought "Oh, how charming!" but today I think "NO! My head is pounding and I need a rest!" This is made worse by the fact that I know this is a small town and our campsite is probably less than five minutes from here. The directions I have to the site are now useless as most of the roads are closed for the event – I need to wing it.

Let me tell you more about our "Welcome To Onzain" experience. We drive at a snail's pace through the square, a foreign car in a mob of bicycles, but not just any car – Clancy. The families on their bikes give me sideways glances – this is their road today but eventually I manage to break free of the mob and the police, and make my way down a side street. This is where I spot a young chap leaning casually against the wall smoking a cigarette. My gut feeling is that he has an air of arrogance and perhaps will be a little rude but I give him the benefit of the doubt – if he's local, he may be able to help. I ask where the Siblu campsite is and he shrugs and laughs (gut feeling confirmed), and he then waves his arm towards another side street which is even narrower; against my better judgement, I turn left as he suggests. Fifty metres later I am met with more barriers and more cyclists – this is a dead end and I have to do a ten point turn to get out of here!

Note to self, listen to your gut feeling!

Cursing under my breath, I drive back down the street and am relieved to see he is gone. I feel a little silly and don't want to see a smirk on his face as I drive past.

I see another man walking his dog, newspaper and baguette under his arm. He looks so much more approachable and I manage to explain to him what I am looking for. Perhaps it is the visible clues – old car, child, English – must be in need of a campsite. He gives me directions, which although understood don't feel quite right because they send me out of town towards Blois. Nevertheless, I trust him and sure enough soon see a big yellow sign on the road out of Onzain – I realise that this is the redirection I am looking for.

This lane is even smaller than the last one but finally, I see the sign for Domaine de Dugny. It is surrounded by sunflower fields opposite a big billboard picturing a large goat! Apart from telling me that there is a local farm making goat's milk products nearby, it is also a good reminder of which of the many bends in the road I need to turn off at in the future. My heart skips a happy beat when I see that the location is gorgeous. Despite feeling as though a truck load of cement had been poured over my head, I can at least smile. We've completed the driving for today.

Clancy rolls over the gravel driveway to our campsite. It has been hard to hear myself think under the noise of his engine at times today but now, at a slower speed and with my window open, I can hear the gentle crunch as his heavy old diesel body delivers us safely to our destination. To the left I am greeted with a spread of yellow and green across the seemingly endless fields and ahead I see the barrier to the site. We pull up, I exhale and take a moment to relax back into my seat and momentarily close my eyes before Lola says –

"MUMMY we're here! I can't get out – let me out!"

My moment of peace switches to motherhood and I climb out and help Lola out of her seatbelt. My legs feel like jelly yet the tension in my muscles is asking for a good stretch. Despite my relief at reaching our destination, it has been eight hours since we rolled off the ferry onto French soil and the anxiety and tiredness has resulted in me feeling nauseous – or is that the fact I need food? Putting the feeling aside, we walk across to the lovely timber huts which turn out to be offices and introduce ourselves.

The welcome we receive upon our arrival is lovely. I instantly feel relaxed and the anxiety starts to drain at the sight of a smiling face. The location here is stunning – tall trees and sunflowers, what more could you want?

Once we have our welcome pack and the keys to our cabin, we wander back to Clancy. The pace of life seems incredibly slow here – I think I like it. We pop our code into the barrier and slowly coast along the gravel track. We drive through a tunnel of tall trees, the odd leaf floating onto the windscreen as a gentle wave 'hello' from the nature of the Loire.

Our cabin is easy to find and there is a sheltered parking space for Clancy to take a well-earned rest in the shade. It is half past four now, so I am ready for a cup of tea and food. We open the door to the cabin to find it spotlessly clean, with tea and coffee on the table together with a bottle of wine – of course Lola won't be having any, but actually, nor will I.

Perhaps I'm a little paranoid but travelling alone with a child makes me acutely aware of my responsibility. Yes, I could have a glass of the wine but I'm feeling a little overwhelmed about the task ahead and can only think of every possible scenario, one of which is being required to drive somewhere in an emergency and therefore having no alcohol. I think the wine may be coming in the suitcase instead.

I manage to squeeze in a cup of tea before parental responsibilities resume and we set off on foot to explore our home for the next three days. It is a small and friendly site and within a few minutes, we find the facilities and pop in to the little shop to get some milk and order bread for the morning – it is ordered from a local boulangerie, so we choose a baguette, a croissant and a *pain au chocolat*. We will figure out which is best tomorrow when we get to sample it!

From the door of the shop we see the bar and restaurant and entertainment rooms. It appears there is plenty to do and it's nice to see that the buildings are in keeping with the local style. Lola sits down with her ice cream just in time to see the children's club finishing up for the night – she had spotted the sign earlier but this is the first sign of any activity.

Siblu Holidays have three well run clubs to keep the little ones occupied. Lola is the right age for Bubbles Club which they may attend (with a parent) up until age five. After that come Pirates until age eleven, then Barracudas for the older kids. I ask for information, even though I've never been a fan of these clubs because I like to think that holidays should be shared time. Nonetheless, I have to bear in mind that Lola needs some time to play and enjoy herself on this trip. We are in the car more often than not!

Armed with the knowledge that Bubbles Club will be on tomorrow morning, I agree that she can go. It will give me a break for an hour and I can see that the room is well equipped with plenty of games and craft activities. Now it's time to head back to the cabin – I'm starting to feel particularly peculiar.

An exhausted Lola and I have a light dinner and a cuddle out on the deck, sheltered by a yellow and white striped canopy. We sit and nibble our food, with neither of us having much of an appetite. The temperature is perfect, warm with a gentle breeze stirring as the sun sinks lower, leaving a trail of orange and pink in its wake. I carry a sleepy Lola inside, lie next to her on the bed and in moments she is gone, off to the land of princesses and castles. I am not going to be far behind her. My head is pounding and I feel like the cabin is moving beneath me – not enough water, Emma, take your own advice! So far, so good though, my little girl has been in the car for eight hours today and there hasn't been a hint of tears. I am a lucky mummy.

As I sit on the deck and take in the last of the evening sun, I try not to think too much. It's sinking in now that we're actually doing this and I have a month with Lola and Clancy to take care of alone in a foreign country. How do I view it? Let's not think about that too much or I may scare myself. I'm following my heart and embracing whatever gets thrown at me. Wouldn't life be boring if I didn't do that?

Lovely Loire

I wake to darkness. It is silent apart from the sound of Lola's heavy breath – she's still asleep. The plan for today is to get out and have a look around the area but not to go too far. Yesterday took a lot out of us both, the lacklustre sleep on the ferry not helping matters. Throughout the trip, the plan is to get out and about in the mornings and make sure we're off the road by mid-afternoon so that Lola has time to play in the pool and we both have a chance to recharge. To be in the car any longer would be unfair and I don't think Lola would stick out the whole trip very well if she didn't have the opportunity to enjoy herself too.

Clancy has only used half a tank of diesel and we have travelled 293 miles, and I'm feeling pretty good about that as it means I'm doing more to the gallon than I estimated in my budget. Funding this trip has been just one of the elements I had to consider, and I spent hours poring over routes, ferry crossings and accommodation trying to minimise costs while also being sensible and safe. It's too late to think about that now, so we just have to get on and hope that our pre-paid visa works in the French fuel stations!

The shop opens at eight o'clock which seems like the middle of the day to me, but will it be worth the wait for our baked goods, I wonder? With a very excited child on my hands, we walk to the shop in the chilly autumn air. The sun is barely up and in contrast to yesterday afternoon, I have a scarf and jeans on. I love this time of year – fresh air and sunshine!

After successful collection of our breakfast, we walk back through the crunchy sound of fallen leaves. Lola's head is already in her brown paper bag, her teeth pulling the flaky, buttery goodness away before she gets to the chocolate centre. I am a little slower and manage to apply some butter, rich and salty, before eating my croissant with my second coffee of the day. We have a stovetop coffee pot here which makes a wonderful smooth drink, and it's worth the wait.

With full bellies, it's time to walk back down to the entertainment area – this is doing us good already, plenty of walking so far today. We meet Charlotte, the English girl who looks after the little ones in Bubbles club. Lola takes to her immediately and they dance, do jigsaws and play some French board games. I sit and watch and although I need to be present, it does give me some time to relax a little. Charlotte tells us that there is a talent show tomorrow. Being end of season, most of the guests left yesterday and Lola is the only child of Bubbles age at the moment. Lola is unperturbed by this and together with Charlotte, she learns the song and dance which they will do if she chooses to do the show. I have mixed feelings when I hear it isn't until half past eight at night but I am prepared to see how it goes – if Lola gets to have a nap, we could possibly stay up a bit later.

The hour flies past and soon it is time to say goodbye. Our next job is to head off in search of sunscreen and a few bits of shopping. I also need to fill Clancy up and test the pre-paid visa at the automatic pumps. It's niggling me not knowing whether it is going to work or not.

There are two supermarkets which I spotted whilst negotiating the Fête du Vélo on the way here – a Lidl, which of course we are familiar with in the UK; and a Casino, complete with fuel, chemist and pretty much anything else you might like to buy.

The Casino is just around the corner from a Peugeot garage – not one that you may imagine with shiny cars and a well lit showroom, but a proper garage; this is a mechanic who appears to have been here years and just happens to have a Peugeot sign outside, by the look of it. It reminds me of my dad's house – he too has a few old Peugeot signs hanging around inside and out, so I feel safe in the knowledge that if Clancy had a mishap this chap could fix it. For those who have questioned my sanity around driving a forty-year-old car with 1 million km on the clock around continental Europe, this is why I am not concerned. If I had a modern car, this man would shrug his shoulders at the sight of a computer – a good old diesel, however, is a different story.

But back to the moment at hand, I decide to try Lidl first because, if I am honest, the huge Casino is a little daunting when I am feeling a wee bit weary. On arrival, I find that it is not quite the same as the one at home; there are some similarities but the quality of the fresh produce is far superior, but what did I expect? We are, after all, in a country which prides itself on good food.

I buy only enough for two days. We are driving to Les Landes in what is predicted to be high temperatures later in the week, and it would quite simply be a waste of money and food to buy any more than the essentials. Coffee, sugar and fruit are staples to tide us over. I still have enough of the sensible food and snacks that I brought from the UK to keep us going in the car during the drive.

Leaving Lidl and heading into Onzain in search of sunscreen, we find it is past midday. The table-lined side street next to the square is buzzing with the relaxed chat of locals embarking on the tiresome journey of a lengthy lunch – the shops, however, are closed! Sunscreen is off the list, but Lola and I remain unperturbed and take the opportunity to go for a wander and soak up the ambience of what is a daily occurrence here: long lunches and time with friends and family. Being September, there are few tourists around and the locals are just doing their thing: eating, drinking and, noticeably, smoking!

Ten minutes later and we are back at the car. It's a beautiful little town, but with everything closed we are limited to what we can do. I must say that the car park, cobbled and shady from trees, is essentially the town square and would have to be the prettiest car park I've ever come across. I could very easily stay and take it all in, the slower pace of life, the appreciation of taking time for the little yet important things – lunch with friends, idle chit chat and relaxation. Unfortunately, the midday sun is upon us and Lola has other ideas, specifically jumping in the pool!

Lola greets Clancy with a bonnet hug and a kiss. She is very attached to this old man and I manage to catch her on film when her affection for the car keeps her lingering there a moment longer, just enough to press the shutter.

With a final glance and a little envy I say a silent farewell to the diners who are unaware of us departing, or so I think! As Clancy moves over the cobbles, my eye catches movement to my right. In the nick of time, he halts, obedient to my speedy reactions and my right foot! A man jumps in front of Clancy, waving his arms frantically and speaking in rapid French, grey ruffled hair and tawny brown skin barely visible under his wide brimmed hat. His wife stands mildly by his side smiling and waving and after the initial shock, my concern passes. He is pointing at Clancy and then his camera – he simply wants a photo. After a pause to allow him his artistic licence, Lola and I have a giggle. It's only our first day and already we've encountered mad cyclists, police and an eccentric photographer – I wonder what is ahead!

The journey back to the site is pleasant. After we roll off the cobbles onto the smooth tarmac, our longer detour sends us past the tiny railway station and over a single file bridge which perhaps may not support anything bigger than a car. An elderly man on a bike with a baguette under his arm and dog running next to him is the extent of the excitement but it makes me smile. I often refer to slowing down, taking the enjoyable route, not the fastest, and making the most of the world that surrounds us. The simplicity of a gentleman riding an old bike complete with dog, baguette and cap epitomises the reasons for us being here.

Onzain is a small rural town – a lovely place to be based, in fact, because it is the surrounding area that makes this a perfect location for us. We are in Châteaux country and I have a little lady who has a vivid imagination, one that has princesses living in these stunning buildings, driving to work and getting stuck in traffic jams. Listening to Lola's musings over whether the Princess was late for work because of the traffic again brings me back down to earth with an emotional bump. I am so lucky to be able to share the gift of travel, and teaching her about the world and hearing and seeing her absorbing it all like a little sponge and then creating her own reality is just wonderful.

Driving back to campsite is a joy; it's a shame we weren't here a couple of weeks earlier as the fields are full of sunflowers, miles and miles of them. Even now, as they are starting to wain it is still a feast for the eyes – miles of long, flat roads fringed by the now hazy yellow hue as the flowers bow their heads with a farewell nod to summer. These giant flowers still remain bright enough to give a stunning glow and contrast to the clear blue sky above, the odd tree breaking the yellow horizon with such a beautiful silhouette.

Yes, I definitely feel like I'm in France. The scenery, the nonchalance of the locals, the elderly gentleman; it's our first full day in Onzain and despite feeling more than a little tired and queasy, I am overwhelmingly happy to be here.

One o'clock and I am instructed by Lola that we must go for a swim. In cozzie and wellies, she leads the way without a care in the world, enjoying just being here. We wander the gravel tracks lined with tall poplar trees to find the swimming pool, me following her marching ahead, preparing for her mission to drain every ounce of strength I have by jumping on me one hundred times from the side of the pool. At times like these, I switch between loving being a single parent and occasionally thinking how nice it would be to have a spare pair of arms to catch flying Lola approaching at high velocity! Of course, when you look back at these times they are the ones that stand out, to hear the shrieking and to watch the excited jumping up and down is a wonderful memory that will stay with me forever.

We approach the pool and I can hear nothing but the sound of the breeze in the trees and Lola's marching feet, red wellies on crunchy autumn leaves. The pool is closed. I smile to myself despite being overheated and a little disappointed – of course it is, we are in France and it's one o'clock in the afternoon, and why would I expect the pool to be open when it's thirty two degrees, after all! It turns out to be normal: the facilities are open all day during peak season but as we are in September, we must fall into the shoulder shrugging "it's the way it is in France" pattern that we have very rapidly become accustomed to. We will come back later when the pool is open again, and it will be nice then to cool off after another hot day under the autumn sun.

It isn't the end of the world because this campsite has many play areas which are well-shaded, in addition to pedal cars and bikes, so there is plenty to do. Even just walking and exploring is enough, if I am honest. On this particular occasion, Lola and I walk back under the canopy of trees, catching falling leaves as we go. Once back in our cabin, we lie on the bed, tell stories and fall into a deep and peaceful sleep.

Four o'clock and we wake, ready to sample the delights of the pool complex. The set-up on this site is great: retractable roof on one pool as well as another outside with slides for the older children and adults. There is a paddling pool (which Lola has decided she is too big for) as well as the indoor pool. For the next two hours, I am the equivalent of a floating springboard, Lola landing on me each time she launches herself from the side of the pool. Eventually, a promise of ice cream is enough to tempt her away from the fun, and we walk back through the mesmerising autumn trees to our cabin via the little shop where we buy ice cream and order our bread for tomorrow.

Sitting in the warm evening air, we enjoy our dinner, basic but delicious – ham, cheese and bread, with fruit salad made by Lola to follow. At last, my body starts to let go of some of the tension it holds, reluctantly but noticeably, and the depth of my breath changes as I appreciate the stillness and peace. I can feel my heartbeat and consciously inhale and close my eyes, succumbing to the slower pace of the Loire. Lola had gone inside to find a book a few minutes ago and it occurs to me that it's very quiet – in bare feet, I tiptoe in to find her lying starfish on the clean crisp white sheets.

Taking advantage of this little surprise, I pull out the maps, wondering what tomorrow will bring and reflecting on what today has given us. I feel better, my head is clearing finally and the jumble of thoughts that have been jumping around in my mind seems to start to form an orderly line. Yes, I am relaxing at last.

The silence of the Loire Valley is broken by noisy chatter right next to the cabin – my dozing brain cannot compute but finally I click to the fact that Clancy is out there and a crowd is not walking past but stopped. With a degree of nerves, I poke my head out to see what is causing a stir. Clancy is surrounded by four French men pointing and chatting excitedly. It is the men I had seen around the site and it appears that they have hunted us down, having seen us driving around. I always see heads turn, first to the sound of the engine then to the vision of our dear boy, but to make a special effort for us, I'm flattered – I think.

I weigh up the odds – the chances of one of them speaking English are pretty slim, so I put on my best French and introduce myself. They only have eyes for Clancy, and my invisibility cloak must be brilliant, so I decide to shed it and venture closer.

"Bonsoir!"

Nothing.

I am tempted to break into song but fortunately before I get the chance, one of the men turns to see me – their ears can thank me later. I explain the car is my father's, and there's no point in going much further when the response is a huge grin spreading over the brown friendly face I see in front of me. Nicotine stained fingers juggle a beer, a roll-up cigarette and a mobile phone, and finally the phone is pushed into my face (well, two inches away from my nose). I sway backwards, partly because I'm nearly knocked over but also because the man still has his lit cigarette in his hand, and I want to keep my hair, please! Once back on two feet, I see a picture of an old 504 pick-up on the screen and whilst I don't understand the rapid patter, the beaming smile and banging on chest tell me all that I need to know – this man has a car he is very proud of and he wants to share it! I reply with lots of nodding and a "Wow, *c'est bien!*" and this seems to do the trick in calming his eagerness to share and set me on fire. I attempt to make my excuses to leave, and then realise there is no point as the man has already regrouped in his huddle of friends, lighting their next cigarettes, and sauntering off to go about their extremely important evening business – boules and beer, I would imagine! Chuckling to myself, I retire. I'm exhausted but at least my headache is gone.

The Unpredictable Beast

This morning, I'm feeling much better – almost rested, after a wonderful sleep in a peaceful location. Lola and I have our hot drinks and wait for the sun to come up and the shop to open. Yes, it's only our second morning in France and we're settling in nicely. There is a distinct air of autumn, and while the days are still reaching high temperatures, these mornings are a little chilly but the clean, crisp air is so refreshing. It is a pleasure to walk to the little shop to collect our croissant and baguette, fresh and delicious – just asking to be devoured.

Rather than walking straight back to the cabin, we sit under the trees in one of the playgrounds. Watching Lola so carefree overwhelms me with emotion, and I can feel something welling up in my chest which I think is a combination of relief, pride and happiness. Whilst this trip has come about for a reason which I would prefer not to have to deal with, I am also mindful that I must make the most of every moment. What a great gift to a child, devoted time from someone who cares for nothing more than to make her happy – to live in this moment and to cherish it.

As I suppress a tear that has come to my eye, I take a deep breath and decide that this baguette can't wait for our return to the cabin, it must be eaten right now out of the brown paper it is wrapped in and oh my goodness, it tastes so much better sitting in beautiful surroundings with a loved one than it could ever do sitting at home! The crust isn't too hard – in fact, a little chewy – and it tastes delicious even without the addition of butter!

Ten minutes running in the early morning sunshine and Lola returns to me, very excited but also scratching her tummy complaining that it feels very itchy. A sinking feeling arises and the momentary pleasure of perfect fresh bread is soon a distant memory. These are not the words I want to hear so early in our trip: she suffers with eczema and a severe flare up could impact our plans, but more importantly, she would be in pain and unable to sleep. Eczema is horrible and both Lola and I have had many sleepless nights when she was younger. These days, she rarely suffers but the heat and change in the environment are something for this condition to thrive upon.

We walk back to the cabin hand in hand where I investigate the tummy and find she has a rash covering her. I think it is a reaction to something, and it certainly looks very uncomfortable. Though she tries to remain calm, I can tell she is suffering. In addition, the headache which consumed me when I arrived appears to have crept back – it's going to be a close to home day. I don't want to be worn out or sick so early in the piece: everything was very rushed in the last few days before we left so I need now to be sensible.

Safety is paramount on this trip and I need to be in the best possible state, mentally aware and physically strong. The plan to drive down to the Aquitaine in a couple of days is one that has tormented me a little because I know it's going to be hard. The need to reduce my time away, due to a change in personal circumstances, means that I don't have the three days I had initially planned when I was mapping the route. I need to rest, get rid of this headache and nausea but most importantly, be Lola's mum while she too is suffering with her health.

After covering Lola's tummy with cream and taking pain killers myself, we decide to go for a little walk around the perimeter of the campsite. I had hoped to visit the mini châteaux park just outside Amboise today, not too far from here, where you can walk around perfect tiny models of the castles of the Loire. I ask Lola whether she wants to go.

"No mummy, I want to stay here, I like it."

Would taking her out in the heat in the car with an eczema rash on her tummy be a good idea? I think for a moment and realise of course it could have a knock-on effect. Driving when it isn't a necessity would just be silly, increasing her discomfort and possibly making it worse. I've been through that with her when I drove from Brisbane to Sydney a couple of years ago, all day in the car when she had eczema flare up on her ankle. Despite being bandaged, she managed to scratch and to this day still has a scar as a reminder. It's not sensible, simple as that; with unfamiliar roads, a bad headache and a poorly Lola, it's a recipe for disaster! I need to try to get on top of things before we head south.

It's not the end of the world to be confined to barracks today at Domaine de Dugny. The location here in the Loire Valley is nothing short of beautiful. We are surrounded by fields of sunflowers, and to the rear of the park there is a small lake. Lola and I take our stroll and she is happy to find another play area just to the side of the water. During the high season, you can take pedaloes out but given that it is September and the end of the holiday season, activities are winding down. I prefer this, to be honest, having the peace and quiet to enjoy our surroundings, and I count myself lucky to be able to enjoy it with Lola.

I am grateful to have Lola distracted by climbing frames and swings as I try to consume as much water as I can. It has just occurred to me that this headache is probably a knock-on effect from having been in the car for seven hours and not drinking enough, being so focused on finding my way to Onzain and not paying attention to my own basic needs. I should know better, having suffered severe dehydration and a kidney infection when I lived in Thailand, but this is a timely reminder of the importance of staying hydrated while driving in the heat. The reminder of course also applies to Clancy, who needs to have his fluids checked every day. We're not so different to vehicles, are we? A shared need for fuel and fluids and some tender loving care to keep us in top form!

As the morning heat increases, Lola asks to go for a swim. I am a little concerned about allowing her to go in the swimming pool with her rash, but let's be honest – how am I going to get around that! As we walk back through the site and approach the pool, she can hear the other children (and adults!) screaming with delight as they splash around in the sunshine ,so I am going to take her for a dip; it might get rid of my headache while I am at it! Today, I am pleased that the pool closes for a couple of hours at lunchtime as I know that the best thing we can do is get some sleep.

Having walked, played and swam, I convince Lola that a nap is needed and we both fall asleep, hoping to wake up feeling better.

Staring at the ceiling, my head is swamped with thoughts of what lies ahead. The drive down to Parentis-en-Born, approximately five hours if you use the motorway, is one of the routes I have agonized over because I know that taking the old roads this time will be slow. There are many small towns, which will mean roundabouts and traffic lights, and although on the map the road looks straight, it will be a long drive. In addition to this, it is a shame that I won't be able to explore the area south of Poitiers a little more. I had hoped to spend a couple of days in the region between the Charente Maritime and Poitiers enjoying the countryside and villages, but unfortunately that isn't going to happen, as far as I can tell. Worst case scenario is stopping half way in a motel, but despite my rational mind telling me this, I can already feel the anxiety starting to build around meeting our next target. Who on earth thought setting goals was a good idea, anyway!

My train of thought is broken by movement on the bed as Lola starts to scratch her tummy. Eczema, for those who don't know, is an unpredictable beast, and just when you think you've got it under control it rears its head and lets you know –

"I'm still here! Didn't think you'd get rid of me that easily, did you?"

Once Lola awakens properly, she clicks that tonight is the night of the talent show. It's not often I get to go out at night – in fact, I can't remember the last time – so tonight I have agreed to let Lola do her little dance at the talent show. It sounds very grand, doesn't it, but actually there are very few people around and this holiday park is so relaxed it's more like popping out to meet your neighbours and friends for a coffee. There are only a handful of children here, so the entertainment team have decided to do the quiz and show in the bar.

The sun hangs low over the flat landscape surrounding Domaine de Dugny, with shades of orange creeping up to meet the intense blue of the sky of the Loire. This is a real treat for me, as I am usually restricted to barracks after bedtime but I'm not complaining. That said, I'm a bag of nerves as we approach said bar, amazing when I think of the nonchalance I used to exhibit just a few years ago when I travelled alone and thought nothing of going out late at night in cities around the world. It's an open air bar, comfortable seating offering views across the neighbouring fields and a beautiful sunset. A balloon is passing, low in the sky close enough to see the faces of the people in the basket. We wave and Lola decides she must go for a ride soon – perhaps when you're a little bit bigger, darling.

I order a coffee, while Lola has water and we sit and wait, enjoying the surroundings and listening to the chat of the locals who are slumped in the large white sofa in the corner. From the right, an oversized parrot by the name of Patch the Pirate emerges, who is one of Siblu's mascots. Lola's head becomes glued to my chest and she refuses to get down from my lap. I try to prise her away to at least get her to look at me but she is clinging like a limpet. Fortunately, the human operator of said parrot realises she is petrified and wanders off to find another child – one that is not scared of oversized cuddly toys..

Will she recover in time to do her little dance? Charlotte appears and asks us if Lola is ready, and the rigid fear that had engulfed her moments earlier disappears as Lola smiles and shouts out.

"CHARLOTTE!"

Lola slides from my lap, takes her hand and they go to take their place, ready to perform.

With shaking hands, I press record on the camera. My little girl has only practised this dance twice and whilst I know she picks things up quickly, I wonder whether she will be nervous – maybe she will freeze or just forget the steps. None of these things happen and she, without a care in the world, does her thing and receives a round of "aahs" and applause. Yes, I have a tear in my eye and can't talk because I will sob my heart out. A lady next to me asks, "Is she yours?" I splutter a "yes" and wipe my eyes. She asks if we'd like to join their table, but I decline – it is nine o'clock now and bedtime for a very happy little girl and her proud mummy.

8

Trapped By Doodingues

Having had a couple of quiet days, I'm determined to get out and about today. We aren't going to get to the attractions I was hoping to, but I am happy just to saunter around the local villages taking in the scenery. Before we do this, I need to top Clancy up with fuel, ready for our drive tomorrow. We will stop at the Casino where they have 24 hour pumps, which will be the test of my pre-paid visa, loaded with my fuel money. I've kept this separate and specifically for this purpose so that I have no concerns over running out of fuel money. In addition, I have my cash float which is for food, with my budget worked out down to the mile and a daily spending amount, so I have to be vigilant.

It's midday and we are ready to head off for an hour or two, first stop Casino supermarket. Lola and I enter the Hypermarket with some trepidation – these things are huge, selling everything you can possibly imagine you might need. We are only here for some fruit and croissants, so it is hopefully going to be a quick visit but while we are wandering the wide aisles, I have to admit that a little more money to spend on some of the beautiful produce on display would be nice. I remind myself that tomorrow we are driving all day, so it's pointless anyway.

Meanwhile, Lola becomes distracted by a French children's brand exclusive to Casino, "Doodingues", and I have to drag her away from the colourful display. Despite my belief that I have managed this successfully, after negotiating the self-service checkout, pleased not to have had issues with my card, we approach the automatic doors and she sees another splash of colour right next to the door.

Not to be beaten by cartoon characters, I continue through the doors, assuming she will follow. To my horror, I turn to see she is on the other side of the huge sliding doors, which have closed in seconds once I passed through them. Being so little, she doesn't have the size to trigger the sensors to open them. It is like slow motion – I see her little face crumple when she realises she can't get out. My heart is in my mouth and I am almost in tears searching for an emergency button. Before I find it, a customer comes through and the doors open – that was the longest few seconds of my life. Insignificant to some, but seeing my child look so helpless and scared and not being able to get to her was not something I wish to repeat. I didn't like that one bit and don't think Lola did either: next time we are in a supermarket, she will be pinned firmly to my side.

Back at Clancy, Lola is still upset and tells me she was very scared in there. We take a few moments to have a cuddle before going to get our diesel. At the pump, I make sure I have selected *gazole* and enter the pin of the card into the keypad. After a few moments, I receive a message to tell me that yes – I can have up to one hundred euros in fuel. This is a relief – it works and the budget is intact!

All fuelled up, we set off to drive through Onzain and out onto one of the local lanes. No maps today, I'm just randomly driving. It soon becomes clear how rural this location is, after driving for about an hour to see nothing but fields and tiny villages, most no more than a bend in the road. A restaurant with a large "closed" sign hanging outside and a bed & breakfast with no vacancies; fields of corn and sunflowers standing tall to attention – akin to a guard of honour, and as we pass, I feel a sense of being protected. Approaching a junction signposted Blois, I make a snap decision. Lola is still a little unsettled from our earlier door incident, and my mum instinct kicks in: she needs me this afternoon not to be stuck in the car or dragged around a busy town, however beautiful the Château de Blois may be.

I think I need to accept that the first few days are not going to give me what I was expecting. The Loire Valley will still be here next time – we will definitely be back and I will spend a couple of weeks doing all the things I had hoped to. The mini châteaux, the picnic on the riverside and the afternoon tea in a local château will have to wait, but next time I will photograph all of those wonderful things and take the time to enjoy them. I'm learning lessons pretty fast on this trip!

9

From Châteaux to Truckers

The darkness is soothing. It is eerily quiet and the Loire continues to smother me with a healing blanket of serenity. It feels almost uncomfortable to be in such a peaceful location – scared to breathe, perhaps. At home there are street lights and the night sky has a bluish hue, yet here, it is pitch black. The stars twinkle like a million diamonds sprinkled on black velvet.

I have come outside before Lola wakes to be able to reflect and cherish the moment. Today has come around far too quickly, and with so much to explore in this area, time and health have not been our friends. The purpose of this trip is to inspire others whilst doing a very personal challenge as well as sharing an experience with Lola, and though of course I can return to the Loire another time, I nevertheless wish we had more time.

It's seven in the morning and the sun is yet to appear. Plans to be on the road by now have been changed because of the time difference and the fact that it doesn't get light very early. My new departure time is eight but the goal of being off the road by mid-afternoon remains so that we have a chance to relax. We have a lot of ground to cover and the drive is not something I'm looking forward to. What I had envisaged as a leisurely drive through rural France is now likely to be a long haul, driving to Parentis-en-Born, which is south of Bordeaux. The first half of the drive down to Poitiers is going to be slow but one thing that is for sure, if I see a half decent toilet along the way, we will be stopping!

"Where are you mummy? It's dark, mummy! MUMMY?"

Lola's face emerges from the long, dark hair which has being fashionably styled into a mop by her deep slumber. She plonks herself on my lap and tells me it's cold. The stunning show of stars seems to have distracted me from noticing this, but now I shiver and venture inside to find my jacket. It's time to load Clancy, but at twenty to eight, my eight o'clock start is not looking promising! The target is to be at our next location by four o'clock, which should be within reach even if we leave a little later. After all, it would be wrong not to enjoy our hot chocolate and coffee ritual before we set off, or our last chance to sit on the deck and listen to the early autumn sounds of the Loire before we embark on the next leg of our journey.

There is a chill in the air as we pack Clancy. My route card sits on the passenger seat and Lola has snacks, drinks and things to do next to her.

"I miss Charlotte, mummy. I don't want to go."

It has been a flying visit but she has formed an attachment nonetheless.

"It's OK, we'll keep in touch. We have her email."

"But I don't want to go!"

It is worth taking five minutes to reassure her, and in the scale of things, it shouldn't make a lot of difference to the drive today. The usual cuddle and a promise of fun later is enough to set her mood back on track and as we break the morning silence with the meaty noise of Clancy's engine, it's time to go.

There is a soft thud as the key drops into the wooden box outside the office. My fingers linger just a moment before I let them go, sorry to say goodbye so quickly. The barrier slowly rises for the final time as Clancy begins the next leg of his journey. If he could talk, he would tell us about kangaroos, lizards and snakes and rattling over unsealed outback roads – the thought occurs to me that this gravel track would make him feel quite at home, for when he lived in the outback this would have been normal, if a little tame. My father's friend, Graham, owned Clancy prior to dad, and his daughter worked as a relief teacher in remote outback settlements. For six years, Clancy covered one thousand miles a week every week and it was at a time and in a place where tarmac didn't exist. After that, he was driven to and from vast copper mines by Graham's son-in-law, who is affectionately known as a lead foot – it's amazing Clancy didn't surrender to the torture!

It's comical to see road tests of modern cars in such extreme conditions. Clancy, with a few practical modifications to his old body, has driven the equivalent of twenty-five times around the world, yet the presenters on popular TV motor shows take a sharp inhale of breath and say –

"It will only last 1000 miles out here."
"The suspension will be ruined!"
"It'll never survive."

At least it gives dad and me something to chuckle about.

Driving down the tawny coloured track, it is difficult not to smile. To my right, the sunflowers are the colour of caramel, their yellow petals wilted; their seeds, ready to be harvested by the farmers, are the colour of dark chocolate, scorched by the summer sun. I will remember to come a little earlier next time, but that means high season – am I prepared to brave thousands of families on holiday for the sight of a field of sunflowers? Probably not here, but perhaps I can find a place to have the best of both worlds without the madding crowds. Perhaps that will be my next adventure with Clancy, in search of secret sunflowers.

The goat on the sign reminds me that I didn't get the cheese as planned, but this is France and there will be cheese in abundance to be enjoyed later.

"Stay on the right, mummy!"

Lola is a very good back seat driver. I thank her for the reminder and slowly take the lane down to Onzain, and after a left at the main road and passing under the railway bridge, a stunning sight awaits us.

We approach the river and are greeted by the lovely Château du Chaumont; if you stay in this area, you really should visit this beautiful 10th century fortress. In the 15th century it was burned down and restored and it has a wonderful history through the generations – but for me, part of that wonder is simply the way it rises from the horizon, sitting proud overlooking the river. If driving from Blois towards Amboise, you will pass it on your left, and from Onzain, it is on your doorstep. The château conjures images of battles faced in the past, and stories to be imagined of what happened behind those walls over the last thousand years. It also has stunning grounds to be enjoyed by the family and has five restaurants. I'm a picnic girl but certainly afternoon tea in such gorgeous surrounds may persuade me to part with a few euros!

I smile as the sun is just poking his nose over the horizon and a now familiar golden glow lights the land. A solitary campervan approaches on the long flat road ahead, our only friend here for now as we join the D952 to Amboise.

Once I manage to take my eyes off of this landmark, glowing in the morning sun, I turn my attention to the road. I guess I have forgotten that life occurs for locals each day and today, being a Thursday, I meet this head on at half past eight. Until now, traffic is something we have managed to avoid but here, as we drive the northern banks of the river, I am a little perturbed to be met by approximately ten vehicles. Ten vehicles! I hear you ask, but let me assure you, in the past four days I have seen empty spaces and very few people – this is somewhat of a traffic jam for us.

At Amboise I am torn, distracted by the Château Royal d'Amboise dominating the river to the south. It is incredibly tempting to stop and explore but to take a break so early in the day would not be a clever thing to do. In other circumstances, yes, but today I am on the road with a mission, and this is already turning into a learning experience for me: three days in one place is simply not enough. I have a thirst to explore and learn with Lola, to write about what we learn with enthusiasm. For now it must be sideways glances whilst being the driver, for today my challenge is to drive safely and knock off another milestone on our journey.

In a split second decision which is largely influenced by the flow of traffic, I decide to stay north of the river and say a wistful farewell to another beautiful building. We continue towards Tours and I instantly regret my choice – we are stuck! Such is my disbelief at the volume of traffic that after twenty minutes at the pace of a tortoise, I am convinced it must be road works or an accident. Not a good start so early in the day with 500 km ahead of us but soon a school crossing appears – it is simply a matter of bad timing and once we are through

43

these lights we start to make traction. I shall remember in future to avoid towns at nine o'clock – well, at least those of any size.

We pass Tours and I feel happier. As you know, I don't use any modern navigational tools but instead have hand written route cards. Those, together with the visual picture in my head, allow me to set milestones to mentally tick off and we have just passed one. The next one is Poitiers and the goal is midday.

The A10 south from Tours is the motorway that runs down to the Aquitaine, which would see us at our destination in five or six hours, but for us it will be the D910, which runs parallel. It is a long, straight road but now the landscape has changed to agricultural. Judging by the huge, cylindrical metal storage bins on the horizon we are in grain country. The dust and steady stream of trucks confirms this as we continue on our journey south. There is a trickle of local traffic and as expected, we are met in the small towns by roundabouts and traffic lights. This is actually a tiring drive and I feel like we aren't making a lot of progress at the moment.

Lola is happy in the back of Clancy, singing away and playing in her own little world, but she has also made her first reference to the need for a loo! I'm hoping Poitiers is not too far away and that I can find somewhere quickly. I have no intention of getting tied up in town centre traffic, so will take my usual route of "*toutes direction*" which invariably sends you the quickest way through the larger towns. I have also learned that these towns have commercial areas on the outskirts generally accessible to motorways and other major routes; these areas are a sure fire way to find an overnight stay in a Premiere Classe or Novotel and there is usually a McDonalds around too.

Now, here I would like to say that Lola and I are not fans of McD's but my goal is not to feed us but to use a decent toilet and have a break. Fortunately, my gut feeling is right. I trust my instincts and keep on driving south until we hit the commercial area filled with accommodation and takeaways as expected. If you are driving this route and want to somewhere to take a break, just stay on the D910 and you will find this area easily.

As we pull in, I am pleased to see that it is just past eleven, almost an hour earlier than I thought. It's taken two and a half hours which is not too bad considering the hold-ups we had along the way. We enter the fast food place and order a happy meal and a coffee – the food not important, but Lola gets a toy, which she is extremely happy about (we don't do this at home!). Very nice toilets and an outdoor play area allow us to refresh for a while. Lola tries to talk to a little French girl and I watch as the two of them communicate through their own sign language while they play happily.

Surrounded by people who have their heads in laptops and phones, it is easy to see that the art of conversation over food that the French do so well appears to have been left on the doorstep when they crossed the threshold of the big yellow arches. On the plus side, it is a pleasant surprise that Lola's happy meal has a yogurt drink and fruit included so perhaps the French have managed to sneak a tiny piece of their reputation for good food in here after all.

The chicken nuggets and chips are non-descript but I eat them anyway. It's certainly not the French food experience I crave but it will fill a gap. The coffee is welcome but not enough to quench my thirst, so I re-fill my water bottle from the fountain. The challenge of getting Lola back into the car is perhaps the hardest of the day so far – under duress, I finally manage to prise her from the slide and we return to Clancy. I shall have a quick look at my maps and route cards before we set off. Angoulême is ahead, then we get to Bordeaux – the last two milestones to pass until we arrive at our destination.

Maps do a funny thing to me – they stir up a little excitement, a desire to turn off and explore – and the region we are entering now is one which I had intended to spend a few days in. There are small villages and yet it's not too far from the coast. Getting lost here for a while would have been nice, but it is not to be this time. I snap myself back to the task in hand, mental notes and estimated arrival times. I think two hours to Angoulême then another hour and a half to Bordeaux, so we're not even half way there. I say out loud –

"Don't think about it, Emma – Just Do It!"

"What, Mummy? What are you doing?"

"Driving, Lola, that's all. Just driving."

"Oh, OK. I knew that."

In my thoughts, I carry on. Yes, Lola, though I'm worried it's a long

45

way – probably another four hours and it's getting hot now, approaching thirty degrees. If I'm honest, I am a little concerned about both us and Clancy getting overheated.

Meanwhile, happy with my answer, she chants her Michelin Man song:

> "The Michelin Man
> He's the Michelin Man
> He's a funny old Grampy
> Like my Grampy"

I smile – Grampy is never far from her mind, and in case you wondered, Clancy has Michelin Man stickers on both front doors, not to cover any dents from donkey kicks in Turkey – just because he has.

My mind comes back to the prospect of this afternoon. Before we left Domaine de Dugny, I phoned dad because I had noticed that even driving locally in the sun, the temperature gauge was creeping up a little and I could hear the fan starting up. Clancy is of course used to extreme conditions, having lived in the outback and travelled across land to the UK from Australia – in fact, this pedigree has me putting my total trust in the car, more so than I would a modern car. The good thing is that the car has a manual thermostat and an electric fan to keep him cool, so when I phoned dad he just gave me instructions to turn the thermostat down a little so that the fan kicked in a little earlier. You see, this road trip is not all fun and games, and I have had to use my 'practical single mum on a mission' head on more than one occasion already. If I were scared to lift the bonnet and apply basic mechanical checks, this trip would not be happening. The idea of breaking down has been pushed to the back of my mind, as it just isn't an option – we are going to successfully complete the challenge, whatever it takes.

The road south from Poitiers offers an easier run, being the old road to Spain and the one preferred by the truckers. I know that running with the trucks is a safe way to go, since if I needed help someone would stop – but also, if you stay in the flow of the traffic with them, you keep up a consistent and safe speed. This afternoon is turning out to be an enjoyable drive, with roads which are undulating and tree-lined, and drivers who are friendly and accommodating.

There is none of the anger and angst of the motorways in sight, only beeps and waves to cheer us along. Granted I'd rather be taking it easy on the minor roads, meandering through the surrounding countryside, but today we need to get to our next satellite before dark, which means full steam ahead, Clance!

The sun is now high above, punishing us with its ferocity, so I decide to open my window a little more. Until now I've had the passenger side windows open to let the air circulate but have avoided having mine open any more than a crack to keep the noise down and excessive wind at a minimum. It is well over thirty degrees and as we know, Clancy has no mod cons, and we need some air. I'm kicking myself for not buying a net that slides over the door like we had in Australia – a great, simple invention that allows the air to flow without letting the dust come in.

As I am thinking about buying one of said nets, the inevitable happens and I hear a shriek from Lola. Let me rephrase that – there are hysterical tears from Lola as a piece of grit must have landed in her eye. I assess the situation, travelling at speed in convoy with trucks on a single carriageway, tree-lined road. There is no way I can stop safely to help her and I can't help but think of how painful it must be to have something in her eye like that. I'm taken back to a time when I was at school that I got grit in my eye during a netball match. The pain was awful and I remember dad taking me to the doctor's to have it swabbed clean. Poor Lola must be feeling something similar. I wince at the memory and only want to cuddle her, to soothe her. After a couple of minutes which seemed to last an eternity, her tears must have washed the dust away. This is the first time I've had real tears from her and considering we've been in the car now for almost five hours, I think she's doing really well.

Fortunately, moments later we come across our first truck stop. It is very basic, not much more than a huge car park with little shade, but nonetheless, it offers a chance to check Lola is OK and to take a break from driving. Thirty minutes of cuddles as well as a little walk and I notice that the landscape is changing, sandy and dusty in the warmth of the afternoon sun. We return to Clancy and I feel like we're on the home straight for today, at least – Bordeaux is within reach at last.

This next part of the drive is one I'm comfortable with. It appears straight-forward, to get on the Bordeaux ring road, find the junction, get off – easy! This is until I approach the ring road. I am greeted by a crazy junction and a choice to pick a direction. In my planning I didn't think to familiarise myself with clockwise and anticlockwise and no, it isn't as simple as left or right! I go with my gut but soon notice that we are heading south-east which means I am going clockwise, and that wasn't the plan. A few seconds of anxiety pass before I think –

"It's a ring road, Emma! You'll get there either way!"

I must be getting tired and stupidity is creeping in, but at least the panic is over. There is more traffic on here than we have seen so far, mid-afternoon on a weekday, with typical idiots switching lanes and cutting people up. I stick to my guns, coast along the inside lane with my eyes peeled for the right junction. In reality, I can't really go wrong as we're heading to Spain, which funnily enough is fairly well signposted.

So, we're on the final stretch and it's only about an inch on the map. I vastly underestimated this last bit. The drive to Parentis-en-Born seems to be the longest of the whole day despite only being forty-five miles. It is an eternity before I finally see the sign for the D43 and it then dawns on me, after all of my efforts to avoid tolls, there is a barrier between us and the junction! My plan has been foiled! I cautiously move towards the big orange "T" that tells me my tag will work here and watch the barrier rise as we go through the toll gate to the sound of my Sanef tag beeping. At this point, although initially somewhat annoyed, I really don't care. At least we know the toll tag on the windscreen is working.

Finally, we turn off, heading west to our next stop, La Reserve, a lakeside park once again owned by Siblu. This drive is long and flat but now we are fringed with pine forests and dust. We are now in Les Landes. This time there is no Fête du Vélo to greet us, and I find the site easily. To be honest, I'm exhausted, and in fact I could cry at the sight of the reception, with relief setting in that I get to relax for a while. It has been extremely hot this afternoon, though surprisingly, Clancy's sheepskin seats are brilliant for high temperatures. It got decidedly sweaty today in full sun with little cool air circulating, but the covers, rather than making me hotter, absorbed the heat. Right now, though, all I want to do is have a shower or a swim and a cup of tea, to stretch my aching body.

After a warm welcome, we find our cabin and park Clancy up. As expected, it is spotless inside and I am over the moon to once again find a stovetop coffee pot, and within minutes our cabin is filled with the aroma of fresh coffee!

It was always going to be short lived, that moment to relax and have a drink. Thirty minutes later, Lola and I set off to explore a little. This is a big site, and we can walk through the huge pine forest surrounding us to get to the lakeside beach but we need a map to get through the little roads and rows of cabins. Eventually, we emerge from the cool shade of the trees to be welcomed by the clean white sand and a gentle breeze. The sun is now sitting lower in the sky. In the blink of an eye, Lola's shoes are off and she's gone! Who can blame her, after almost eight hours in the car. As I watch her play, oblivious to time, unaware of the significance of this journey, I feel at ease despite being extremely weary. I sit with a bottle of water and some bread, feeling the ache of my neck from a day at the wheel, yet also feeling the stiffness drain from me. I know we have a couple of days here to rest and I know that one of the drives that was concerning me most is over. Right now, I am feeling invincible and seeing Lola – hair blowing in the wind and running barefoot in the sand – reminds me to be present, to take mental note and commit this to memory.

This is why I am doing this: life should be about shared experiences and appreciation of them, about not only enjoying our time but also making that time available.

Families are coming down to the beach with picnic baskets and who can blame them. The sunset is promising to be beautiful, but for us it's been a long day, so as the sun starts to sink I persuade little Miss Sandy Hair to come back to the cabin with me. After initial protest, she is persuaded by hot chocolate and a hunt to find the swimming pool. We stroll back to what is to be our home for the next few days, chatting about why the lake isn't the same as the sea and why the sun goes to sleep and the moon wakes up. Simple pleasures.

As we approach the cabin, we are greeted by shadowy figures on the sandy ground next to us and I see boules. I hadn't noticed when we arrived, as it appeared as an unused area of ground and nothing more, but now we see numerous bodies in the dying evening sun. Some slouched with cigarette in hand, some more animated, with arms gesticulating in disgust at their latest throw, and of course the chatter in a language familiar to me yet too rapid to understand.

We wander past unnoticed and I let Lola into the cabin before unpacking Clancy. He has cooled down nicely and I pat the bonnet and give him my thanks for delivering us safely once again. Rain is forecast this evening so I take everything we need inside, as it looks like we're in for a stormy night.

We settle down for a chat and a cuddle and the next thing I remember is being woken by thunder. The rain on the roof is deafening, yet Lola is in the land of nod. My brain adjusts to the rhythm of the drumming on the roof and eventually I fall asleep.

Rain

The night is somewhat disturbed, with thunder, heavy rain and winds throughout, and it is a relief when I can at least get up and have a drink. Sleep deprived but excited to start a new day, we have our ritual hot chocolate and coffee, and are feeling optimistic that the rain will stop. We sit, we wait and I give in to the iPhone to keep Lola entertained – it's torrential out there.

At half past ten, we are offered a reprieve so decide to venture out, Lola in her trademark red wellies and me in flip flops, as we pick our way through the puddles. It's remarkably quiet and I realise that people are probably looking out of their cabins thinking "they must be Brits!"

What our observers think makes not the slightest bit of difference to me as Lola revels in muddy puddles and giggles uncontrollably.

Whilst contemplating where to drive to today the skies darken again and we retreat from the attack of torrential rain and poor visibility. My sensible head says this is not a day for driving, but a day for staying put and waiting for it to pass, so we do. With steaming fresh coffee in hand my thoughts turn to the surrounding area and the places we may explore once the weather improves.

Bordeaux is the entrance to this unique part of France. Les Landes is extremely flat, yet you are lulled into thinking differently as the landscape is famed for immense sand dunes and dense forests with trees towering all around you. Many crops are grown in the area, which is interspersed with lively seaside towns, oyster farms and extensive cycleways. This really is a wonderful region to explore with children or alone; our site, La Reserve is situated on the edge of Lake Bicarosse near Parentis-en-Born with a lakeside beach and cycle paths on the doorstep. Within a few minutes, you have Mimizan Plage or

Bicarosse Plage, should you wish to get out and explore the beautiful Atlantic beaches. The cycle paths and watersports bring many visitors to the region and I can see why. It is wild, beautiful and seductive and offers something for all ages.

To the north is Dune de Pilat, which I plan to visit tomorrow if the weather is better. Although we are not too far from Spain here I think heading over the border will bear little fruit in these conditions, I also think that the Basque region is worth a visit of more than a mere few hours. In contrast to the sunny Spain we imagine, this area is green and rainy but it also has great food and a rich cultural history to explore. Originally, I had planned to drive down the coast into Portugal before going to southern Spain. That route down the Atlantic Coast and inland heading south-west was on my itinerary to get to Casa Annette, a small guest house in Cortelazor and I still hold a strong desire to see inland rural Spain to spend a few days immersed in the simplicity of the Andalusian hills. I will plan it for another time for it would be a shame to rush – instead, I intend to embrace the journey across the Pyrenees which are only a hop, skip and a jump from us here. These mountains have captivated my imagination for many years and I am finally going to get to drive from the Atlantic to the Mediterranean, a dream come true.

Dune de Pilat

"Mummy, where's the sunshine gone?"

Good question, Lola. It appears to have been swallowed up by a big cloud of mist, never to be seen again.

Despite the grey outlook, I am determined to go somewhere today. Dune de Pilat is nearby and I believe will be a good place to go in search of – after all, how hard can it be to find a sand dune that is 500 metres wide and 2.7 km long? At 110 metres high, I should be able to spot it even in the mist, and Lola plus sand equals entertained child for a while.

It's still quite warm but decidedly damp so we take a jacket and jump in Clancy. We're heading north along the coast road towards Bicarrosse and I think it will take about half an hour to reach our sandy destination. Mr Reliable starts at once and we set out. I've done my route map, and it should be a breeze today as we're not going far at all.

Driving along the roads in this area is a little lacklustre; it is beautiful but because the roads are flanked by tall forests you can see very little. This continues so far that I wonder if I am ever going to find this sandy monument – I guess it's on the other side of the trees, but how do we get over there? Eventually, I can see sand above the trees – just a glimpse, though, and soon it is gone. But I need not have worried because shortly afterwards we are met with the signs. The signs that tell me I am not going to casually stroll up this dune and enjoy its peace and quiet, the signs that yell –

"I'm a tourist attraction – not just an incredible freak of nature!"

Well, we have come this far, so I turn into the car park which is carved in between the trees of the forest with plenty of narrow, muddy tracks to park in. Potholes are in abundance and puddles rise up to our ankles from the rainfall of the last 24 hours – heaven for Lola and her favourite foot wear.

"Muuuum. Can we just jump in the puddles? I don't want to go to the beach, there's one at Siblu."

"Lolly, there's a car coming! It's a car park!"

Fortunately, the speed of oncoming vehicles is less than five miles an hour, the bumpy ground rattling even the best suspension money can buy.

"Ohwa – but Muuuuum!"

Her lovely turquoise and white striped dress is now fully customised to blend in seamlessly with our surroundings, perfect shades of brown splattered like the mud on Clancy's mud guards. She loves to co-ordinate, does our Lola.

Eventually I convince her to come with me. There is a time and place for puddles – I have been known to jump in a couple myself – but for now we have a sand mountain to conquer.

Walking to the dune is not quite what I expected, and after I have figured out the parking situation (pay on exit and it's free if you can run up the dune and back in 20 minutes) we pass multiple gift shops and cafés. It is a shame, but I guess it has its place and it helps reduce the destruction of the forest. Having a controlled entry point is probably a good idea, but a little more subtlety than tacky gift shops would be nice, though.

The views once we reach the top are outstanding, even in the mist. It was hard getting up here – it didn't seem too bad from the bottom but I mistakenly chose to "take the steps". These steps are unstable, slippery and basically dangerous, with each step almost as high as Lola's legs. It was hard trying not to slip myself and even harder trying to hold on to Little Miss Lolly.

The lush green forest which we have just walked through seems tiny as I gaze inland; the trees appear like a close knitted blanket, and a solitary house is dwarfed by the enormity of the sea of dark emerald it stands in.

Out to sea, the view is quite different. The Atlantic has been stirred by the storms of the last two days and still swells, with white foam rising atop a grey mixing pot of wet, salty depths. Waves fascinate me, they always have, and from here I am captivated by the sheer drop of the sand meeting the endless expanse of grey. Blue seas and skies are beautiful, but here today I am pleased to have seen the power of Mother Nature as she reminds us that beauty comes in many forms. For a few moments, watching the waves is enough to distract me from the mist and the tourists that have engulfed us, but then I turn to look at the dune to see human ants – black dots following each other along the sandy ridge formed into a sculpture by the wind.

Next, I turn to see Lola – the boots are off, so is the jacket and she's rolling in the sand. It's going to be a messy day! She takes great pleasure in running back down the dune and amazingly, both of us remain upright. We walk back through the tourist shops and I succumb to postcards, a chicken baguette and an ice cream for you know who. Was it worth the walk? Well, yes, it was and when we go to pay for the parking, it is only a couple of euros, so I am happy.

The weather is still miserable and as we drive back to La Reserve I have a niggling feeling that these storms aren't going to be leaving us anytime soon. I think I may need to leave a day early if I am to cross coast to coast to the Med.

Fog Bound in The Pyrenees

Well, it's Sunday, and we've been away a week and today is the first day I've decided to change the schedule. The weather over here on the Atlantic coast isn't improving and I am anxious about the drive east over the Pyrenees to the Mediterranean. It's going to be a two day drive rather than the one day I'd planned. Now that I understand the time it takes in good conditions, I know that taking on a drive through the mountains in poor visibility is going to be hard. There is little point in sitting here in the rain worrying about what's ahead, so I am better off leaving a day early and taking it slowly. With the plan of a quick trip over the border to Spain for a day foiled by the storms, I must accept that we aren't here for a holiday, we're here to complete a challenge. The pressure that I'm feeling at the moment isn't very pleasant at all – I am trying to make the most of the time with Lola and ensure that she has a wonderful time but inside I am starting to wonder what I've got myself into. Perhaps it's just tiredness, but either way, I have to press on. Clancy won't drive himself home, will he?

On the plus side, I get to visit the Pyrenees, which is something that has been on my bucket list for many years. There is a distinct possibility that I won't see much in this weather, but even if I can take in some of the small villages and stunning scenery I will be happy. I have my fingers crossed for a ray of sunshine, in more than one way, for the descent to the Mediterranean.

The plan is to cut across country, head south-east on a diagonal and hopefully get past Tarbes, which sits near Lourdes high in the mountains, before we search for a bed. It would be lovely to stay in a nice *chambre d'hôtes* (B&B) for a few nights and explore the mountains but this time it will be a cheap overnighter.

We're starting out later than usual because it's Sunday and the shops aren't open yet. Although I can get fuel at the self-service pumps 24-7, we do need a few provisions for the trip, so we'll stop in to the supermarket too. I'm just about to give the cabin a good clean, which is a requirement to get your deposit back. Tip – when staying in a particularly sandy campsite, you should keep on top of the sand on a daily basis so that you won't end up with a dune in your bedroom. It seems to multiply from in between one's toes to create a mountain!

This is the first change to our planned schedule, the weather is dismal, there is a chance of more storms and I'm hoping I can run away from them and leave them breaking over the Atlantic coast as I head to the hills! I'm looking forward to the next couple of days – to stunning views and an air of anticipation – and though I am a little nervous as I have visions of narrow, twisty mountain roads, it has to be done. Worst case scenario, we have to take cover somewhere and there probably isn't a nicer place to do that than in the Pyrenees, so all in all there is nothing to be concerned about. Let's see how far we get.

At the fuel station I am once again the centre of attention. It's funny how people just assume I am fluent in French and launch into conversation with me. Perhaps it's the old Peugeot, which to be honest is not uncommon in France, or perhaps it's just the way people are – I'm not sure, but it's fun. My French is limited but I can understand a reasonable amount – well, that's if it's not fired at me like a machine gun, of course. This particular instance involves a gentleman with wispy white hair ("he's got silver hair like Grampy, mummy!") and a berry brown complexion, the lines on his face akin to a road map of his life. Perhaps he just wants a chat?

I manage to talk to him for about five minutes, and I'm not sure whether he is understanding anything I say but I am left with a big smile on my face and a feeling of calm. Isn't it strange how some people just have that air about them, the ability to almost suck the stress out of you just through their presence? This man was one such person and I am left feeling ready for the drive ahead. I'm also happy because the diesel is 6c a litre less than it is 200 metres up the road. I spotted the difference yesterday afternoon, and though it may be small, it will add up to the cost of a croissant at least.

As I think about filling our tummies using the money saved at the pump, I remember to write down our costs. Being on a tight budget for this trip, we don't have the luxury of eating out and buying whatever we please. I have a preloaded travel Visa and when it's gone, it's gone. It's a week into the trip – I'm keeping a manual record of everything we spend on a daily basis because I would hate to find myself stuck in the middle of nowhere unable to get myself out of a sticky situation. For all of the excitement that surrounds a trip such as this, the reality that is in the forefront of my mind more often than not is that I am travelling alone with Lola, and money is a concern, as is health of both us and the car. Driving for miles at a time without seeing a soul is pleasant as long as you don't let the niggling awareness of "what if" creep into your mind.

Today is going to be challenging – a dream coming true, yet I am a little scared. The roads I have taken so far haven't been motorways but they have been main roads, while today I will be weaving through minor roads, traversing the plains of the Midi Pyrenees and I don't know what to expect. Cows and sheep, I am sure; services and toilets, I think not. Yes, today is going to be a big challenge indeed but I have to do it.

Clancy is full, levels and tyres checked and we're good to go. Lola is set up for the trip, *pain au chocolat* and milkshake in hand and I've bought her an app for the iPhone to keep her entertained. She's been incredibly good and I really want to knock out a few miles today. She knows that it's going to be another full day in the car, so the least I can do is make it more bearable for her. I have resisted the urge to buy WIFI access until now but I think it may be a blessing for her to have something to keep her busy, so I bought half an hour of internet and downloaded a game.

The forecast suggests that I may be driving in thunder and lightning today, but at least doing it this way I am breaking up what could be a long trek – my idealised view of this part of the trip is rapidly becoming a distant memory. In future, I will limit myself to spending more time in one region so that I can explore properly. This particular region has so much to see and do, and from a personal point of view, to awaken to a view of the mountains – shades of green against clear skies and simply to be able to meander – would be a dream come true.

But today is about covering ground once again – the plan is starting to unravel! It's not a bad thing, it just sets me a little challenge of finding somewhere to stay on the hop. I have noted the larger towns which house roadside motels such as Premiere Classe and Formula One and am sure we will find one considering it is low season.

The route for today is seemingly simple: cut across the E5 motorway and head south-east using the minor roads. As we do so, the skies become increasingly heavy, as a mist which I'd hoped to leave near the coast is now becoming dense and all encompassing. It is going to be a long day. Despite the poor visibility, I remain optimistic – in my mind is a vision of the pretty villages and communities which fill these foothills, but the reality is that I am traversing some remote areas and there aren't a lot of towns or people! Can you picture it, the village square adorned by a post office and town hall, with the statuesque steeple of the church standing proud in the centre? There is a buzz as locals chat in the street on their way back from coffee and bread collecting duties. A chicken flaps across the road, followed by a goat and a lumbering dog and children play in the fields happily.

Well, I could picture it but I'm certainly not finding it! Not even a place for a coffee so far, and then I remember the Sunday rule. Note to self: based on previous experience, Sunday is great to drive but useless for finding anything open!

Finally, I come across a town with something open – Roquefort, where my initial thought is "Ooh – let's get some cheese!" My moment of excitement is short-lived when I realise that this is not the right Roquefort – the one famed for its AOC *(Appellation d'origine controlee)* fromage is Roquefort-sur-Soulzon and it lies in the south of the Parc Naturel Régional des Grands Causses. It is still in the Midi Pyrenees but much further north-west in the Aveyron. If I manage to get across to the Millau Viaduct it may be somewhere we can go, as I remember hearing the legend of the cheese and it has always teased my imagination since.

> *The legend has it that a love-struck shepherd… in order to follow a shepherdess, supposedly left some bread and sheep's cheeses in a Combalou cave. On returning some time later, he found them covered in mould. He tasted the cheese and loved it. Roquefort was born. Guardians of this savoir-faire maintain this tradition in the deepest of these caves – it seems the miracle is still performed to this day*

59

With Clancy resting in a scruffy looking square, we get out to stretch our legs. The little place I originally thought we could pop into is not at all appealing. There are elderly men smoking, reading newspapers and drinking beer, not coffee. I appreciate the authenticity of the shabby looking establishment but choose to walk across the bridge in the other direction. There is little else here, some pretty gardens on the banks of the river below us but not my little Pyrenees dream village, by far. We return to the car, wondering if this time perhaps I have gone a bit too far off the beaten track. We'll see.

As we roll through the miles I am thinking of what may lie ahead. I imagine the sun breaking through the stubborn mist and the beautiful panorama emerging slowly… at first, a shadowy and sinister outline of the peaks high above and eventually, the impossible colours of the mountains win against the millions of droplets of water that are blurring my perfect vision. I wish I had a cloth and that the road ahead was a steamed up window, and I could simply wipe away the fog to reveal the stunning landscape unfurling in front of my eyes.

Although this would be a wonderful scenario, the cloud does not lift and the time is approaching to look at the map because these roads are narrow and there is nothing around to tell me where I am. I haven't seen a car for a while or a house for that matter – in fact, I can't even tell if there are sheep or cows in the fields that line the roads. Yes, it's that foggy.

The roads have a deep gully running along each side and then a field – no hedge, fence or road markings. Driving today in thick fog is like walking a tightrope: I have to trust my judgement and just stay out of the gutter. Once again, I allow my mind to wander, imagining the scene on a sunny day with views to die for, of cattle grazing in the lush landscape with the mountains as a backdrop. Or perhaps a farmer trundling along on a little old red and rusty tractor – you know, one of those with the bouncy seats and squeaky wheels.

"I need a wee, mummy." Lola is squirming in her seat as she announces herself back from the world of the iPhone.

My daydream is abruptly ended and it's time to look for somewhere safe to stop because this particular road is definitely not an option in fog. I hope that we soon find some kind of village or road with a bit more space to pull over, but the time drags on and it crosses my mind that I may be going around in circles in the mist. Finally I see a sign on an unannounced crossroad which indicates that Tarbes is not too far away. There is a grass verge on the narrow road opposite, so after Lola is relieved of her discomfort, I take a moment to look at the map. The good thing about the detailed Michelin maps is the ability to see these tiny roads. I find the crossroads and realise that I am not off track but I would be better heading east towards Saint Gaudens – the main road is closer if I head that way, and right now I need some easier driving and a bed for the night.

After what seems like hours, I finally reach the D817 at Lannemezan and also welcome a clearer sky. We have come onto the road further east than my goal of Tarbes, which means I will happily be off the road soon. I feel a huge sense of relief to see a sign for Saint Gaudens, which is a good place to stop because it will give me the option of heading to Toulouse and Carcassone in the morning or taking a different route if I feel like it. I haven't decided which way to go because although I am interested to see Carcassonne I am also aware of the fact it will be very busy. As a World Heritage Site, it is likely that within the ancient walls we will unfortunately be confronted by a blaze of tourist shops, so I need to think about the practicality of it. Will Lola enjoy it? Do I have time? Is there a better option? At the end of the day, I can reach the place easily from Canet Plage should I choose to do so for a day trip, and perhaps that will be a better option.

The trouble with doing these lengthy drives is that you really just get to the point where you need to rest – you lose interest in what is around you and focus on the goal. In Saint Gaudens I keep my eyes peeled for a sign leading me to a motel. I'm sure it is a lovely little town but all I can think about is a bed, and I could not tell you if the town is quaint, busy or quiet but I do know there is a roadside motel around here somewhere. I may not be able to absorb my surroundings, but the big McDonalds sign next to a smaller one for the Hotel Ibis tell me to head out of town. Somewhat on automatic I do as I am instructed, but after a few minutes I can't find either the golden arches or the motel, and the only thing in sight is the sign for the motorway – I don't want that! After a split second of panic, it occurs to me that these establishments are strategically placed, so the search is not abandoned. We continue following my gut instinct and sure enough, sitting on the roundabout exit to the motorway is our destination – well, Lola thinks McDonalds is where we're stopping and expresses her disappointment when I pull into the carpark of the hotel. Let's hope they have a room!

This is our first experience of such a motel in France. It's clean, efficient and does what it says on the box – a bed for the night with a coffee and snack machine in the foyer. These hotel chains have varying standards: some have restaurants, but most are here to cater to the driver or business person, perhaps. They are priced accordingly, this one is fifty-five euros plus five for breakfast, and Lola doesn't get charged as she's under five. Of course, it is possible to find a bed and breakfast for a similar price in some regions, but for the purpose of tonight, a roadside hotel is what we need. Anything more would be a waste of time and money.

Checking in is easy, and we take one bag upstairs, leaving the rest in the boot with Clancy parked under the security camera. The room is clean, with a large double on the bottom and a single in bunk bed style above. The TV is set to Madagascar in French to keep Lola happy while I have a welcome shower, easing the tension from my shoulders. I hadn't realised how much driving in that fog has taken out of me. Keeping my wits about me while trying to talk to Lola and keep Clancy out of the gutters all came together to give me a challenging day. Alas, my dream introduction to the Pyrenees has not quite met my expectations but tomorrow is another day – one which I still haven't planned but have high hopes for.

The Best Pain in the Neck I Ever Had

It is six in the morning in an Ibis twixt the motorway and a drive-through McDonalds. Not quite what I had in mind for my overnighter in the Pyrenees, but nonetheless a good stopping point. The room serves its purpose as all of these budget hotels do. I have to say that the bed in this place was very comfortable and it was quiet, which I didn't expect given the proximity to the motorway. Unfortunately, my vision of enjoying a leisurely drive through this region with time to explore has been somewhat clouded for two reasons, the need to cover ground more quickly and the underestimation of the time travelling these national routes takes.

Actually, let's make that three reasons, for despite the lovely comfortable bed, I have woken up with a crick in my neck and it is fairly painful to move my head even slightly. This causes me to pull out the maps and look at the planned route to Perpignan. I had been in two minds about a stop at Carcassonne, knowing that it is a tourist trap but swayed by the fact that it is after all, a World Heritage Site. The reality is that I certainly won't be taking the *autoroute*, which would have been the quickest option to get us to our final destination in one day. I am not stupid and whilst I use my mirrors intensively when I'm on the road, I also always glance over my shoulder before changing lanes, and there is no way that is going to happen today. This leaves the D117 and on reflection, I am very happy with this decision – the ability to stop at will and to enjoy the Pyrenean scenery, if I'm honest, is far more appealing than thousands of sweaty tourists in a walled city! This, for me, is a classic case of embracing change and being flexible along the way.

We have woken up to an improved outlook. We left the West Coast because the weather was not particularly good and we are looking forward to what has been promised – the return of the sun. After my deliberation over the route, I pack up our overnight bag and head down for our all-you-can-eat breakfast. It's good that they don't charge for Lola, as she nibbles some honey cake, eats a pot of apple puree and some cheese. I feel that it is of course only fair for me to enjoy the croissants and bottomless coffee on offer, despite it not being of the standard of our patisserie from Siblu Domaine du Dugny.

With breakfast over, it is time for us to get back on the road once again, this time for a drive which entices me with excitement rather than apprehension.

"But mum…. What about McDonalds?"

As we roll out of the car park, Lola protests that we have not gone to McDonalds, despite it being ten metres away. She doesn't like the food but the idea of a happy meal is far too tempting for her little mind. Sorry, Lola! Mummy's in charge and we're going mountain hunting – you never know, we might even spot some goats and find a hot chocolate along the way.

"WEEEEEEEEEEE!"

Once we are on the road, her grumbling lasts just a minute or two, and then as I navigate around the roundabout she squeals and leans into the bend in her seat. This seems appropriate for corners and roundabouts and is something I'm going to be hearing a lot as we traverse the landscape of the Pyrenees.

As soon as I turn from the roundabout on to our planned route, I know this is the right choice. I am filled with anticipation because I know from my maps that this route will take us further up into the mountains. The motorway would have simply taken us north-east to Toulouse and then south-east to Carcassone and to be fair, that would have been a little boring! The good thing, we are on the main road and it is a good surface to drive on, gently undulating and sweeping its way deeper into the scenery. I am starting to feel a little nervous excitement in my tummy; blue skies meet shades of green, as the landscape of the Pyrenees unfolds ahead of us, and at this point I am very grateful that the decision of which road to take was taken out of my hands by a sore neck! Indeed, this is the best pain in the neck I ever had!

There is little traffic on the roads. I have seen a couple of trucks and a handful of campervans but that's about it. Clancy is happy to coast along at 40 mph, occasionally we reach 50 mph, but with no pressure on me now, we can for the first time really enjoy the ride.

Our first stop is not far into the drive. I made a conscious decision this morning to take frequent breaks in order to limit my tiredness and neck pain. If it happens that I don't make it down to the Mediterranean and Canet today, then so be it, there will be places to stop if I need to along the way. In all honesty, I don't think that will happen as it isn't actually that far, just 163 miles, but I am prepared to stop if I find the going gets tough. Clancy appears to love this terrain, being such a heavy old boy he just kind of rolls along the miles, with such great suspension, comfortable seats and none of the hard ride you experience in modern cars. We pass St Girons, and roll into a small town called Castelnau Durban, which feels like a good place to take a break. Not only is it picture perfect but I am feeling the need to walk and stretch; what better than at a place next to a babbling brook in the mountains.

Lola and I both fall instantly in love with this little village for different reasons. I love the simplicity of it, how as in many French towns at ten in the morning there isn't much going on! Lola, on the other hand, has spotted a school with a playground complete with children and she likes the look of it – I have to say I can't disagree with her. It would be a wonderful place to go to school, surrounded by nature. The school building is typically French in appearance, colourful shutters on the windows set off against the backdrop of the lush green pastures of the Pyrenees.

"I want to go to school there, mummy. Can we go to talk to them?"

Oh, if only it were so simple – but who knows what may happen in the future!

My eagle eyes spot a toilet block in the car park and not wanting to miss the opportunity due to the scarcity of such things in France, I cajole Lola into leaving the oh so pretty school in order to visit said conveniences. It takes a little blackmail, a visit to the shop while we're here, but eventually she agrees to come with me. Why do I mention the toilet? Well, this particular drive is one that I would recommend to anyone and with that in mind I should also let you know where you can find toilets! If you take this route, be sure to stop in this little town, take in the surroundings and use the facilities as you may not see another until you reach the Med!

The little shop next to the river is obviously geared towards tourists but fortunately it does not suffer the invasion of tack that many such establishments do. There is a deli and a lovely selection of artisan products, ceramics and crafts here. I don't mind paying for quality and can't help but imagine that the sheepskin slippers that Lola has her eye on have come from a sheep that wandered in the fields above us – extra thick and fluffy to cope with the cold and wet which it has endured.

Yes, you've guessed it, I buy those little boots for her and feel happy but also a little guilty; this is the first time in the trip I've spent money on anything other than food or fuel! I'm so paranoid about running out of money that I'm too scared to spend any! This little treat costs me twenty euros, and I could very easily spend a fortune on local ceramics here but once again remind myself that there will be a next time, and at least I know where to come now!

Forty-five minutes later we head back to Clancy where Lola greets him with her usual bonnet hug. I take a picture for the memory – she is fully embracing this trip with me and these little moments are incredibly important. Neck stretched, a brief look at my maps and route card and it's off we go again. I think if I have the opportunity in the future, I would look at staying near here, as it's so central to the region, offering hiking and skiing or simply driving and enjoying the scenery. It is a stunning area on all accounts.

The scenery starts to change as we drive and my "wow"s get more excitable.

"Look at this, Lola! Wow, that's stunning."

These words are continually falling from my mouth as we creep ever closer to the silhouette of the mountain peaks to the south. I come to a junction, one which says "Andorra" or "Foix". My heart is screaming at me to take the route further south to Andorra – traversing the mountains across to Spain would be incredible. It is the most I can do to take the road east to Foix but with a last longing glance at the lane winding up in the distance, I do so. I remember that I have a destination and a goal and a brief detour to Spain would be not be that at all – I could well be gone a couple of days! I don't have the time or money for that luxury but the strength of the feeling to explore reminds me of the fact that I am my father's daughter and that it is getting lost off the beaten track that truly drives me. I see no sense in sitting on a motorway, mindless and boring, whilst missing the special bits in between. Life is an adventure and although we could never take every single side road that appears on our journey, we can have a damn good try and see where it takes us!

Ten minutes down the road I see a view that I can't help but stop to take a picture of – the peaks of the mountains are providing a stunning backdrop to the pastures in which cattle are grazing. Yes, it's a cliché but I don't care. The stark contrast of the now bright blue sky and the multi-faceted greens of the land are too inviting to miss. Thanking my lucky stars for my neck pain once again, I remember that on a motorway I would not have the luxury of stopping to take such a photo: in fact, I wouldn't even be able to see it, would I, driving at 100 mph, eyes forward, watching out for speeding drivers of fast cars on mobile phones!

If you are the owner of a fast luxurious car, I apologise for putting you in a pigeon hole but I'm afraid I could write a book about the experiences I have had with erratic lunatics driving cars with little respect for the rest of us on the road. My experience is of agitation and impatience, always wanting to get there first – why don't you slow down and just enjoy the ride?

Well now, I have probably successfully offended a small part of the motor world, so shall I continue? You didn't expect a girl in a very old car taking the back roads in France to be a fan of flashy cars, did you?

Back to the latest photo stop, Lola and I enjoy the view alone until a couple of other cars pull in and of course spill out with their picnic baskets. This is one of the things I love about doing this: we are not in a designated rest area, just pulled over on a grassy verge with a small layby, yet the French manage to lay out a full picnic – wine included – and treat it as if it were a ten course degustation. Lessons to live by, I feel.

Of course Lola and I do not have the beautiful wicker basket, the wine or the cigarettes for that matter but we are happy with our bottles of water and baguette to tide us over. Are we hungry? No, not really but we don't need to be, since for once we are just sitting looking at the view.

Unfortunately, we can't sit here forever and I want to take a minor detour into Foix as we pass through towards the blues of the Mediterranean. Once again, I reluctantly strap Lola in and get back into my armchair, patting the steering wheel as I tell Clance we're off again and he obediently jumps to attention. Next stop, Foix, then Perpignan, before we continue to Canet en Rousillon, where our next accommodation awaits. I may need some paracetamol along the way, as my neck is starting to hurt more and a niggle of a headache is trying to sneak in. I tell it to go away – there is far too much beautiful scenery to look at, and there is no time for headaches.

Foix is a small and intriguing town worth a visit if you are passing. It has an air of calm and the locals appear to have a permanent smile affixed to their faces. I pull Clancy into a gravel car park – or at least that's what I think it is. There seems to be no reasoning around the positioning of the other cars, just a case of squeezing into the gaps. Strolling across the road to the path that goes along the river, we wander in the lovely, warm sunshine. The sound of running water is music to my ears, and the little bubbles are so clear we can see the pebbles below, their shades of brown catching my eye momentarily with a glint of sunshine. Sitting on the bench next to river, we are sheltered by trees. A gentle breeze whispers through their leaves and as I take a deep breath, I can smell nothing but fresh air – not even bread! Looking up, I see that we are overlooked by the Château de Foix sitting high above the town. I can see why in medieval times it was said *El castels es tant fortz qu'el mezis se defent* ("the castle is so strong it can defend itself"). Comprehending that it has been here since the year 1000 reminds me of the emotion I felt whilst in a lesser known museum in Venice. It was the only time I have ever been brought to tears in a museum and was scared to breathe for fear of breaking the silence. This castle is not as old as the paintings on display there, nor is the silence so loud, but the feelings it evokes, and the idea that there is such great history still surviving to inspire us always stirs something deep within me.

This time, more so than previously, I feel a desperate desire to spend more time here but am mindful of the time escaping us today. If I continue to stop every ten minutes we'll never reach our destination. Regrettably, it is time to leave Foix and leave the rest to my imagination, but I am very pleased we stopped here – it further reinforces my desire to spend more time in this region – to share it with others and to introduce Lola to a world beyond anything she could learn in a school classroom.

When you're driving up in the mountains, it's hard to really get a feeling of how high you are – that is, until you reach a peak and are able to look down on the road you need to traverse to get down. This happened to me as we abridged the summit above Quillan. Of course, we had to stop for photos but it was at this point that my father's words echoed in my head. When I was learning to drive there were two things I remember very clearly:

1. You can be the best driver the world, but it's all the other drivers (I won't use the exact words!) you have to worry about.
2. Use Your Gears.

Never more than now, as I see a steep descent ahead of me with hairpin bends to negotiate, will this resonate more. I am planning on not using my brakes unless I have to!

"Mummy – how will we get through that mountain?"

I had been thinking exactly the same thing, for on the other side of the town all I can see is a mountain. I guess we'll have to go around it!

We pull out on to the main road and I am pleased to see a truck ahead of me. He will pace me and hopefully stop any of those aforesaid "others" from trying any risky manoeuvres on these roads. I am very lucky, as Clancy has a low ratio gear box and therefore I can easily drop down a gear to slow him down. It really is possible to drive on my gears with this old man. My Clio back home would not allow me the same security in this situation.

I stay behind the truck as we trundle down this hill. The town awaits us at the bottom and we drive through without stopping, only to be faced by what appears to be a sheer mountain face ahead of us

– it is the same one we had commented on at the top of the hill and I am about to find out how to get around it now!

In the UK we live near Cheddar Gorge, a beautiful part of Somerset where you can indeed drive down through the gorge into the town. Well, Cheddar, as much as I love you, you have nothing on this! We are driving through the rock! The road has been carved to follow L'Aude River and when I say 'carved' I am not exaggerating. At this point, following a vehicle somewhat larger than me is a blessing as it gives me the chance to gauge where on the road I need to be positioned. Imagine looking at a cliff then taking a spoon and scooping out a section from the side to make a backwards "r" shape with a very curled down top! Yes, we are driving underneath half an arch which is carrying a mountain on its shoulders. My scientific and quizzical brain takes a moment to consider the physics behind this before I say out loud –

"Don't think about it, it's been there for years, just go straight through it!"

Today is indeed turning into a memorable day.

Having negotiated this stunning part of the drive, we are now reaching lower ground and the next hour or so is uneventful. The landscape starts to change as we are nearing the Mediterranean. The road is still long and straight but we are starting to see sand muddled with the granite, and the lush green of the mountains is now giving way to sparse shrubs and the occasional vineyard. My thoughts go to visits to Spain and I am reminded that we are almost in Catalonia. The road signs are starting to appear in French and Catalan – this excites me as I am interested in culture and history, and Catalan is one which holds a certain mystique for me. The staunch traditions and desire to be considered independent and the vibrancy yet simplicity of life is intoxicating. Many people think of Barcelona when they think of this region, yet it starts up here in France. The area near the Spanish/French border brings a melting pot of two countries rich and diverse on their own, only enhanced by the common tie of Catalonia. For me, this region is heaven.

70

Our destination on the coast at Canet means that we must get through Perpignan, and as we approach the town it appears I underestimated the task in hand - and the traffic. We arrive at approximately three o' clock, having been on the road since eight, and although I've taken a number of breaks it is now well over thirty degrees and I am stuck in a traffic jam. Typical, to be caught at the last hurdle just as I thought it was almost over! The windows are open because of the heat and we're stuck next to an old bus with fumes bellowing out, moving at around one metre per minute! Just as I am resigning myself to this being a long afternoon, I see a sign which directs us down the path of the river. In my hazy memory I can picture the river on the map and decide to take a chance – I think it may be a way around the traffic – with what's called driving on instinct.

As you know, I don't use any navigation technology, and instead make my own route cards and study my maps intensely, committing the picture and place names to memory. If I am honest, it's one of the parts of travelling I enjoy most, being able to find my way around countries in this way, with the additional help of the position of the sun. Even Lola at three years old understands that I use the sun to direct me in times of doubt. So here in the heat of Perpignan on a Monday afternoon, we are just eight miles from our destination and at a standstill. I am in the far left lane and I need to be in the right hand one to get over to that road; this may be the most challenging manoeuvre to date as the traffic is bumper to bumper, with frowning faces to be seen all around me.

I make my move and smile at the truck on my flank as well as shrugging my shoulders and pointing where I want to go – step one achieved, as the man allows me to poke my nose in front of him. I do the same to the next lane of traffic and it takes a couple of attempts. The exit is now only a few metres away and I have grumpy people sitting behind me but I'm determined to get where I want to be. One more car and we're there, and I ease off the slip road feeling somewhat accomplished as a stubborn yet sensible driver – perhaps I am more like my father than I realise.

Now what? Follow your nose, Emma. Canet is south-east of Perpignan and the main road runs down the coast so I head to what is unmistakably the sky above the sea, slightly off course from the sun, which is now past its height in the clear blue sky. I am excited to

71

see the silhouette of the Pyrenees as they reach their fingers towards the sea. I can't quite see the water yet but I know that when I can see the fingertips reaching the azure ocean I will be near our destination.

The next few miles is easy going and I find the right road signposted to Canet and follow the road to our home for the next couple of nights. Through two roundabouts, turn right immediately after the second I remember reading and sure enough, we arrive at Mar Estang, Canet Plage.

Relieved to be here, I park Clancy under a tree and take Lola into the reception. As I ask for our reservation, I am greeted with a stiff reply.

"We have no booking for you."

My heart sinks. I have a piece of paper in my hand which says otherwise and suddenly I feel exhausted. It's four o'clock and I don't want to drive anywhere else. The lady at reception is not helpful in the slightest but getting upset won't help. As I start to consider my options, an English speaking staff member calls across and asks if I'm looking for Al Fresco. I hold back the tears and feel the panic that was rising a moment ago start to ease as he tells me things work differently here.

Until now, we have been staying at Siblu sites, which are wholly owned and managed by Siblu, with one reception for all; at the sites where multiple operators have accommodation, there is an independent reception for each. I am directed to the location of said reception for Al Fresco and am not sure whether the tears I can feel welling up are tiredness or relief, but either way, I am happy to see a friendly, smiling face walking towards me waving. He knows my name, he's expecting me and he's called Laurence. He also goes to get me some of his teabags as he can see I am in need of a cuppa - how very English but very appreciated!

Once we're shown to our van, Laurence gives us the space we need and assures us he's there if we need anything – is now the time to cry? Not quite, but it is time to stretch our legs and find something yummy, and Lola and I waste no time in going off in search of food and drink and are pleasantly surprised to find an on-site bakery filled with too many delights to choose from. But we manage it and with a chocolate eclair with extra chocolate inside – almost as big as Lola's head – and a baguette and some fruit from the shop, we walk back to our cabin. As we do so, Lola asks me to tell her the story of how Clancy got his name so while she makes a start on her sweet pastry, I start.

Clancy lived in Australia for a long time. He worked hard driving thousands of miles every month, but eventually he got to the age where he wanted a rest so he started to take it a bit easier, spending more time close to home. One day, while he was resting under the shade of a gumtree, a camel train came past – this was a normal occurrence for him, but today one of the camels was limping and looking very tired. The farmer realised that the camel couldn't carry on, so offered him a home on the ranch for him to rest and get better – the camel was called Clancy. Soon afterwards, the farmer and his wife were talking about how the camel and their Peugeot were like twins, reliable ships of the desert who were now enjoying a quieter life, so when Graham, the farmer's dad, came to take his car back to his house they decided to call him Clancy in memory of the camel."

Lola knows this story well but still loves to hear it.

"He's part of our family now, mummy."

Yes, Lola – he is.

We sit on our deck with our delicious food. The rain we left behind on the Atlantic coast is a distant memory as we enjoy the evening sunshine and though I notice a constant stiff breeze, the air is fresh and warm. Just right, I think.

Clancy gets unloaded and is given thanks before I sort out our sleeping arrangements – it is going to be an early night. Now I've started to relax, I am becoming aware once again of the throbbing in my neck and head. I was so focused on getting here I'd managed to dismiss it for most of the day, but now as the sun starts to set over the lake, I just want to flop. We can explore the area in the morning. Clancy has once again done us proud and will need refuelling and levels checked in the morning, but for now he can have a snooze next to the cabin.

73

A New Direction

The soft glow of the imminent sunrise peeps through the gap in the curtains – it tells me that another beautiful morning is about to start, yet despite the knowledge that the views of the Pyrenees await us, the feeling of isolation cannot be eased.

Yesterday was hard. The anxiety had built over the course of the past week, and a breakdown was imminent – the slightest incident could be the straw that broke the camel's back. That straw came in the form of an orange lady in a hypermarket. I had decided to go out for fuel, ready for our departure tomorrow so as to be able to have a rest today. The 24 hour fuel pumps were located at the huge Casino not far from here so it seemed like an easy thing to do.

Upon arrival at the store we were greeted by something twice the size of my local Tesco Superstore, which would have been fine were it not for the lack of staff present. When we reached the checkout there was not one till manned out of the twenty lining up in front of us. The only option was the self-service till.

As my turn arrived, I became aware of a breath on my neck, close enough to smell the stale smoke – the overpowering scent of perfume mixed with it caused me to feel nauseous. My ears tuned in to sound of tutting and mumbling, and upon turning, my eyes were greeted by a lady who was as orange and brown as a seventies carpet. Her poor application of fake tan combined with years of lying in the Mediterranean sun and smoking made her skin appear like a wrinkled autumn leaf.

I was already feeling anxious before I left the campsite and having this person towering over me in high heels, sunglasses on and bleached blonde hair appearing like icing on a child's cake, only increased the panic I felt rising. For some reason I lost all of my confidence and felt out of my depth – what the hell was I doing? My surroundings suddenly felt utterly foreign and the air of discomfort the women had shrouded me in was almost too much to cope with.

After she had almost repelled me from the till, we walked back to Clancy and I knew that I then had to go for fuel – by this point, I was shaking and almost in tears. We got into the car, where I managed to regain some composure and I drove across the road to the pumps, but this is where I broke down completely. I could see the exit from the roundabout very clearly yet I was unable to work out where to get off! My brain had shut down. Eventually I pulled across to the hypermarket again so as to watch other cars before following suit. How could something so simple bring me to my knees?

As a result of this, I went back to the cabin feeling inadequate, isolated and scared – doubting everything I am trying to achieve.

This morning I am able to re-frame somewhat. After I got back last night, I talked to dad and he helped me to understand something I had lost sight of. He doesn't care whether Lola and I complete the full 3,000 mile challenge or go home tomorrow – he just wants us safe. I have been putting far too much pressure on myself to just get this done that I allowed my health to deteriorate, and what I need right now is to take a step back and be with Lola while I get myself back on my feet mentally and physically.

"Mummy, let's go hunting for some flamingaloes! Laurence said they live in the lake."

Lola's timing is perfect as she jumps up and down before flopping on the bed next to me, her wild hair tickling my nose as I wriggle it and rub it on her cheek. She giggles uncontrollably before reminding me that we have to go now before the sun comes up so that we are back in time for the bakery and I can't really argue with her.

This is why we are here – our lives pass by so quickly and we waste far too much energy worrying about unimportant things. It's time to focus on now and make the most of our time here. So we are going for a walk to see if we can find some flamingos which roost in the lake next to us. *Etang de Canet ou de Saint-Nazaire* is a few moments away on foot and I have an excited little girl who wants to go "flamingaloe" hunting. Her pronunciation of the word is enough to bring a smile to my face and lift my mood a little. I don't correct her – I will remember that moment for a long time as the sense of pride shows on her three-year-old face.

The sun is not yet over the horizon. It rises over the Mediterranean and sets over the Pyrenees, and as for the view, you really couldn't ask for more. As we take our morning walk, I feel grateful to be here, despite desperately fighting the desire to go home.

A bright orange dot sits on the water, its size growing rapidly, changing the colour of the sky as we walk. Once we get to the lakeside, we walk together, talking and enjoying the moment. I take a photo of Lola with the mountains behind her and the glow of the rising sun catches her skin beautifully. The mountains are purple this morning, there are shades of pink in the sky, and the clouds are floating effortlessly with the highest peak stretching high above them. I don't think I will ever tire of this view. After our walk, we pick up our fresh bread and go back to the cabin. I am feeling overwhelmed with waves of emotion and I need to focus on Lola. I'm going to enjoy a day with her today just being mum.

On the beach it is a pleasure to see Lola playing, and she even persuades me to go in the sea. It is warm from the long summer days which have now passed, and the gentle waves are music to my ears as I hear the "swoosh" when they wash over the sand and retreat back to the beautiful blue Med. Turning to walk back up the beach, I avert my eyes from the promenade and its raft of apartments, choosing instead to focus my gaze on the Pyrenees. I'm still exhausted but the view combined with the soothing sounds of the sea help me to relax.

Approaching from the sea is a brown bundle of happiness – brown not from a suntan but because Lola is covered in sand! She is rolling up the beach, attracting sand to her wet body as she goes and her hair is now a tangle of salt and sand, stuck to her face and in her eyes. I can't help but smile, to see her in her element – just being a child, just having fun. These moments give me strength to continue; she is a tonic, there is no doubt about that.

The blue sky is slowly changing to grey, and a few drops of rain tickle my cheek as I continue to watch my little girl play. I can't help but think of how her Grampy would feel to see her so happy. The pang of familiar sadness reinforces the strength that my little girl gives me – there was a reason I started out on this challenge and I will see it through. I am lucky to be here.

I seize the moment, jump up and run down the beach and tell Lola we're going for a swim in the rain, one of my favourite things to do.

"But mummy, you'll get wet!"

I laugh and take her hand and walk to the water – funny child!

We splash around for a few minutes before I have to admit that the rain is now a little too hard to be fun anymore. Our towels are soaking, so we drag our soggy selves back to the cabin to get dry. This turned out to be a fun day once I allowed it to be, so let's hope we can turn this thing around and continue to enjoy the time we have left.

15

Collioure

This morning I have woken up still feeling a little disheartened but comfortable in the knowledge that I am doing the right thing for my health and my family. Making the decision to shorten the route is a hard one, and the visit to the Peugeot museum after passing through the Italian lakes, the Alps and Switzerland is still just about on the horizon, depending on how the next couple of days go. The problem I have is that if I just drive from one place to another, I will not be able to explore and write. When I consider this, I decide safety and a more complete experience for us both and for those who read our story is the better way to go. How can I talk about being on the back roads when I am racing from pillar to post, sleeping in the moments in between just to get through? A shortened route together with a more laid-back approach will allow us the luxury of exploring our surroundings and that can only be a good thing.

As I have mentioned, when I was first planning this route I was hoping to travel down through the Basque region to Portugal before coming across to Andalusia; from there I was to drive back up to France through inland Spain, across to the Côte d'Azur then into Italy. In Italy I considered driving to Le Marche before coming up to Lake Como, Switzerland and possibly even Austria. Our final stop was to be Berny Rivière, an hour north-east of Paris in the countryside.

It was fairly obvious before I left the UK that I wouldn't manage that distance given the time restrictions, so I have already adapted the route somewhat. I'm still hoping that I can make it across to Italy but we'll see. What I can do is enjoy the beautiful region we are in right now, and if I set sensible goals this will give us a shorter drive with more time spent discovering what surrounds us.

So today I am heading in the direction of Spain. I am told that on visiting Collioure you can dangle your feet in the shallow waters of

78

the harbour and little cleaner fish will nibble your feet – I'm not sure about that but it sounds like a nice place to visit anyway! It is only eighteen miles to this coastal town, so depending on how time goes we may even get to Spain. We'll see.

The route to Collioure passes through St Cyprien and Argelès, where I know there is a market today. I am hoping to find some local food and wares. I've not yet had the pleasure of a traditional market on this trip and I am looking forward to it.

We approach Argelès Plage and I am hit by a myriad of colour – unfortunately, bright pink, yellow and orange rather than the preferred colours of nature and history! Undeterred, I drive through and spot a market on the harbour side, and after some negotiating with motorhomes and people crossing the road aimlessly, completely unaware of oncoming traffic, I find a field to park in and walk back down the main road to the market. I learn very quickly that the idealistic view of a French market is not always as perfect as you would like. This particular one could have been in any town anywhere in the world in terms of the stalls on offer – cheap kitchen wear and clothes and little in the way of the fresh produce I had hoped for. A very brisk walk past the stalls leads us to the harbour area, which is a much prettier outlook. Surrounded by waterside restaurants, bars and gift shops it reminds me of Auckland Viaduct, a place where I have spent a fair amount of time – I used to have an apartment on the harbour in the days when I was working in the city, in a life which is a distant memory now that I have Lola. The difference here is the jaw-dropping backdrop of the Pyrenees behind the boats which makes it bearable in the midst of tourism!

Around the harbour there is a mixture of shops and eateries, and my quest for local ceramics leads us into a gift shop which turns out to be an emporium of plastic tat – perfect to draw Lola's undivided attention. I am very lucky with Lola, since up to this point in her short life, tantrums could be counted on one hand, but the tiredness and being in the car so much seems to have got to her today. When I say "No" to a request for a pink plastic monkey, she turns into a crumbling, weeping pile on the floor. As this is so unusual for her, I am caught a little off guard and not sure of how to proceed; the fact that we're in a shop (I am not a shopper!) doesn't help matters! On this occasion she is determined to come out of the shop with something for her. I am very tired but not quite prepared to give in, so we march out of the shop and back to Clancy, a good ten minute walk during which Lola continues to voice her frustrations.

When we get back to Clancy, I feel absolutely drained once again. I know Lola so well and I know that for her to behave that way means she must be exhausted. Once again, the doubts that I had managed to come to terms with start to creep into my mind, and even if I quit now and drive straight back up to Brittany it's still a long drive.

Am I doing the right thing? Is it worth it?

Lola and I have a cuddle on Clancy's big back seat and we snack on croissants. She is calm now and I am feeling better for the mutually beneficial cuddle. I tell her I'm sorry she's sad and I love her, and she gives me a big kiss and says, "I'm sorry too, mummy – I don't know why I cried, I just couldn't stop it". We decide to drive a little further but not too far so that we can get back for a swim and a walk later.

Clancy trundles out of the field and we join the D114 heading south to Collioure. I'm not sure what to expect, but I have my fingers crossed that it will be quiet given the season, but it is a much visited town. We arrive at a roundabout at the top of the town and head down the hill, and on seeing a sign to a car park I take advantage straight away.

It sits above Fort Miradou and a military training camp, and I lock Clancy, having paid two euros for all day parking. We decide to take a look at the coastal path above us before venturing below. It is stunning. From here it is easy to absorb the dramatic coastline and the town below us, and I am pleased we took a moment to do this first. Not only is it a view to remember, but it also gives me a good idea of how far we have to walk. It's not for the elderly or faint hearted but I think we can manage it.

My backpack is well equipped with towels, swimming costumes, water and camera to ensure we cover all eventualities once we get down to the town. I just hope I don't have to carry Lola and wet towels back up the hill!

The walk down is not particularly interesting, with residential properties sitting on a very steep main road, but once we get to the bottom I start to become a little intrigued. I know that Collioure is an artists' haven, with many famous painters including Picasso having lived here, and I am already starting to see why – narrow streets, pretty flower filled window boxes and artist studios entice us in as we start to move towards the water. It is already quite busy – I dread to think how it would be in August.

We browse a couple of shops before being confronted by ice cream, lots and lots of ice cream. Lola chooses a strawberry one and we continue to wander around to the left which takes us to the harbour area. It is when you reach this point that you appreciate the splendour of the architecture here, a fortified town with imposing walls and a tower protecting the shallow waters.

On turning the corner, we find some seats made of crates, painted a metallic grey and backed by artists displaying and selling their wares in the open air. I'm not sure if the seats are supposed to be a sculpture or for sitting, but having just walked down the hill in the sun I'm sitting down anyway.

Refreshed, I realise that the crowds are arriving by the bus load but nobody seems to be making the walk over the little bridge and around the giant walls, so we do exactly that. We are greeted by the sight of a small beach and colourful traditional buildings. Wrought iron balconies and shutters painted bright bring a smile to my face and I realise that despite the crowds, the ambience of this town holds certain romanticism.

Of course, the links to Picasso add to that, and I find myself imagining him sitting here with a Pastis, taking in the clear blue sky and the vivid colours that ensue from the sunshine adorning the landscape – the architecture is, of course, stunning and begs to be painted. I let Lola get her costume on and splash in the water while I just take it all in. There will be wet clothes to carry back up the hill in the bright French sunshine but it doesn't matter – she is happy, I am happy and I definitely understand why so many artists are attracted to this area. I'm not sure that I would feel the same way in the height of summer but visiting in September allows you to enjoy the sunshine and quiet moments away from the crowds.

Half an hour later and it's time to move. Lola would like to stay but once again I'm in single-mum-on-a-mission mode, thinking of getting food, then back up the hill to Clancy so he can take us home to the campsite safely.

Once Lola is dry, we leave the beach and find a small park just above which provides a lovely play area sheltered from the sun by towering palm trees. Lola makes a new friend while I sit and enjoy the view for a few minutes. A little white train passes as I wait for her, and I guess it may be an overpriced tourist attraction but it would also be nice to take a look and see how far it goes. I manage to persuade Little Miss Lolly to come with me and we find the departure point for the train. It travels along to Port Vendres, through vineyards and to a lookout point high above the Catalonian coast. Lola gets to go free, being under four, and it's eight euros for me – not cheap, but I think it will be worth it and now the train has been spotted by my little excitable girl it would be hard not to!

The first part of the trip is pleasant, simply taking us out of Collioure on the main road, but I have to say that it's nice for me to be able to enjoy the views rather than being behind the wheel. I look down to see that Lola has nestled her wet head under my arm and is asleep already, and though I wasn't expecting that, it's a good thing – she must be exhausted.

I enjoy the ride on the train in a welcome moment of peace. My arm is going to sleep but Lola is a picture of serenity – salty wet hair and a healthy glow – a different picture to the shop in Argelès this morning. She stirs on the descent into Collioure and wastes no time.

"I'm hungry, mummy – can we eat now?"

It occurs to me that we haven't eaten since this morning so we leave the train and set out in search of food and whilst there are an abundance of places to eat here, they aren't for us. I can see the wine on the tables, the sunglasses and the mobile phones, and we need simplicity, please.

Rather than walking through the narrow streets around the harbour we take the back road, and are rewarded by more pretty buildings and a small sandwich bar – just what we need. A ham baguette, a cake and a bottle of water is perfect and we sit on the pavement in the shade of some trees and enjoy a delicious lunch. This bread is different to the crustier baguettes we've had so far – it has a softer, chewier crust which complements the salty butter, salad and tasty ham perfectly. The cake is covered in sprinkles. I give in once Lola has had a few mouthfuls of the sandwich and let her dive in to the rainbow of sugar. She looks up and I smile: she has a moustache of icing and little coloured dots and is completely unaware. She smiles back and a little shower of sugar drops over her chin to her lap. She uses her finger to attempt a rescue, picking them up and popping them in her mouth with a level of focus I would use to thread a fine needle. I'm sure we'll both be suitably refreshed to climb the steep hill now. It's decidedly hot but we have to get there somehow – Clancy is waiting for us!

Back at the car and the memories of this morning are distant. We've had a lovely day and I realise that this is what we've been missing. It's time to get back to the site, have a shower and go for an evening walk by the lake.

16

Aaahh. Ceret.

Today I am feeling more positive. I've had a rough few days and I gave in to my sensible head and took some time out to regain some strength and actually enjoy this experience. There have been doubts, tears, phone calls home and exhaustion but I'm getting back on track now. My phone call with dad three days ago made me think about the reality of this situation – I have been so focused on achieving my mileage goal in a limited time that I have lost sight of why I embarked on this journey in the first place It was because I felt helpless and was looking for a way to do something which would make my father happy, to give him something to focus on at a very difficult time.

The fragility of life is something that we rarely face. Whether it is because we are afraid to do so or are just too busy, I don't know, but the reality is that all of us at some point will have to face these fears. Life is not infinite.

Right now I feel like a spring that has been wound tight for a long time, one that is slowly being given a little space to move but yet to fully "boing". I returned to the UK two years ago after living overseas for many years and I am only now starting to see things gradually take shape in my life. Coming back to the news that my father had Prostate Cancer on top of the MS was something I took in my stride at the time, yet I think the cumulation of this together with the upheaval of starting afresh with nothing as a single parent has perhaps manifested now that I am here, miles from anyone I know, facing daily challenges of my own.

My belief has always been that we are students of the world and that Lola will benefit from this trip, not only from having time with me, but by learning about so many things while we are away. Nonetheless, I of course doubt my sanity which has been questioned on more than one occasion. Having said that, while here at Al Fresco in Canet Plage, I have had the opportunity to talk at length to

Laurence, who has been incredibly supportive in helping me to rearrange my accommodation when I realised I just needed to stop. The plan had been to drive over towards Italy and spend a couple of days near Nice but after talking to dad, I realised that spending two days in each place then driving for seven hours was not going to have a happy ending. Al Fresco have been kind enough to change my booking from Frejus and allowed me to stay here for a few extra days to recover fully. This also means that I won't be visiting some of the areas I hoped, but at the moment, I am really taking it a day at a time. The only thing that is for sure is that I will get Lola to Disney for her birthday.

I have gone from having a meticulously planned trip to one which could go anywhere!

Today, however, I intend to achieve two goals: find a donkey and go to Ceret, a small local town that I saw on TV a while ago. I was drawn to the surroundings and the appeal of a quaint and relaxed town in the beautiful Pyrenees. The buildings are old and weathered and the ambience warm and friendly – of course, television can paint any kind of picture it desires with clever editing but having driven through the region on my way down, how could I not take a trip back up to the hills? Ceret is within easy reach, and if my research is correct there is a donkey riding stables on the way! You may think I am mad but I had promised Lola a donkey ride before we left home and whilst I can take her to Weston Super Mare (UK) for a ride on the beach, it's not quite the same as climbing mountains on them. Yes, of course I have a vivid imagination, full of beautiful scenarios, but if we don't dream we have nothing to work for, do we?

I have also decided to ask Laurence to come with us, his girlfriend left last week to go back to University and I think he is missing her. I also know how hard these guys work in the high season, with long days and little praise from demanding tourists – the life of a rep may seem an easy one but I would say it's far from it. It will also be nice to have adult company along the way.

"Mummy! Where is Laurence? We need to find him!"

Lola is incredibly excited at the prospect of having company in

Clancy, and she has already told him all about the car and her Grampy and has enjoyed having attention from someone other than myself. Small things like taking the time to sit down and listen to her stories and dance with her have put him firmly in her favourites category.

I know he has to work this morning as the final few guests are leaving their cabins, but afterwards he has some free time. We walk along to the Al Fresco office and to Lola's disappointment he isn't there, so instead we decide on a little walk across to the beach. As we turn the corner, Lola spots her target and charges head first towards him.

"Laurence! You have to come with us today – we're going to the mountains again!"

He tells us that he'd love to but he needs to finish some work, so we agree to depart around half past eleven. It's going to be odd having someone in the car but a nice change nonetheless. We all get into Clancy and Laurence is kind of gobsmacked – he thinks it's a very cool car and is surprised by the interior.

"Wow! This is such a cool car. Why has it got a furry dashboard?"

I explain that the modification is to stop the glare from intense sunshine reflecting up into your eyes. He nods before asking –

"Why is the car called Clancy?"

I explain the story with Lola's help but she accurately points out…

"But mummy, he doesn't look like a camel."

I admit this is true and say he works hard like a camel – and she seems to accept this.

We continue chatting about the car, dad and why we are doing this challenge and head south to Argelès before turning inland towards the mountains. I have entrusted my map to Laurence which feels very weird, as I think I'm happier following my nose! I have read that there is a horse and donkey stables in a small village on the way – well, not really on the way, kind of around a few lanes off the main road, but in the general direction. We appear to be in the middle of nowhere, on blind bends following gravel roads and with a tendency to meet crazy locals wondering what we're doing up here. My guess is that since it is September they are hoping that all of the tourists have gone home so they can fly around the lanes at their usual speed – on reflection, no, 60 mph is probably normal regardless and it is probably why they drive beat-up old cars rather than shiny new ones.

After encountering several speeding locals, I admit defeat – our search for donkeys has failed, the stables are closed because it's the end of the season (didn't say that on the leaflet) so it's time to head back to the main road and upwards to the cooler air of the hills. It has been hot but extremely windy down on the coast, so much so that it's almost unbearable to walk. Lola has likened being on the beach to electric shocks – not sure how she knows how that feels but she's right, being bombarded with sand in high winds is decidedly painful and annoying. Up here in the hills it seems a little calmer and as we ascend I am excited at the prospect of finding somewhere to have some lunch and a wander. To be honest, I've decided to make today a day out of sorts. It sounds silly when we're effectively on holiday but we haven't done much of the "having a nice time" side of things. Today, I'm having lunch out instead of making our own and I can't think of a better place to do it.

Ceret is a town in the foothills of the Pyrenees with a population of around 8,000. It sits firmly in the Catalan region which is something I love about this area. One of the staff on our site had said, "I am not French, I am Catalan!" I love this regional pride but when I asked him to explain more to me about what that meant to him, we had a problem with communication. A simple understanding of the statement may suggest an arrogance, or perhaps a long standing rivalry with other regions, but his posture, arms folded and shoulders back, together with the amazement that I should even ask him to explain actually says it all. I am either stupid or very brave to question his loyalty and love for his home. I need not ask any more – I get it.

Catalonia spans France and Northern Spain, which again is something I find fascinating, but what makes me even happier is the ham and cheese! You may ask, how can man survive on ham and cheese alone (or woman for that matter) but when you sample Cuit de Jambon so tender that it dissolves on your tongue leaving a trace of sweetness, and you mix it with the mild smoothness of Manchego cheese and simple rustic bread, you will understand. Simplicity at its best. I could very happily live on ham and cheese sandwiches, which incidentally reminds me of a time in Venice when I did exactly that because I could find little else… but anyway, to get back to my point, Ceret is Catalan, in the mountains and near to the sea – it is my kind of place.

We arrive to Ceret fairly quickly and begin the search for a car park. To be honest, I am a little surprised, as in my romantic imagination I expected this town to be old throughout, but here in the outskirts there is modern housing. I am learning a lot on this trip and one of the most important things is that the only way to really discover a place is to visit it yourself – that is, of course, unless you have a wonderful writer like myself to fill in the gaps that the travel and real estate agents miss for you!

There are no spaces here and I feel a little disheartened. I really did want to wander around here and take in the ambience. Not to be beaten, I set off in my usual left then right, follow my gut manner. The worst that can happen is I go up a one way street and a gendarme stops me – ah wait! That already happened on our first day in Onzain, didn't it!

After a couple of dead ends, we decide to retreat down the hill. There must be more than one way into the town surely, and as I creep out of a crazy triangle-shaped junction I catch a glimpse through the trees of some cars parked below the road. If I can find an entrance, this could be a spot to park – it could be someone's back yard but it's worth a try. Out of nowhere we see a gap in the trees and turn right down a narrow gravel track. I am a little dubious about this but I really want to see Ceret so I park up next to a couple of work vans and survey the area. It does appear to be a car park and it is actually exactly how I imagined Ceret would be – I can see the old buildings and narrow pathways above us – and though I have yet to find the path to get up to the town, it must be here somewhere. As I release Lola from her seatbelt, I see an elderly couple out of the corner of my eye, emerging from some trees, and I now see the way up to the town. If I am honest, it is so quiet here that I feel like I am intruding. I notice that the couple are carrying a basket and picking fruit, is it theirs or can anyone pick it? I assume the former and although I would love to sample some, my parents taught me better.

As we wander up this pathway, I can feel the flutter of butterflies in my tummy. This is what it's all about – a little trepidation and a town which has been flirting with my dreams for some time. I imagine that the elderly couple I have just seen have walked this same path at the same time every day for fifty years, that the uneven pathway is this way due to the number of feet which have trodden the soft stone over the years; every tiny dent and crack telling a story of its own. These two people remind me of the importance of not only family but also friendships and with Laurence with us today I'm pleased to feel that Lola and I have a new friend for life.

This area of France is certainly one with two sides: the orange-brown coloured bodies lying on the beaches or driving their expensive cars, walking the beach in high heels; and those who live a quiet and carefree existence just a few miles inland. Worlds apart.

Together with Laurence, we come into the town square and are greeted by multiple places to eat and an abundance of art galleries. The square is shaded by huge trees and the atmosphere is incredibly relaxed but we have a decision to make, where to eat! My usual solution to solving such problems is to use Lola – she picks the place she would like to eat at. Is she influenced by the ice cream menu placed front and centre? Of course, but that's fine, the waiter here is the most cheerful of all of those in the surrounding establishments and welcomes us in. Yes, this is the best place for us.

Little Miss Eyes Bigger Than Belly orders a sundae with pears and chocolate while I pick the only thing I could here in hills near the Spanish border, Jamon Iberico and Manchego sandwich. Notably the menu says *jamon* not *jambon*, the Catalan language overriding French despite being north of the border. I am expecting the ultimate sandwich and indeed I get it. Served on a beautiful dark blue plate, I receive two slices of bread, each an inch thick, filled with the most delicate yet tasty ham and subtle cheese to complement it. The cured meats of this region are outstanding and the bread is really all it needs. Some may call it peasant food, yet to buy this quality of *jamon* in the UK would cost me a fortune. I choose a fresh lemonade to drink along with the obligatory coffee and I sit back and enjoy the

89

ambience.

Laurence proves to be a great distraction for Lola, and I relax – for once I don't need eyes in the back of my head. Glancing over to my right, there is a murmur of noise and I realise the local bank is closing for lunch. It crosses my mind that I could possibly handle a day job here – being able to spill out into this character-filled square for a couple of hours each day is certainly not the same as sitting at a desk working through lunch as I so often did in my professional life. Back to reality, as Lola exclaims that her tummy is full, and what a shame! I will have to finish the monster sundae, but I'm sure I can.

With full bellies and Lola with ants in her pants, I have to say goodbye to this little spot where I could quite happily sit and watch the afternoon go by. Many of the shops are closed as expected but one little gallery remains open. The proprietor looks up over his glasses from his painting to acknowledge us and it occurs to me that he probably doesn't feel much like he is as work; sitting enjoying his craft with the door open, not concerned over whether he gets any customers today. Any that come in and make a purchase are a bonus.

I spend as long as Lola allows browsing the originals and prints on display but refrain from a purchase as I know I can't justify the cost and we're only half way through the trip. I did indulge in a couple of cheap prints in a Collioure gallery which will satisfy the urge for now. If I manage to buy anything else on this trip it will be ceramics, but I have a sneaking suspicion that my sensible head won't let me. Next time I come to this region, I will come with an allotted budget for ceramics and art – oh and a big chilly bin to put some local *jamon* in! It's funny, despite the brazen front of certain coastal areas here, I have ever so slightly fallen in love with it; how could I not with such stunning scenery and vast array of architecture and history. It is confirmed, though, I am an off the beaten track kind of girl – the allure of bright lights and late nights is not for me.

Wandering back to Clancy, I have to wonder if anyone actually lives in these old, narrow streets. The silence surrounds us and Lola's constant chatter and singing seems to echo out across the green landscape. How wonderful yet intriguing.

Fortunately, as we get back to our secret car park I am pleased to see Clancy is still here. I had felt like we were intruding somewhat and had been a little concerned for his safety (mad woman!). After a bonnet hug from Lola, he rumbles to a start, smoke cloud around us, and we climb the gravel track back up to the main road. It's only a short drive back to the coast – it took longer on the way up as I was in search of donkeys and ponies – but this time, it's easy. Again, to compare how far removed I felt up in the hills – surrounded by history and mystique – to the modern tack of the area we're staying in, is a comparison of two worlds, yet only separated by a road and about forty minutes. The joys of driving.

This seems like a good time to touch on exactly that. I know that everyone is different – some like to fly and be catered to, some like to explore – but let me try to tempt you a little. Had I not wandered off to Ceret or taken the minor roads through the Pyrenees, I would have missed out on memories. Yes, I felt out of my depth in thick fog and unsealed roads in the agricultural lowlands; in fact, that's an understatement. I was peering over the steering wheel feeling the full tension of my upper body in my shoulders as I prayed we were nearing a main road, but I knew that if I followed my gut I'd get to where I needed to be. What will Lola remember? She will remember the moment when the fog lifted and we saw the beautiful mountains ahead of us, and she will remember driving down a tiny lane to find a hedge suitable for a toilet stop! Today is similar, and I could easily have been sitting by the pool or on the beach but it would be such a waste. Having the car with us gives us freedom, and it's not just any car but a car we've brought from home.

You see, even if you fly, there is a limit to what you can take with you. When you take a ferry or similar you are free to do exactly as you please – in fact, you can pretty much live out of the car. You just load up with everything and off you go, easy! No trying to squeeze the lid down on the suitcase or deciding what to leave behind, anything goes! Perhaps if you are driving a SMART car that wouldn't be the case but hey, I'm not, I have Clancy, who has a huge boot and seats which fold down into a bed. This car was built for the road and the history is a testament to it, 1 million km and counting – did I mention that already?

But once again, I got sidetracked, and my point is this. Today, by following my instincts, I have had a glimpse into a different life, into the past and into something which I yearn to know more about. It's inspired me to improve my French so that next time I see an elderly couple I can talk to them, if to nothing more than say, "wow, you guys inspire me". If I had not had the car, I would not have had that experience, simple as that, so next time you're thinking of flying to sunnier climes think about the bigger picture, be adventurous and make the most of your time with your loved ones. If you only have a couple of weeks each year to spend with them, even more so, make every moment a great memory to cherish.

Now, after my insightful advice to you, I am brought back to the task in hand and we drive back down to Argelès before heading north along the coast to Canet, passing flamingos on the way back. Laurence heads back to work and we return to being team mummy and Lola. We are back in time for a play on the beach but once again the wind is fierce. There was not a breath up in the hills, but here it's enough to sting your skin as it blows the sand in all directions. Lola says, "It's giving me electric shocks again, mummy" and then yells as sand gets in her eyes. It is not a day for the beach, despite the clear blue sky and tempting Mediterranean Sea. A picture paints a thousand words, or does it? I took a photo to remember the moment, and you would look at it and think "stunning", whereas to be here is quite literally painful. All may not be as it seems in a picture.

Lola and I retire from the beach by way of the underpass that goes under the main road straight into our campsite. There is a security guard positioned at the gate as you exit the tunnel who checks your wrist band; on such a busy beach I would imagine that there would be a lot of unwanted foot traffic in the summer so it makes sense to have this chap sitting here. There are other crossings further up for those who wish to walk along the lake but really, aside from that, all of the buildings are beach side anyway. We haven't really ventured too far along the strip to Canet, and certainly not at night as I'm trying to keep Lola in a reasonable routine, but I know there are some restaurants and bars up there. To be honest, it doesn't really interest me, as I'd rather sit and watch the sunset and hope for a glimpse of a swooping flamingo over the lake. I have promised Miss Lola that we will go to buy some postcards and a new swimming costume while we are here, so we will wander along to the shops perhaps tomorrow – but not until mid-morning, of course, as it will be a ghost town any time before that!

Let's leave it for the night now as it's time for hot chocolate, checking Clancy is locked and cuddles all round. I've had a nice day today and compared to a few days ago it's a huge turn around. I'm trying not to overthink, to leave the maps alone until I need to check them and managing not to worry. The best thing about this campsite is the fact that the internet is so bad – they have a WIFI area near the bar but it's hilarious. As you approach you see a crowd of people huddled around their phones and tablets trying to get a signal. The signal is poor anyway and twenty people in a ten foot square area is really quite funny! You see, although for some it may be a problem, for me, it is good, as it helps me to establish what I hoped to – a disconnect from the online world and reconnecting to precious time with Lola. That said, the blog is not getting updated but hey ho, it's part of the story. The plan was to keep my followers informed as I travelled, but as with many other things on this trip, I can't do it. Let's look at this as something else to add to the story rather than a problem, shall we?

17

Over The Border To Spain.

As I have mentioned previously, we are currently staying at Canet Plage, the beachside sister of Canet en Rousillon. We have kept it simple here, not heading north except to get diesel and essentials at the supermarket.

From our base here at Mar Estang we are within easy reach of the commune of Argelès, which is split into old and new. The old town sits slightly inland and the newer developments on the coast, something which seems common along the coast. The population growth over the last ten years has been huge, with the development of the marina and plenty of holiday and long term accommodation. Personally, I find the strip here a little too full on for my liking but I do feel that it would be worth a visit in the future to give it the benefit of the doubt, and next time I will park up and explore both the inland old town and perhaps sip a coffee while I gaze at the beautiful view.

When you drive south from Canet Plage, you quickly move through St Cyprien before you get to Argelès. You can turn right at the roundabout before you get to St Cyprien if you want to head up to the Pyrenees, but driving through these two towns is fairly painless despite there being many pedestrian crossings – which, incidentally, don't exist according to those who step out in front of your car randomly.

I have driven through the tourist focused area of Argelès on several occasions and you can't get away from the fact that you are smartly hit in the face by bright orange and pink signs and plastic beach fare aplenty. Traditional French establishments are replaced by Indian and Chinese takeaways with the odd Fish and Chip shop thrown in for good measure. From the marina, and much like Canet, the views are beautiful; you can't take that away when you see the mountains sinking into the sea, reflecting and absorbing the light and bringing a new view every day.

However, you can't spend your time only gazing south to the hills, can you? Overall, I think this part of the Pyrenees Orientales is a very good base for families, with the miles of beaches and entertainment on tap. There are numerous campsites, which in true French style are well equipped for you to stay put on site should you choose to. The area is a popular place for retirees too and I can see why that would be the case once the hoards of summer tourists disappear. Being able to enjoy those beaches and views all to yourself during a morning walk and coffee would override the chaos of high season.

The proximity to Spain and the mountains offers huge opportunity to live a full, rich life as well as sampling the local food and culture. For me, as a lover of both France and Spain, this area is appealing. With the road signs written in both French and Catalan, it is a culture standing alone and proud.

I expect the Spaniards living across the border also state something similar and why not? A rugged, beautiful coastline giving way to towering mountains and further south, orange groves and towns such as Girona or Barcelona to entrance you. Barcelona, whilst known for muggings and a high crime rate, is also home to unbeatable architecture and food, and it's a city I could get lost in – but I'd make sure I wasn't wandering the streets at night.

I have to be honest, these past few days have challenged me considerably and I've had to force myself to go out on the roads after my meltdown at the supermarket after we arrived. It really shook me to realise how utterly worn out I was and the memory of the panic rising in my chest when I was simply trying to get diesel – something I've done numerous times, of course – is not a pleasant one. On the plus side, I've learned a lesson here: listen to your body. I wasn't doing that and in the end, my body and mind said –

"No! We refuse to be rational and need to get your attention now!"

Even before we left the UK, I had neck pain and was tired; I was anxious about the crossing because I knew I wouldn't get enough sleep and had a full driving schedule ahead. I felt that I had no choice but to go ahead, despite my gut screaming "it's too much, it needs to be changed", because my head was saying "you have a new job and lots of people supporting you, so don't let them down".

95

In hindsight, I look back and in fact I had lost sight of the fundamental reason for this challenge – to put your family first and make the most of the time you have with them.

So here we are today, sitting in a campsite which is of a good standard, next to main road but surrounded by stunning scenery. This is what gave me the strength to get back on the road, the fact that despite my negative emotions, I am fortunate to be here and have to make the most of it. I have a little angel who I've hidden tears from and who has been so patient, despite being in the car for seven or eight hours a day. My goodness, I am lucky, and the tears come to my eyes with pride. Approaching four years old and able to sit and have a conversation with adults and surprise them with her vocabulary and knowledge, to be able to appreciate the scenery and share her wonder with others. Childhood is a gift and I am here, able to create memories and give Lola all of me. It's enough to kick start my motivation and make the most of it.

Casting my mind over the trip so far, I feel that I have wasted time. I've missed some places and experiences I had hoped to share, yet I know if I hadn't just stopped we would have been risking an accident. It is a bitter sweet moment as I think of the excitement I felt when I found the mini châteaux park and told Lola that we were going on a Princess trail; that was several months ago, before I took my job and when I had more flexibility. Three days in the Loire Valley with Lola's eczema and my headaches did not lend itself to the round trip exploring the Loire I had planned but at least now I can focus on where we are, Catalonia.

We've woken today to a chill once again, which is a good sign as it means the sky is clear, and a perfect morning for a stroll by the side of the lake. It's difficult to describe this walk, as it changes every morning. Despite there being a reasonably busy road between the lake and the beach, the view somewhat compensates. We have done this walk most mornings since our arrival in Canet and each day brings another stunning outlook, with the Pyrenees showing off a different colour, shades of purple and orange, and the definition of each peak highlighted in a new light that is really a feast for the eyes. Honestly, what more could you want than to wake up to the Mediterranean on one side and the glorious mountains on the other?

Which way do you look first? The sky changes at every glimpse as the sun rises over the sea, casting a comforting glow over the land.

We have stayed here for longer than I intended and the reality, as you know, was that I needed to take a break. It leaves me a little sad that we won't get to visit Italy and Switzerland in our limited time frame but it also is a testament to one of the things I was trying to relay in this whole challenge. Life throws curve balls and all the planning in the world may not come to fruition. The ability to stop, take stock and embrace change is crucial; what would be the point of me driving day and night? It certainly would not give Lola and me the memories to cherish and I would be in no position to write this book.

So today I am planning on a perfect scenario, as we are off for a walk to enjoy the beautiful landscape and are then going to drive down to Spain – that is, of course, after our obligatory visit to the bakery. We have definitely slipped into the French lifestyle, waking later than we would in the UK, and since it gets light at around half past seven, we go for our walk at quarter to seven in order to enjoy the relative peace and beauty of the sunrise. We are back just in time for the bakery to open, after which we sit with our fresh croissants and hot chocolate.

It sounds a bit too good to be true, doesn't it? Four days ago I was desperate to go home – I was exhausted and tearful and the reality of what I've set out to do hit me hard. I'm very lucky to have arrived here, to have had support from the staff at Al Fresco holidays and to have been able to talk to my dad about the situation. I was so focused on doing exactly what I said I would do and didn't want to let him down. The tiredness clouded my judgement and I feel very fortunate to have been able to see through that fog and talk honestly about my concerns. Now, I have breathing space and I am going to do today what I wanted to from the start – explore a little and take a day off. I am not taking the motorway, but driving the coastal route which looks extremely wiggly on the map. I'm anticipating a lot of concentration and a long day but I think it will be worth it.

I shall leave you now as the sun is starting to peep over the horizon and I don't want to miss the always changing feast of colours that her rays display for us.

18

And Then I Fell in Love With Catalonia

Fiercely independent, Catalonia has me captivated. I love the simplicity of life, the beauty of the landscape and the call of the past which entices me to learn more. We know Barcelona for football and Gaudi, for the long tree-lined Las Ramblas which I could get lost in forever, watching life go by, tasting my way through La Boqueria (central market) but although the capital of the region has much to offer, it is when you go off the beaten track that the true intimacy and beauty appears. This is so well captured by a book I read recently, "Two Wheels over Catalonia". Richard Guise took the coastal route much the same as we are today, which delights me – to read a book and be able to relate to it is wonderful. He did his trip on a push bike but it's a hilarious book with also just the right amount of interesting facts woven into it.

So today, although we have a choice, it's a simple one – take the easy route and see nothing or wander the coast and possibly still not see much because my eyes will be fixed on the road. Of course my choice is the latter. I could be in Spain in forty minutes but it would be boring, and were I attempting to get to Barcelona or beyond it may be different, but today is about exploring.

The road on the map appears to be a succession of hairpin bends following the coastline of the beautiful Mediterranean. I have written my usual route card with town names and road numbers for quick reference and we are ready to descend on Spain. It is a tiny fraction of the Spain I had hoped to see but it will be worth it, I'm sure.

Heading south once again, we pass through the nearby towns before picking up the D914, which will take us all the way to Spain. I would like to get down to Roses and if I could manage Figueres and the Dali Museum it would be even better. My experience tells me that that a road which looks similar to one of Lola's scrawlings when she was a baby may just mean that I am setting my hopes a little high. I could end up staying in a B&B somewhere high above the Med if I'm not mindful of the time, but I still have my strict rule of being off the road by four o'clock to stick to if possible. We'll just have to see what the day throws at us.

The early part of the drive is pleasant but familiar. We have already visited Collioure and taken a little train down the coast to Port-Vendres, so it is the road from here onwards that things get interesting. It starts to meander more and follows the lay of the land over hills and sharp descents, offering endless views of vines appearing in perfect, straight lines cut into the steep, windswept slopes. The wines of both Collioure and Banyuls-sur-Mer are AOC (Appellation Contrôlée), which means they can only be produced here. The soil is poor and the vines grow close the ground, requiring a lot of care. In fact, the grapes are manually harvested and produce a very low yield per hectare. That said, it is reputed to also produce great wines – perhaps having to battle the constant winds makes the plants stronger and more resilient, slow growing with time to develop flavour.

Please note, I am not a wine expert by any means, and these are just my thoughts when my eyes are filled with the shades of green and brown across the land. I think of mountain goats who cling to sheer rock faces, defying the laws of physics – these vines must have strong roots and diligent and passionate owners in order to survive.

The next town we arrive in is Banyuls-sur-Mer, and as we come over the hill we are greeted by the now familiar frontage of the beautiful buildings of this area. The local tourist board have a slogan for this little town, "between sea and mountain, where the sun and wind meet." I like that, as it describes this stretch of coast very well. On this occasion I am not stopping as we have only been on the road around thirty minutes, but another mental note is made on the ever increasing list in my head of places to return to.

From Banyuls it is only nine miles to Spain but I have a feeling it is going to take quite some time. It appears that there are no towns between here and Cerbère, so I imagine the road and terrain is such that is does not lend itself to settlement.

The driving now demands my full attention, as the road is not only full of twists and turns but is narrow in places. As I have learned on several occasions on this trip, the locals don't share the same concern as me over little things like overtaking on a blind bend with a cliff face on one side and a steep drop on the other. I am amazed to be passed not only on a bend but also on the peak of a hill – madmen, I feel.

I manage to catch a glimpse of the road ahead and am gripped for a moment by anxiety. I can see the road spiraling down to the sea before it climbs in a zig zag up to the next peak. The moment passes quickly when I remember that this is what it what I'm here for, pushing boundaries and getting off the beaten track. Granted, it would be much more pleasurable if there were less nutters on the road with me, but it comes with the territory and I am learning more about driving and myself as each minute passes.

Once again, as with during the descent from the Pyrenees, I remember to drive on my gears and use the brakes as little as possible. Clancy is made for this kind of driving – I am very pleased I don't have my little Clio with us today!

The border between France and Spain sits between Cerbère and Portbou, and between the two, you drive along to the end of Cap Cerbère before doubling back on yourself and climbing the hill to the border. In times gone by, I'm sure things were different but today the only indication of it being a border is the abandoned graffiti-covered booth and a small, square EU sign telling you that you have arrived in España. There is a layby just across the border so I stop to take a photo, and there is a moment of relief as I know the twistiest part of the drive is over. I am now on the N260 and have at least made it to Spanish ground.

Sitting here, high above the Mediterranean, looking at the jagged peninsulas ahead, I feel on top of the world. The sea shimmers a deep blue tapestry of mesmerising calm, and the rugged landscape of the Pyrenees as they meet the sea is a multitude of the colours of nature; there are browns, greens and greys which blend to a perfect view. The simplicity and solitude offered by this region once again stirs emotion in my belly and a tear in my eye as I appreciate the moment.

I wish I could stay here longer but we have a long way to go, so I shift Clancy into gear and start the steering wheel gripping descent to Portbou. There are a couple of hairy encounters on the bends – I think driving downhill on these roads is more challenging than up, perhaps because you can see how far it is to get down!

Once we are through Portbou we pass through a tunnel and now are approaching Llançà, a town where I need to make a decision. Do I go off on the even narrower road to Roses or cut inland to Figueres? The time is approaching two o'clock so I choose the latter: Lola is getting edgy, and I am getting tired, so continuing further off the beaten track would be unfair and risky.

Llançà is a small town which I think I'd like to stop in next time I come down here – today, on a Sunday afternoon, it is quiet. A quick scoot around looking for a parking space has left me with nothing so I decide that it's another one to add to the list.

The drive from Llançà to Figueres is a boring one because we are now back on the main road, and as we approach the town I turn north on to the N11 and start our trip home. As we start to roll along the straight tarmac I realise that once again today has not turned out quite as planned! Yes, as expected the road was very twisty, the views stunning – but of course I wasn't able to enjoy them as I was in the driving seat. This is a road that I would love to drive again, but next time I will allow more time and make more stops along the way, and it would be even better if I had a chance to be in the passenger seat and enjoy the scenery! Perhaps I need to recruit a travel buddy to enable me to do that!

I had a desire to visit Girona today but it was unrealistic given the time I had, so instead I end up just driving. Not that driving is a problem, I love it – but it would have been nice to stop. I am learning a very big lesson today, though. Do not take the N11A via Jonquera on a Sunday afternoon. Having taken two and a half hours to get to the end of the coastal route (you can't get off it, you have to reach the end!), I decided to drive back up the main road. I didn't take the motorway which would have seen us home in less than an hour and because I didn't check first, the border town – which is a haven for people buying cigarettes and alcohol – has caught me out. We have queued for an hour and half just to get up to the town, and it turns out that the problem is that once you decide not to go through the toll booths and you turn up the hill you are stuck, and are going to La Jonquera – the land of crazy tourist shops and crazy people.

I guess if you like shopping it's a nice place to go for a Sunday afternoon, filled with outlet stores and a selection of bars and restaurants, and perhaps it's worth the sit in traffic for some. The problem we saw today was pure volume of traffic. I thought it must be an accident but it is vast numbers of people trying to fit into one narrow road. The benefits are here, I believe, for French people because the prices are considerably cheaper if you cross to Spain. In fact, Laurence said that he has done a couple of tobacco runs with friends to save a few euros but for me it's an enormous NO! Perhaps I should come here on a weekday morning and see if it is as bad, but then again, perhaps I can find something much nicer to do with my time like drive on through and find a picturesque spot to relax and have some local food.

Anyway, having had the two extremes of car travel today – beautiful twisty coastal roads versus traffic jam from hell on a steep hill – I am very pleased to be back in our little cabin. Catalonia has captured my heart. I have been before to Malgrat de Mar and Barcelona, but today was different – today I saw a glimpse of something I wish to learn more about. I stopped to take a picture of the view back up the coast at one point and although it was cloudy it is still stunning, the dark outline of the coast speckled with white houses and terracotta roofs, apparently clinging to the side of the cliffs, ready to fall into the sea. In fact, I think I will paint this scene, as it makes me smile to write the words and imagine the view that those houses have. I wonder if they have pigs that close to the sea and whether their *jamon* would taste different because the animals eat different vegetation to those roaming around in the hills. Hmm - something else to ponder, perhaps I need to write a book about tasting *jamon*? It would of course mean another trip here but that wouldn't be so bad.

19

A Night Out

Last night Lola and I had an adventure. I bent my rules and we went out because there was a family disco in the bar area of the campsite, and as you may imagine, my little girl has never been introduced to the multi coloured lights shining their patterns on the ceiling so she was very, very excited. Despite it not being dark, she had a wonderful time playing with some other children – dancing and running around while I actually had a chance to sit down and have a chat!

I have to admit, I started out as a completely paranoid mother, and despite being just a few metres away, I was worrying about her and thinking about bedtime but after a while I accepted that this is what happens for most people on holiday! In all honesty, I had to let go a little last night but once I allowed it to happen it was quite nice to feel like a grown up individual rather than a full time mother!

While Lola danced, I talked to Laurence and it was a conversation I will always remember. With Lola out of earshot, I could talk about what I'm doing, the challenge, the emotions and of course being a single mum. I was amazed to hear that he thought what we were doing was brave and admirable – I simply have been looking at it as a way to create a memory for my father whilst raising some money for charity. I hadn't really considered how it looks to an outsider, so it was incredibly humbling to know that people do care and believe in us.

During our conversation Laurence also talked about his own mum, how she too was a single parent and worked two jobs, and how he had spent a lot of time in his youth being angry and resenting her. He'd never had the chance to talk to her about how he felt or to be able to understand how hard it was for her or why she had to be at work most of the time. Through talking to me, he felt that he could see why she did it a little better, but the most poignant memory of the night for me is this.

He had been watching the way I interact with Lola, the way I talk to her and include her in everything and talk openly and honestly to her, despite her being three years old. He said that he wished that his mum had spoken to him in that way and that he felt that if they had that relationship he would not have wasted so many years through resentment.

I was speechless. I know I rant on about the importance of making the most of the time we have with our loved ones but perhaps I just assumed everyone thought I was a little bit mad! To hear him say this was enough to give me the extra boost I needed to complete this challenge. I always said if I can inspire one person I will be happy – apparently, I have.

Today is our last day here so I'm taking it easy to prepare for the drive. I am leaving tomorrow with the extra bit of confidence I needed, so Lola and I will stay close to home. We will take a walk along to the shops at Canet, have a play on the beach and perhaps a swim in the pool if it isn't too cold.

We take the underpass to the beach for the final time, listening to the traffic above and walking towards the light at the end of the tunnel. It is nine o'clock and the road is quite busy but the beach is clear. I look to my right and behind me and once again a smile can't help but cover my face as I see the mountains behind us – they really have me hypnotised. This morning they are not the shades of purple we see as the sun rises but a dark mysterious tapestry of greens. The occasional cloud creates a wave of the lightest grey across their faces, the summits rising high, reaching for the sky above.

This beach is beautiful, there is no getting away from it. We walk north towards the town along the promenade and are greeted by a couple with their little dogs and a couple of cyclists – it's still early and most of the coffee shops are still closed. I am about to give up on our mission to find a shop open, thinking they've all gone south for the winter, when one gift shop opens its shutters with a rattle and a clank just behind us.

Lola has asked for a new swimming costume and her crocs have broken, so today I am spending some money. I have been very careful so far and have stayed well under my daily budget, getting by on around ten euros a day – this is because we haven't eaten out, we've shopped locally and prepared our own food. I looked at the menu in the campsite last night and nothing really appealed, but Lola would rather have fun than sit and eat a meal in a restaurant, anyway!

So into the shop we go – I am psychologically prepared this time after the meltdown we had in Argelès. I have a limit in my head, Lola can take as long as she likes and we'll all be happy! Fortunately, on this occasion she is back to her usual self – she finds a swimming costume immediately, a hat and some shoes and we're done. All reduced because he's closing the shop for winter too, so all in all it's a good morning.

On the way out we see a wall of pink – no, it is not pink bricks but ninety-nine fluffy flamingos. These birds have been a central part of our stay here, from the large statue of one on the roundabout, the morning walks to find them, to the eventual sight of them taking off in a sea of pink. The "flamingaloes", as Lola calls them, are a memory we shall take with us – so we buy one.

Having done our shopping for the day, we walk back along the promenade. The skies have turned grey yet there is still clarity of light to be admired. It's a silver grey rather than the murky brown shade I am used to at home! The mountains now appear dark and sinister but the contrast between the sky, the mountains and the bright white canopy on the beach bar is astounding. It is like somebody is shining a torch on the bar – I wish the dull days in the UK were like this.

As we walk along the seafront, the gentle breeze is starting to become more vigorous. We had respite for a while but it seems it is coming back, and I just hope it blows the clouds away for us so that we can go for a swim.

Back at our cabin, we sit on the deck with our bounty in front of us. Lola has changed into her new costume and hat. I have a flamingo sitting on my map book, a baguette, butter, cheese and ham in front of me waiting to be dissected. I tear the bread, as it's so much more satisfying than cutting it, and prepare my mid-morning snack – happiness right there.

My mouth is watering as the tasty treat approaches my mouth, I bite – I chew – I stop. I can feel something very hard in my mouth and it isn't long before I realise it is tooth. Not wishing to alarm Lola, I discreetly take my tooth from my mouth for inspection later – I have a big hole on the right hand side of my mouth. There is no chance of me going to the dentist, so I pretend nothing happened and carry on with my bread. I know somebody else who lost a tooth to a baguette, and I think of my dad as I push my tongue through the very strange feeling gap in my teeth – I know how you felt now!

Once we have cleared up our plates, Lola is very keen to go to the pool to test her new costume. We haven't been in there yet so I've agreed despite it still being a bit cloudy. The pools here are great, with slides for the adults, and smaller pools for the children – much like we have experienced elsewhere.

Upon entry, we are required to take our shoes off, leave them on the shelf and wash our feet. I can't help but stop to take a photo when I see some black stilettoes gracing the wooden rack, and I giggle as I remember seeing an orange lady with white blonde hair competing with the sand in a similar pair yesterday on the beach. A stark reminder that we are in the south of France! Thank goodness we can escape inland!

The pools are cold – Lola thinks otherwise and I manage to stay with her for half an hour before it starts to rain, which gives me an excuse to head back to cabin. We walk back, soggy and shivering and decide that a sleep may be the best idea this afternoon. Our little night out earlier in the week has taken its toll on us so we need a re-charge. Clancy will also need his standard checks carried out to ensure he's healthy for tomorrow, so the rest of today is set to be boring but relaxing, and I'm sure you don't need to read about that, do you?

20

The Dreaded Motorway

Today it's time to move on. My decision to cut out Italy and Switzerland was the right one given the circumstances, but this morning I find myself a little wistful as I had planned so many things for Italy. I was hoping to visit the birthplace of Maria Montessori together with the museum, as well as stopping in the Italian Lakes on the way up to the Alps. I now understand that another trip is required for that – perhaps two, in fact. To think I was contemplating Puglia, the heel of the Italian boot, in my planning! Optimist, Naive or Crazy? Now there's a name for the book, perhaps – they are all words that were tossed around by people before I left.

I am taking the easy option today, driving to Fontvieille in Provence, and rather than taking the inland route I'd wanted to, I am opting for the motorway. My confidence has taken a knock and I think I am still a little shell shocked from the extremity of the exhaustion I experienced after the first few days. Today will test my wellbeing and conserve a little energy to enjoy a couple of days in Provence before I start the long drive back up. We only have ten days left now and a large chunk of that is going to driving days, so I'd like to experience the legend of Provence for myself. I'm sceptical but hoping that it being September, I will miss the influx of crowds and traffic which the region attracts in the summer months.

So, it's time to say goodbye to Canet Plage and to Laurence. Lola is sad as he has been extremely kind and helpful while we've been here. Clancy is packed, the cabin is cleaned and the levels checked ready for the next leg, which may be boring as we cover the miles on the motorway. There are many little towns I'd like to visit along the way but time does not allow, so we'll earmark them for next time. I will return to the region as the scenery and climate are wonderful, but I don't think it will be Canet – somewhere a little less touristy, away from the main road would be nice.

The drive is uneventful – oh wait, there is one big continuous event – the wind. We've suffered these winds throughout our time here but today driving along the E15 is exceptional; the sight of wind tube flags positioned frequently along the motorway tells me that this is normal, and today they are blowing perfectly horizontal without a flap, the wind harsh and constant. I have to be honest: it is hard work just to hold on to Clancy, and I am aching through the necessity of holding on for fear of blowing across the lanes into other traffic. I'm pleased that the road is fairly quiet today, as my full concentration is required at all times, with no let up. To my right and the south I catch a glimpse of the *etang* (lake) and dots which appear to be flamingos, brought to my attention by Lola – but Clancy shouts louder, demanding I grip the steering wheel with all my strength. You think I'm kidding? Try driving this road in high winds – I promise you it's a challenge.

My mind contemplates whether the decision to take this route is the right one. Inland, I would have had an easier time on the back roads but it would have taken all day, and likely into the evening as there wasn't a main *Route Nationale* to get me where I want to be. This way, I think will be three hours, and I can handle that.

For those of you who wonder about my timings, let me enlighten you. If you plug in your requirements to Google maps it will give you an estimate of driving time; if you plug those same places into Via Michelin it will give you a more realistic estimation; and if you are driving a thirty year old diesel car it will take you longer again. Clancy will only go so fast, slow and steady, but fast enough for us. Now consider that I don't take the routes they recommend anyway; this is why it takes me so long but is also the reason that we get to enjoy the country and experiences that motorway service stations don't provide. If you're one of those who rushes from A to B, think about what you're missing – what's the worst that could happen if you explored a little? Get out of your comfort zone and make the most of the big wide world, and take the drivers' seat instead of being a passenger for a change (pun intended).

So, back to the drive – against my usual tenacity and my unwillingness to take a break less than two hours into a drive, I have to pull over when I see a rest area. This wind is really testing me today and I need to refresh a little, so we stop for a break and I take the opportunity to phone Pierre, our host in Provence, to let him know where we are. I know him from my days living in Thailand and it has been eleven years since we last saw each other. He is at work and the conversation is difficult at best. Here we have a clear lesson – when somebody speaks with an accent or in another language, face to face it is quite easy to understand and communicate, but when they are on a bad connection on a telephone it is impossible. I leave the phone call none the wiser to what time Pierre is finishing work, and I don't have an address to go to but I know the town. How hard can it be?

As we walk back across to Clancy in the empty car park, I can't help but smile a little. I don't know what this car has but he always makes me smile. When I sit in the comfortable seats and hold the oversized, worn steering wheel I feel like I'm in a safe place. I can't explain that feeling but Lola has the same affinity. When you sit in a modern car, the seats are firm and the ride is usually too hard, yet in Clancy, the seats are soft and comfortable. Some things are not improved by modern advancements, I can assure you.

Ready to get back on the road, I open the passenger side window just a crack as the sun is now right above us. By doing this, Lola gets no dust in her eyes and I don't have hair in my face, but air circulates nicely – Clancy's own air con. Next stop, Fontvieille; let us hope we can find Pierre.

This little town is a short drive from Arles in the Bouches de Rhone, Provence. It has become a busy tourist centre in recent years and is well-situated for exploring the wider area.

I find the town easily, having written my obligatory route card, but that is when the trouble starts. I have to phone Pierre again now to find out where he is. Enter the phrase – never assume anything. You see, I assumed that Pierre's brother's restaurant was in Fontvielle and because of the phone issue I missed the small fact that in Bistro du Paradou is actually in neighbouring Paradou. Funny that, hey. I know what the establishment looks like because I have seen pictures but it doesn't look much like the town centre of Fontvieille, so I decide to drive out and look further afield. Low and behold I come across Paradou, a tiny village which is home to the bistro. Pierre is standing outside waiting for us in the shady courtyard and I feel a huge relief. I haven't seen him for eleven years yet he hasn't changed much. Last time I saw him he had bare feet, a mop of curly, sun bleached hair

109

and quite possibly a beer in his hand. Today I realise that both of our lives have changed considerably since living on Koh Tao; I guess I too have the lines of experience to be proud of around my eyes. (Only a few, though.)

He sees us approach from the narrow lane across the road, jumps in his car and heads off – we follow to our accommodation for the next couple of nights. On the way we stop in to collect his children, who are being looked after by his parents. Their home is beautiful, but what I would expect of Provence, with outdoor living in abundance. A balance of shade and sun and a welcome that almost brings me to tears – perhaps I am more relieved to be here than I realised!

From here we follow Pierre once again and turn down a little lane. "Where are we going now?" I wonder. Off this road and on to a quintessential gravel and sand track which takes us to Pierre's home. With Clancy parked up, I take in the location, which is lovely: beautiful gardens and some respite from the wind. As we walk across the gravel, I realise that I am being taken to a house. I had thought we were staying with Pierre, not in a house to ourselves.

At this point I really must take some time to express how I'm feeling. You will have seen a picture of a typical Provençale Mas, perhaps – the huge old houses with shuttered windows and a heavy wooden door inviting you to knock. I am now feeling like a child in a sweet shop. This door is huge and heavy; even the key weighs in my hand and as I heave open the door, I'm bowled over by what lies behind. Beautifully furnished with traditional fixtures and fittings, the attention to detail is wonderful. I later learn that Pierre's mum is responsible for everything here. She must have had a wonderful time collecting antiques and soft furnishing alike and I can only imagine how long it would have taken her to do so. From the copper pans in the beautiful kitchen to the ornaments in the living area, I am in love.

Pierre has to go back to work shortly but tells me that his nanny is coming to look after the children and we will be eating with them. I have no option but to accept, and it will be nice to have some company for both me and Lola. She is looking forward to playing with somebody other than her mother!

21

In Search Of Lavender

Yesterday was the first day that I opted for the motorway and if I am honest, I am pleased I did. It was not on the cards at the beginning of the trip but having learned how tiring and slow some of the old routes can be, this was the best decision. On this particular day, if I had taken the old roads it would have been six hours compared to two, and with only five days until I am due in Berny Rivière near Paris, I had to make a snap decision. There were a number of places I would have liked to visit but there is time to do that on another trip. This, in reality, is turning into a "just get there" trip to a degree but by taking the easy (if expensive) option yesterday I am not as tired, so I can now use the couple of days I have here to actually get out and explore.

I am extremely lucky, since when we arrived here yesterday my expectation was of a sofa bed or the floor, and yet we have a whole house to ourselves. There is a stunning garden and pool and I am pinching myself just a little. Provence, funnily enough, was not high on my list of desirability, so I am pleasantly surprised. I have mentioned in a previous chapter about the colours of the Mediterranean and here is no exception.

I actually got up this morning and wrote in my diary –

"I get it. The colours here are as vibrant as they were by the sea, despite us being inland; the clarity of the sky is perhaps helped by the wind that blows, gently today, but at times of Mistral, ferociously."

I had heard of this Mistral, which is rumoured to be the reason for Van Gogh's madness and the removal of his own ear, and having experienced strong winds since we arrived on the Mediterranean coast, I can see why! Provence seemingly gets the worst of it but even in Canet, Laurence said there had been very few days without wind all summer.

But it is thanks to the wind that this morning is clear. The clarity of colour has me inspired – it is a day for lavender hunting.

Before we left the UK, I asked dad what he would go to see if he were able to go back to France and his answer was lavender fields. So today, Lola, Clancy and I are off in search of lavender. I think we are too late for the vivid colour we often see in photos because the harvest is done in August, but we may catch a field by chance if I take the back roads.

My plan is to head over towards Digne-les-Bains and the area which is famed for this wonderful scented plant and although it's unlikely we'll make it all the way, I'm hoping to at least enjoy a lovely drive. Our target area is the Plateau of Valensole which sits at an altitude of 500 metres in the Alpes-de-Haute-Provence; it covers an area of 800 square km and is famed for lavender as well as being home to many perfume houses.

Lola is now running around in the garden between the hedges of lavender and rosemary, with her hair flowing like a wild thing. I manage to capture her in a couple of pictures and to see her joy at the simplicity of running in the fresh air sniffing flowers is such a huge reward. It seems a shame to bundle her in the car to go exploring but who knows what we will find – this region is adorned with many sights and experiences which I am hoping will be quieter now we are nearing the end of September. I actually a feel a little like I'm on holiday for the first time (don't think about the next leg of the drive, Emma!)

Days like these are when I feel happy to be a single mum. Because I have relaxed a little, I have been able to enjoy my time with Lola, and I've been able to sit back and observe her a little and my attitude has been relaxed and happy.

We head out of Fontvieille north on the D33 before turning right towards Saint-Rémy-de-Provence and Cavaillon – the roads are narrow and tree-lined, and the shade is welcome in the rising heat of the Provençale sun. My plan is to continue east until I decide to stop, so it is to be a day for meandering and enjoying whatever we come across. Although I know it's unlikely we'll reach the ultimate destination I can enjoy our journey in search of lavender. The miles roll by until I pass a tiny sign on the side of the road which says "Musée de la Lavande" and in a snap decision I turn around and go back to the crossroads in Coustellet and follow the sign.

This museum is linked to the Château de Bois, a family farm set high in the village of Lagarde d'Apt, in Vaucluse county, a tiny place with a population of perhaps thirty. The farm is located on the Albion highlands at 1100 m altitude, between the majestic Luberon range and the mighty Giant of Provence, Mont Ventoux.

Far from all pollution, they grow over ninety hectares of true lavender, or "population lavender", on their 300-hectare property which equates to more than 10% of all French true lavender production. We learn that they rotate the fields because lavender must be uprooted and burned after ten years.

It is a lovely museum and after wandering around and taking in the various exhibits we stop in the shop and of course, we buy some lavender and soap to bring home. Lola gets a free jigsaw puzzle which she wants to try "right now, mummy" and we venture out to the seating area outside.

It's beautiful out here, the surrounding scenery is calming and although there is no café as such, I get Lola a hot chocolate from the vending machine, which of course comes in a plastic cup. The notorious wind referred to earlier is blustery and with Lola's hair flying free, she is now waving her arms around, trying to see through the mop.

In a split second, her hot chocolate flies across the table, landing right next to my phone. This incident shall forever be referred to as 'choccyphone'. I manage to mop up the liquid quickly, but what I wish to share with you is the way I handled it.

When I am stressed I tend to react, as we all do, but in this moment I see that Lola is devastated about her chocolate and my phone and so I simply give her a cuddle and get her another drink. I tell her that my phone is replaceable but the memories we make together will last forever. Yes, I know it may sound like a cliché, but right now sitting in the stunning scenery of Provence, I think we both need a quiet moment and are slightly overwhelmed.

Surrounded by a backdrop of the Alpilles, on our own just being together – nothing else matters apart from the fact I am cuddling Lola. She instantly relaxes, no longer concerned about the drink or the phone.

I have to remember that she is yet to turn four; she has spent many hours in the car with me without a murmur, simply happy just to be with me and Clancy, which to her signifies a connection to her Grampy. I am incredibly lucky to have such a tolerant child, so receptive to the world around her and such a pleasure to spend time with.

At times when I feel ready to scream, I must try to remember this. Even when I was holding back the tears in a hypermarket in Canet, she was calm and still such a good girl. She patted me on the arm and said –

"Don't worry, mum, we just won't come here again."

The old head on her young shoulders astounds me at times. Her simplistic answer to my frustration with the lack of service in the supermarket could not be argued with, and I'm sure we will probably laugh about the orange lady with the bad temper in France in later years.

We leave the museum and head south, back towards Cavaillon and Saint-Remy before I turn off on the D5 south – a drive which takes us over the Massif des Alpilles towards Le Baux-de-Provence. The scenery is once again breath-taking and the stark grey sandy granite creates a stunning contrast to the dark green vegetation that surrounds us. To think that I nearly didn't come to Provence; there is so much to see without needing to spend a penny (except for fuel!) and for those who appreciate the visual delights that nature offers this really is heaven.

I turn right once we have reached level ground again and start the ascent to Le Baux-de-Provence. It is one of the most beautiful villages in France and as we approach I have no option but to stop for a photo. The road twists ahead of us, empty but for a cyclist and as my eyes travel towards the sky, I see the ancient ruins sitting high on the hilltop. With obligatory photo taken we continue up to the top where we are met with the reality of this little place – even out of season there are cars fighting for spaces, people wandering aimlessly in front of said cars. I have to wonder how long it would take you to find a space in the summer, perhaps you may go insane before you do so!

With that said, it is worth a visit if you are of a patient nature. I would plan a day trip and spend some time taking in the exhibits which are on offer for a small entrance fee. It makes sense to get there early to simply enjoy it and if you time it right you may even be able to escape before the onslaught of tourists.

We descend from the pretty village and find ourselves just a few minutes from our temporary home and are easily back in time to enjoy the late afternoon sunshine in the garden. I like this random exploring, it's what I set out to do and I'm very pleased that finally I'm able to do it. Tomorrow we'll head south in a similar manner and it's something to look forward to – a visit to the Camargue and the sea is likely but let's wait and see. If I get distracted by an enticing view we may end up somewhere completely different!

22

The Camargue. Where Graffiti Meets Greatness

Being here in Provence is wonderful, and until today I had been in a somewhat comfortable environment, one where I was able to communicate largely in English and essentially operate as a tourist. Now that I'm staying in a French home and we have to work at speaking French, I wish we had more time here as this is where my heart lies, learning about other cultures and getting to know the locals. Pierre's children speak Thai, French and some English, and are eager to communicate. As adults, perhaps we lose the confidence to attempt to speak for fear of getting it wrong, but isn't that the best way to learn? One thing for sure is that if I don't speak and get corrected, my pronunciation will never improve. It's not a lot of good being able to read French if I can't ask for what I need.

Yesterday was a lovely day. Despite missing the lavender season, we still had a pleasant scenic tour around the area. There is so much to see here, yet it is mostly just simplicity and simple living; I wouldn't like it so much if I were sharing the roads with thousands of others in the peak season, but now, as the last rays of summer are cast across the Provençale landscape, I love it.

With the simplicity of the region comes, of course, the clean yet rich taste delights, conjured up with just a few basic ingredients. Perhaps it is the long sunny days that warm the tomatoes on the vines, I don't know, but I am sure that the tomato salad I ate was the most delicious thing I've ever eaten, and I don't really like tomatoes that much. The sweetness of the huge fruits dressed in a freshly made herb vinaigrette tasted quite unlike anything I've ever had. I like the fact that this salad, which was prepared for us by Emma, Pierre's girlfriend, was served prior to our main pasta dish rather than on the side. Of course, this is standard on the continent, where food is savoured and treated with respect and as such it is the central element of life. The two hour lunch, which many tourists complain about because the shops are closed, is such an integral part of their existence and I believe is so important. Spending time with friends and family, enjoying life and not rushing; I'm not so good at it myself but I'm trying and it's what I strive for in my life with Lola.

Being able to experience a glimpse into the daily life lived by the locals is wonderful and I wish we had longer here, but we are due in Picardie in three days and I know that I am not going to make that drive easily, especially if I'm taking the long route. I am pulled to heading back over to the West, to be able to drive the Millau Viaduct. But as much as my heart wants to do it, I know it's completely impractical. So today I'm just going to hit the road and head to the Camargue region.

The Camargue is the southern flatlands region of Provence, famed for black bulls and white horses. It holds a certain mystique but I am very aware that the traditional element of this history has possibly been replaced with tourist focused shows and the like. I hope not, but I am heading out for our drive with an open mind towards Aigues-Mortes. I'm not sure which route I'll take, so today is a chance to wander a little and of course pray for toilet facilities en route! Don't fancy using a hedge with a bull charging from behind, after all!

It is an absolutely stunning morning. The house we are staying in has a ceiling-to-floor window on the large upstairs landing, and as I stumble out of the bedroom, having had a wonderful sleep, I am met with the sun rising and shining its golden glow across the gardens. These memories will stay with me forever. I take a deep inhale and appreciate the moment. Lola appears and she just wants to go and run around the beautiful garden. I have no reason to say no, since if it's cold she'll come and ask for a cardigan; if she chooses to run around like a wild thing while she has the chance, who am I to argue!

So as she runs around, hair flowing in all directions, I sit with my coffee in the early morning sun (it tastes so much better here). There is a chill in the air and the wind that I'm now accustomed to is still constant, but I am fascinated by the light surrounding me and it's lovely to watch Lola relaxed and happy. When I was planning this trip, I had visions of sitting in Provence and in an inland picturesque village in Spain with my pencils, committing the images to paper and enjoying the quiet. What was I thinking! One, I have a three-year-old on board. Two, I don't have time! Another thing to add to the list of things to do later.

My frame of mind has changed so much since the day I arrived in Canet Plage. As you know, I was exhausted and wanted to go home. Today, I am daunted by the prospect of the drive back up, which is of course marred by the way I felt in Canet, and yet right now I am feeling a kind of uneasy calm. I am anxious of what is ahead but I want to take time to remember the little moments. Let's look at this trip as a trial run and note that I can always come back. Today, I am going in search of a different landscape to that which we saw yesterday. Rolling plains, granite outcrops of the Alpilles and shaded town squares will give way to salt marshes and perhaps a gateway to a Provence of the past, or am I just dreaming?

We leave home at eleven o'clock, turning south on to the D99 towards Arles – a place we had been invited to explore with Emma which would have been lovely, but again, time is our enemy. Instead, I am skirting the town and crossing the motorway to the southern wetlands of the Camargue. Within five minutes we are greeted by a fox running across the roundabout without a care in the world. Mental note made – today I am taking in all the little details and trying to enjoy myself, as it seems that the days I do this are those that bear the greatest fruits.

The change in the landscape is almost immediate, giving way to a sparse stillness, as we leave the Alpilles behind us. We appear to have entered campervan land – I guess these people also wanted to avoid the crowds and take things slower, and I quite fancy that myself. There is a wide acceptance of motorhomes in France and the facilities provided for free are great, so it seems like a no brainer (we'll worry about the cost of said vehicle later!).

We drive for what seems like miles without seeing any glimpse of life, passing abandoned buildings standing lonely on the horizon. I guess these are the homesteads of the past, and the families perhaps moved to the cities, searching for something, saying goodbye to the simple life that I so crave. I wonder if they are sitting in their one bedroom apartment in Paris, longing for the space and light of their home, yet unable to break the pattern as they are committed to a lifestyle they have created. Unable to walk away because they have overcommitted financially, they can't see a way forward to return to the land of their youth. I am sure those thoughts must pass through their minds; it did through mine while I was working and earning well in Auckland. Money is no good if you are unhappy, a reality that many choose not to face.

These huge beautiful buildings are scarred by graffiti. I expected this area to be different to the guide books to a degree but somehow I didn't expect this. Imagine that image of Provence you have in your head, a lone weathered building standing proud against the colourful landscapes we all associate with the area. Now picture street art plastered all over the front of building – does it appeal? Perhaps the artists who capture these scenes choose to leave out the detail, but I certainly have never seen a painting of Provence with a graffiti strewn Mas sitting pretty amidst the lavender. Perhaps that's a picture I should paint myself – this is, after all, a trip of realities, not of glossing over the blemishes.

It's a sign of the times – modern life on one side of the road, and a man with a cart full of melons for sale, apparently snoozing under his shabby, faded blue umbrella one hundred metres down the road. I'm not going to stop now but if we come back this way I will be stopping for one of those for afternoon tea. I'm pleased I've seen this side of what is sold as a "perfect" tourist destination. There are those who will say otherwise, but this actually is what I wanted: off the beaten track and telling you a story of the real France, warts and all.

Clancy rolls on, enjoying the easy ride today and I start to notice something about this area. Our old 504 must feel at home here, since there are very few new cars but plenty of beaten up old Peugeots and the odd tractor, aha. Real France. As I consider the orange glow of the bodies on the beach in Canet, the high heels at the swimming pool and the aloofness I experienced in the supermarket, I smile to myself. This is more like it. For those who think 'South of France' and associate it with money, let me tell you that just a little diversion from the tourist route will take you to a different place entirely.

Yes, I have talked about graffiti already, but now we're talking about life. The people here seem to have set their lives to run in first gear, trundling along at a pace I could handle, taking time to talk to each other – gesticulating, laughing and frowning, but if I could choose one word to describe them it would be *living*.

We are prone to just existing, but these people are living and enjoying their lives. As I sit patiently in Clancy, waiting for the chap in the battered 205 in front to finish his conversation with his mate wandering past with a baguette, I'm not bothered. I don't have the urge to beep my horn aggressively, I just enjoy the moment. Lola notices the baguette and decides she needs some food; at least she doesn't need the toilet!

The men bid farewell to each other and we move on, not particularly fast, but we are moving. I'm used to being the slowest car on the road and now I feel at home amongst my car peers, and I like this area, it interests me. I wish I was fluent in French and could talk to these elderly people and learn about their families, their history and day to day life. Much like in Ceret, I start to consider what they will do later today – gardening, harvesting or perhaps just a snooze in the afternoon heat of Provence.

My train of thought is broken as I notice that we are finally free from the elderly gentlemen and we start out on the road to Aigues-Mortes. One minute in and I see a tractor, not just any tractor but one which I think may have been manufactured in 1930! It is tiny but has a huge piece of machinery attached – it's amazing that it is still upright! I realise that the roads have now changed from long and straight to winding, undulating and narrow – in other words, not ideal for overtaking in a right hand drive car with an old diesel engine! There are two choices, get frustrated or sit here and travel at ten miles an hour until he turns off – of course, the latter is the only way to go. Eventually, after about ten minutes, the tractor slips off down a gravel track and I almost have the urge to follow him, to get an insight into rural life, but I decide it would be impolite, so in search of black bulls and white horses we go.

And we find them. I am pleasantly surprised that my first sighting is of a bull with a seagull perched on his back. I am gutted not to have been able to capture this on film as it is probably one of the few quintessential things that you'd like to see but would never get to. Lone seagull sitting proud on lazy bull on the Provençale skyline; although a shame to not have it saved on film, it is firmly imprinted in my mind.

On we trundle and soon enough we see what I expected, a ranch which has been adapted for tourism. Beautiful horses stand grouped in the shade, ready to entertain the passing trade. I had images of seeing herds of these animals charging across the plains, wild and free, but unless I spend a good few days driving, I think this will be the limit. I am not altogether disappointed, though; my recent thoughts of the abandoned buildings and the families who have left allow me to appreciate what these people are doing. They are using their heritage to create a lifestyle for themselves in their beloved homeland, and you can't criticise them for this. We all have to survive and as one of the world's most famous tourist regions, why would you not make the most of the glorious surrounds?

As the miles roll by, we enjoy the late summer sunshine and the breeze which cools us through Clancy's wide open windows. My mind is now focused on finding our destination and soon enough, I see the sign and we drive in to Aigues-Mortes. The name of the town translates as Dead Waters, apparently a reflection of the surrounding marshes. In my imagination, I had hoped it was something more sinister than this, perhaps a historical event of significance, and yet now I've driven here, it makes complete sense. The land is flat and marshy; it's as simple as that!

The outskirts of town here is a commercial area. Again, I mention that these areas also are home to low cost hotels, which are easy to find and a safe bet if you're in need of a bed. Here, we are soon into the old town and it is extremely picturesque, and also incredibly busy. The words 'tourist trap' spring to mind but I am also intrigued by this place, having read about it.

Our first challenge is finding a parking space. I follow the signs to the car park along a road which crosses a small bridge over the river, decorated with brightly coloured boats bobbing up and down. I soon realise that the seemingly easy task of following a sign to a car park may be more difficult. As we turn left and expect to see a wide open space full of cars, I am greeted by a car park which lies between two roads where we must parallel park – it being tree-lined on both sides, I now need to find a gap between the tall heavy trunks to start the search for a space. Well, I suppose the abundance of shade from tall trees provides a perfect place in the heat of the summer sun.

We finally park for one euro (woohoo!) and we head for the fortified old town. I'm planning on getting there via the side streets rather than the main road. It's a beautiful day, cooled slightly by the breeze, and I'm actually a little excited about being a tourist for a moment. Lola and I walk down cobbled residential streets, with coloured terraced houses sitting pretty against the almost steely blue of the sky. Who would know we're just metres from ancient ramparts and the thousands of tourists within them.

We turn the corner and at once we are in tourist land. I see a toyshop with beautiful handmade pedal cars outside. I know this will be expensive but I can't resist, so Lola and I go inside. After several minutes of admiring the wooden toys, I ask how much a doctor's kit is. I try to hide my surprise at ninety euros! I thought perhaps forty, but ninety! I smile and say we may come back, but the sweet judgemental smile I receive has me almost ready to pull out my wallet to prove a point, before I remember I need that money! Who are they to judge!

Built in the thirteenth century, the walled city is considered one of the best examples of medieval military architecture. Despite my urge to run away from the swarms of tourists, I have to take some time to appreciate what is before us, as it is awe inspiring. Lola and I spend the next half an hour wandering around this little town on the river. We have an ice cream and then we head back to Clancy, who has been resting quietly in the shade, lucky boy. Where next, then? I get the maps out and work out where we can go, and I don't really want to go back the same way, despite the roadside melon seller, so I choose a route to Saintes-Marie-de-la-Mer. Here we go again.

I haven't done any research about this place but it simply looks like it will be a nice place to stop once we've driven deeper into the Camargue. Much of this region is protected, so you need to be careful where you take your vehicle. I think sticking to the main roads is a good idea today. The landscape changes to a decidedly marshy, flat one and as my daydreams and thoughts wander off to my own little world, I hear a shriek from the back.

"Mummy, flamingaloes!"

Lola is beside herself, having fallen in love with these beautiful birds in Canet. As we move along the marsh-lined roads, the horizon opens up to a hazy sea of pink and white, sitting strikingly against the muddy colours of the landscape and the azure of the Mediterranean sky. Another moment where I wish I could take photos on the go but

I can't, and I am looking forward to the time when Lola can be my partner in picture crime, stealing photos as I drive us on our adventures.

Unable to stop on the side of the road, I finally manage to find some form of a layby and snap a shot of the scenery. I would like to come back here again, I think, taking more time to appreciate the history that is so rich and proud in the Camargue. I don't want to be a visitor – I want to stay a while, with perhaps a romantic notion of finding some "Guardians" to talk to about the lifestyle here. These cowboys largely work on the ranches, and of course there is an element of tourism, but I can't help but feel they are in touch with their heritage and the land as well as their animals. This is another reason to improve my French, to come back and learn about this area and its people, to eat the simple, yet delicious food and appreciate life as it is.

This area produces salt – in fact, half of the French supply comes from here, and it's refreshing to know that there is a sustainable income aside from tourism. Speaking of which, I should mention that I received a hefty warning from Pierre with regard to parking the car pretty much anywhere in Provence: don't leave anything in plain sight, as there is a huge car theft problem. It sounds obvious, doesn't it, but I would imagine that those who visit Provence with rose coloured glasses – or in fact, anywhere in the world that is famed for a laid back lifestyle, beauty and history – will find themselves in the perfect picking place for thieves. It would be lovely to think that crime does not exist, but these regions are a magnet for those whose ethics are somewhat different to our own.

As we approach Saintes-Marie-de-la-Mar, I feel like I am entering another world. Beyond the untouched beauty of the marshlands, where I imagine things haven't changed for many years, I find a busy seaside resort. There is plenty of parking along the sand dunes as you approach the town, and this is the perfect place for thieves, as Pierre mentioned – beach on one side of the road, marsh on the other, and once you're on the beach, you can't see over the dunes. We drive into the centre of the town and meet with a traffic jam and a busy seafront café scene. Not really my cup of tea, to be honest, so after navigating the one way system and having a little tiki tour of the local residential area, I head back to the dunes. I have sensibly left most of our things at Pierre's and only have my backpack with us, so I park up and Lola and I head through the dunes to the beach.

On the flip side of the risk of theft when you are out of the main town is the benefit of quieter beaches. Here Lola and I have the sandy playground to ourselves, so we make the best of it and paddle in the sea and make sandcastles. Simple pleasures equal happy child, which in turn, of course, means happy mum.

After our little break, it's time to get back on the road and hunt for those roadside sellers. Being on the beach has helped me work up a thirst, and watermelon is up there with the best of them when it comes to refreshment. Fortunately, within ten minutes I find what I'm after and also pick up some giant tomatoes warmed by the sun and with my renewed faith in the taste from our meal last night, I buy both and head back towards Arles.

Clancy is ticking along nicely and Lola is visibly wiggling in her car seat. It's time to let our ride deliver us safely back to Pierre's, where Lola will run free in the garden and I will possibly partake of a glass of wine. I haven't had anything to drink on this trip, much as I feel that I am on a twenty-four hour shift in case of Lola having an asthma attack, but here, where I have Pierre next door and his parents up the road, I feel able to relax a little. I know that Pierre only has an hour or so from when he comes home to going back to work, but it will be nice to sit down and have a proper catch up before I have to leave.

Pierre and I have changed somewhat since Thailand, at which time we were both travelling and had got stuck there. We were both working in a dive shop and burning the candle at both ends, and how things have changed.

Now, we are both in effect single parents, with the other parent living in a different country, and it is good to talk to somebody who understands that situation. Pierre works so hard for his children, and he must be exhausted working early in the morning until late at night, but he is very philosophical about it and humble about what he is doing. He simply wants the best for his children.

23

The Road to Lyon

When you think of Roman architecture do you think of Italy? It's the obvious choice, isn't it, but in fact the legacy they left behind is visible across the reaches of the old Roman Empire – including, of course, in Bath, my home city, which is famed for the Roman Baths. Here in Provence there is plenty of evidence of their reign here. In Arles, which is just a few minutes from Fontvieille, there is a huge amphitheatre and of course there is Pont du Gard (Gard Bridge), the unmistakable World Heritage Site just north of here. Even in the back roads surrounding these areas, there are ruins of ancient monuments. We've stumbled across a couple just by taking a drive down the country lanes, the ones which you would not see if you were staying on the tourist route.

Today, we are leaving to drive towards Lyon, but on the way I will be taking a minor detour and visiting a jaw dropping aqueduct before we head north. It will be a great learning experience for Lola and it is perhaps one of the few things in the world which may not be fully appreciated if you don't stand under the huge arches.

Standing 49 metres high (from the water below) and spanning 274 metres, Pont du Gard is worth the visit despite the visitor centre and entry fee. I guess to maintain this beautiful feat of architecture and to protect it, there is no reason why we shouldn't contribute. There are three rows of arches, each different sizes and heights, and really there is just one word to describe it – monumental.

It would be a great shame while we are here not to visit – it is out of our way, but only slightly, and the opportunity to show Lola a World Heritage Site and also teach her about aqueducts can't be missed. It's a stunning morning, with blue skies, and the wind has dropped a little so I think it will be a great little diversion.

With that said, I am sad to be leaving today – I love it here despite my reticence before I came. I felt that perhaps Provence had moved away from its roots and was going to slap me in the face with commercialised tourism, but now I have been here I am pleasantly surprised. Two weeks ago may have been a different story, but I am pleased that at least there are places which have kept their traditional feel. I haven't felt overpowered, oversold or overwhelmed by pushy traders and tacky shops as I'd imagined. That is probably largely due to my own method of travel and exploring: I haven't gone to the obvious places, I've managed to keep off the beaten track with only a brief flirtation with some tourist areas. If I had seen even a glimpse of fluorescent pink, I would have had Clancy turned around in a flash, off to find a shady tree to recover under!

We are leaving Pierre's and it almost feels impolite because the welcome has been so great, but the rest of the trip awaits us. It is less than a week until we touch back down on British soil and this is the first time I've really felt like I don't want to go home. I have a long drag back up to Berny Rivière and I know that I'll need to stop; in my head, it will be around Mâcon, but we will see how the day pans out.

Before we leave, Pierre brings me an espresso and we sit for a chat out in the morning sun – I could handle this more regularly, for sure, as it's not often I get drinks made for me. We talk for a few minutes before he leaves for work and I am left hoping that it won't be another eleven years before we meet again. He reminds me that if we stop in Tarascon to be careful – it's another theft hotspot and Clancy is, after all, a big advertisement for "I'm on the road". This really solidifies my plan to go straight to Pont du Gard, and to keep it simple, especially on a day when I don't actually know where we'll be sleeping tonight.

Clancy is packed up once again. He has been resting in the shade, his tyres and levels are checked and we're set to go. I will need fuel so will stop as soon as I see a station which is not on the main road: as mentioned earlier, the price differences are significant, so I will fill up when I see a good price. As we pull out of the dusty track which leads to Pierre's house onto the D99, I feel a tug of wistfulness. Perhaps Provence in not the demon I had created in my head after all, but could I live here?

It's a straightforward route north-west from Fontveille to Pont du Gard – I'm reckoning on about an hour to get there but I guess there will be minor roads to negotiate as we approach. I suppress a little anxiety, a nagging in my mind that I really should be heading straight up to Lyon. I should remember that this is about Lola, too, and she will be a very lucky girl to see such a great monument at her age. Stick to the plan, Emma!

As you approach the location of Pont du Gard, you have a choice of which side of the river to drive along. In hindsight, I'm wishing I had researched a little more, as my option to stay on the east has us being directed to the main visitor centre. I had hoped to almost be able to do a drive by and stop for a little walk but it seems that is not possible, so I pay for our parking and entrance and in we go. We are early in the day, at only a little after ten o'clock, so the car park is quiet but there is a steady trickle of cars and coaches arriving behind us. I hate to imagine this in summer. Lola and I check that Clancy has nothing left in plain sight and then start the walk to the vast structure of ancient times, which turns out to be further than I thought!

It takes us about ten minutes to get the aqueduct and I am surprised that we are actually allowed to walk across the bridge – it's breathtaking. The view from the bridge down to the river below is just stunning and the depth of dark blue that meanders against the sandy inlets, granite and dark, lush green of the vegetation is almost too good to be true – picture perfect under another clear blue sky. Still the wind, though! I'd heard about the mistral but it's been windy since we arrived in Canet! Please – give it a break Monsieur Mistral!

We cross over to the other side of the water where we find a restaurant and a small takeaway – Lola, of course, opted for the ice cream option, and me for the coffee. Not the best coffee I've ever had, to be honest, but still – we have the chance to sit and admire the view, with a perfect photo opportunity to capture Lola against a stunning backdrop. There will be no question of "where was that taken?" for sure.

Twenty minutes later and we're returning to Clancy and as we approach the visitor centre, we are greeted by a swarm of tourists, so I'm very pleased we got here early! Fighting our way through the crowd, we hop back in Clancy and are back on the road again. Next stop, diesel, then north we head. The N7 runs alongside the A7 motorway, which I fear is one of the busiest in the country. I know that the tolls on the motorways from Arles to Calais come in at around ninety euros and it's probably one hundred euros in fuel, so I suppose this is why many choose to fly with budget airlines – fifty quid versus several hundred if you're doing a round trip. It's certainly a cost I'd rather not incur and fortunately, I like driving, so taking the slow road is perfect for us. I do think that the old road on this occasion could be very time consuming, so it's going to be a suck it and see day. As long as I get past Lyon I'll be happy, as psychologically it's a milestone.

I find diesel in the town next to Pont du Gard and fill Clancy up. The signs of more traffic are appearing and I don't like it! It could be a long day. Despite the A7 motorway probably only taking about three hours to Lyon, from here I've opted to take the N86 before joining the N7 later. On the map, this appeared to be a good run parallel to the motorway, but within twenty minutes of getting on the road I'm feeling a little anxiety. We are passing through little towns and the road is not as straight as it appears, and this is going to be a hard drive. I will persevere for now, but there is no way I am going to reach Lyon let alone Mâcon at this rate, though perhaps it will improve.

As we move past midday, I feel as though we are getting nowhere fast, which is not helped by the fact that I have seen a sign for the Rhone about twenty times, which makes me feel like I'm going around in circles; there is bridge after bridge crossing the river, interspersed with roundabouts and traffic lights. The towns I have passed through are not really appealing to my "oh, that was worth going off the beaten track for" side. There is only one thing for it – I am looking for the dreaded blue sign, the one that points me to the nearest motorway. The road to Lyon is a long one and I think I need to make it shorter.

This decision is easier said than done as now I spend half an hour waiting for the sign. I see it and am about to join the busiest road out of the south of France. This is my worst nightmare – a road full of shiny big cars driven by people with egos big and brash.

Yes, I know that is a sweeping statement, but as I potter along at 55 mph in Clancy, I receive more than my fair share of scowls and impatient drivers sitting on my bumper. I'll be honest, I am not comfortable on this road. People who drive so erratically and are more interested in their appearance than their safety should be pulled over and charged with stupidity.

I can see the face of the person in the car behind me – I can't see his eyes through his sunglasses but I'm sure that if I had time to look in the mirror long enough, he would be driving close enough for me to see the hairs of his perfectly trimmed goatee. Once again, I am gripping Clancy's wheel and concentrating hard, and this time trying to pay attention to the speeding, reckless idiots that surround me.

The meandering River Rhone and the many bridges spanning its varying widths which were frustrating me an hour ago would be welcome now. I would willingly take an extra day to escape this madness. I see Montélimar services ahead and decide to take a break, even if for nothing more than to look at my map and assess the situation.

This is a new experience – this service station is more like a small town. After five minutes driving around, I find a parking space. Oh please, take me back to my quiet little Onzain. I am learning very fast that I was right in my assumption that I would not enjoy the motorways. This is horrible.

Lola and I venture towards the main building to be greeted by crowds of people – the glass on the windows has been smashed and remains broken and taped off. The entrance to this part of the services is not accessible, forcing us all in to one entrance. It is like being at a concert, shunted around in a crowd, when all I want is the toilet and a snack.

Eventually we get inside and I decide that I am going to opt for McDonalds for coffee, since I want to get out as soon as possible. Even at the McDonalds outlet, it is mayhem, but I quickly realise that this is probably normal for this place. There are staff moving quickly through the crowd, taking orders on their handheld devices. This is new to me but as I move forward with the wave of people, I magically find that when I arrive at the counter my food is waiting – the system works.

We are herded like sheep with a tag on their ears to identify them, but rather than being pulled through the sheep dip, we are pushed through the exit funnel to the side of the counter where the poor soul behind the counter gives us our order.

As we exit the building, I feel confused – almost as when you leave a dark room into sunshine and have to blink to adjust, and here I have to ask myself what just happened. I feel like I have been a robot on a conveyor belt, being served by another robot who gave me food. I shudder and commit to memory that Montélimar services are not for me.

This is turning into an interesting day. In the space of a few hours, I have seen a world famous monument, crossed the Rhone ten times, skirted the Alps and been introduced to the reality of continental *autoroutes*. My god, imagine this in the summer. The thought horrifies me.

OK, so it's time to look at the map and take stock. Driving west and into my safe place, the beauty of the Loire and the relative sanity of its roads is not an option; I curse the timetable I am committed to as now more than ever I'd love to go wandering and find a little *chambre d'hôtes* for the night. Focus, Emma, you have to get past Lyon and in a couple of hours this hell that is the A7 will be over.

Breathe, Emma, just breathe.

I realise on approach to Lyon that this is a road I haven't researched at all, since I had no intention of using the motorway to get here and I certainly had no plans to get tied up in traffic. On the map it looked simple – the motorway passes around Lyon and I can continue north to Mâcon where I can perhaps stop.

I decided against a break in Lyon, despite hearing that it has a reputation for the number of high quality restaurants you can choose from – this is not a place to enjoy with Lola, this is a grown up destination. Right now it's starting to look like no kind of destination as the traffic is getting slower and slower. I haven't seen any indication of an accident or diversion but I am feeling a little uneasy. It's well over thirty degrees outside and I don't fancy sitting in traffic. We've used a lot of fuel today and because I err on the side of caution, I don't like Clancy to go below a quarter of a tank. Just as I was starting to consider taking the next exit to escape the traffic (how hard can it be?), we grind to a halt – and that, my friends, is it for the next two hours.

When we finally start moving at a snail's pace, I have had time to look at the map and find my escape. There is no way I'm getting as far north as I had planned but at least if I'm off this motorway, I'm moving. There is a junction about a mile ahead but the impatient, annoying drivers of the species are coming up on the hard shoulder and trying to push in, and it's just causing more mess.

Fortunately, the truck drivers, my allies throughout this journey, are not best pleased either and they skilfully manoeuvre to straddle all

130

lanes, blocking those idiots from coming through. I giggle and can imagine my father or brother doing much the same if they were in a similar position. I feel all warm and fuzzy and looked after in a funny kind of way, as Clancy is once again protected by fellow drivers – real drivers, that is.

Another thirty minutes pass before I reach the junction and it is only then that we see that the road is closed for road works – all three lanes, with no prior warning, but surely it's OK as the result of such activities is a beautiful, smooth driving surface. At least in France they do a complete job rather than filling the holes in the tarmac, which are then washed away at first sight of rain in the UK.

Can I tolerate road closures to have beautiful roads to drive on? Yes, I think I can. Can I tolerate the French 'shrug of shoulders' when questioned about such actions, those which include blockages at ferry ports and the like? Well yes, I think I can because it appears to get the job done and, once again, I say "when in Rome…". If you are in France, expect and accept their culture across the board – don't complain or don't come back.

Of course, this incident has not really made for much progress today but, again, I am reminded of Lola's brilliance. Not a squeak about being strapped in and stuck on a motorway, and how many children would be OK with that? We've had a sing song, played eye spy and talked about some memories of the trip so far, so all in all it's been a nice chance to have a bit of a chat. Always look on the bright side!

So we head east towards Switzerland, and I was supposed to be on the other side of those mountains but it was not to be. I am happy to be back on a deserted road, but I am also aware that it's almost six o'clock and we've been stuck in that traffic for several hours. I don't want to be driving around in the dark in an area I am not familiar with.

I'm keeping my eyes peeled for a sign to a town I recognise. If I keep going east I'm in the mountains again, so I make a decision to take the next left and I see as it will start to take me north again that this is where I need to be. This road turns out to be the right one, as I eventually find a sign to Bourg-en-Bresse, which is a town that I'm familiar with. I know there is accommodation here, I just have to find it and it has to be fast as the sun is starting to dip behind the trees on the horizon. Luck is on my side as I see the sign for a hotel and we pull in. I haven't let Lola see how anxious I am feeling but I can tell you that finding a bed is a massive relief – doubt was starting to creep in.

24

Giant Chickens and Champagne

Well, after yesterday and the mountain and river saga, I am keen to get the job done today. We were on the road for ten hours and with my rule of being off the road by four o'clock each day breached I want to make tracks fast. It's Sunday, so if we leave early I think we can get up to Berny Rivière by early afternoon; experience tells me that Sundays are a good day to travel, often alone on the roads, occasionally accompanied by trucks, but always enjoyable on the great French roads.

Last night we eventually arrived at a town called Bourg-en-Bresse which my research tells me – wait for it – is famous for chickens! There is even a huge chicken to celebrate on the side of the road as you approach the town. This was another time when my months of research paid off because when I was first looking at the route and where to stop I was quite keen to explore the area to the south-west of Paris. Unfortunately, I'm not here long enough to go to the Melun Brie festival but while digging around in Burgundy and the surrounding areas, I did come across this town we're in.

Before we left Provence, I went through the roadside hotel websites and looked at the towns in which they have sites between Lyon and Paris. I had committed a number of those towns within a hundred mile drive to memory so that I knew that, dependent on where I got to, we had a bed for the night. I had hoped to reach Mâcon but the light was failing as we approached here last night and I didn't know what was ahead, and to say it was a relief to find the hotel is an understatement. As you know, I took a punt, following my instinct yesterday to get out of the traffic in Lyon, and it took us along an absolutely stunning route where, much like in the Pyrenees earlier in the trip, I felt the urge to abandon the schedule and turn off into the mountains to explore.

Guess what I'm going to say next? Yes, you've got it. Had I stayed on the motorway, I wouldn't have seen the beautiful scenery and been able to add this to the "must come back to explore" list. Yes, it was a little stressful not knowing where we were going to be staying but the day really encompassed what this trip is all about. Adapting to the situation and embracing it, you never know what's around the corner. I also learned that Montélimar services is a place that I never wish to visit again, and it was good to see that side of driving in France but wow, won't be stopping there again any time soon.

I find it somewhat amusing that my love of mountains and rivers for the first time was tested as we crossed the Rhone so many times. As we passed over each bridge I thought "How can we be crossing the Rhone again!" I imagine that on closer inspection of the map it will look like it is plaited with the road we were on, at least that's how it felt. Of course that was the main reason for choosing the option of getting on the motorway, since I knew it was going to take all day and we were unlikely to even reach Lyon if I stayed on that road for too long. Another time, perhaps, but with just a few days left until we're due home, I couldn't afford to lose that time.

But now, having had a restful sleep, a skype call to dad and a lovely sunset to watch from our hotel window, we are ready to make our move. I would like to have a good look around the town but I want to be on the road by eight o'clock. I need to find fuel and am told there is an unmanned station just up the road so that will be easy.

The breakfast is as we expected – honey cake, croissants and unlimited coffee as well as condiments, fruit and yoghurt, and it's enough to set us up for the day. There is a thick mist hanging over us – significant, I feel, as we have crossed into different terrain now, from the Mediterranean climate to the more temperate northern region. Now more than ever I understand those artists who speak of the clarity of the skies to the south, which I could look at all day.

We load up dear Clancy who had a rough day yesterday, thirty degrees for ten hours and stuck in traffic for two hours in Lyon, but he survived and thrived; he is the ultimate touring companion.

Today there is a need for warmth so I tuck Lola under her blanket in her seat and put her special slippers from the Pyrenees on – she is happy, I am cold. Clancy takes a moment to get going too today, and he seems to be saying –

"No – don't like the cold, thank you very much."

I talk to him, telling him it will be warmer once the mist lifts, giving him a pat on the dashboard.

"Come on, Clance, we're nearly home now."

Yes, I do talk to the car, as does Lola – he is part of the family!

The fuel station is easy to spot, just five minutes down the road, so once full to the brim, Clancy retraces his steps past the hotel and onto the motorway. This particular hotel sits on the roundabout that takes you to the nearest motorway, and as we drive down the slip road I see the toll booth and I twitch, but I know it has to be done today. With our Sanef tag on the windscreen beeping, the barrier lifts automatically and lets us pass through graciously – we'll be charged for that next month on our account.

Here we go, open road, fog and no traffic. I hope the weather improves or it will be hard going. I suspect I have a couple of hours before it does, though, so slow and steady wins the race today. I haven't told Al Fresco yet that we may be there tonight rather than tomorrow as I really don't know how far we'll get after yesterday. I'm also still tempted to explore the region a little, so we'll see how we go.

I've decided to take the A39 motorway for the first part of the drive, before heading towards the Champagne region. There was a choice of two but this one felt better and so far that is proving to be a good gut feeling. I have been on the road about an hour and have seen six vehicles. I'm sure that on a Sunday in the high season this motorway would be like any other but today, as we head towards October, it's mine. It's boring, it's an easy drive and I'm kind of losing interest in mountainous scenery, which astounds me. The temptation arises to divert from my route to go to Troyes, a little town which I know is famed for *brocante* and art shops as well as good regional food. Not today, Emma, this is a day to cover ground, not explore.

As the day continues, we see a little more traffic and, surprisingly, I find myself within an hour of Riems by eleven o'clock. It looks like we are going to make it all the way up, so I decide to find somewhere to pull over to call the campsite. No point in paying for a hotel an hour from where we're going tomorrow if I can avoid it.

No sooner has that thought crossed my mind than I see a sign for a brand new service station, which looks like a good option, since it certainly can't be anywhere as grubby and busy as Montélimar. We pull in and this is great, the car park has three cars and a truck in it, there is a play area, toilets and food. Perfect.

This trip has at times been A Tale of Toilets so why should I change things now? These are brand new, shiny and have laminated doors with pictures of lavender fields on them; sad though it may seem, I am so delighted to have found somewhere that I don't have to blackmail Lola to use the toilets that I take a picture of said doors.

We then take our croissants and hot chocolate outside and I sit on the edge of the play area watching Lola in the morning sunshine that has emerged from its misty blanket. I'm feeling quite relaxed now that the psychological barrier of reaching the northern region of France is gone. I sense relief but it is mixed with a little twinge of regret, feeling that I have missed out on opportunities to see and do more. Some self-coaching talk reminds me that our safety had to be the priority and there is time for Lola and me to go back to the list we have. Being able to write this book and give my readers a list of those places is a bonus, and I hope they enjoy them as much as we did; I hope they perhaps write to me to tell me how much they enjoyed them. Sharing this experience is actually a privilege, I suppose, to inspire you to explore, to encourage you to reach out and to ask if you'd love to travel but are a little bit scared – but most of all, to share it with my father.

Lola's voice brings me back to my senses as she tells me that there's a man standing next to Clancy. Apprehensive to leave my spot, I try to ignore him but Lola persists and eventually I walk over and smile. This chap is trying very hard to speak English to me, which is a change from what I have experienced so far, waving arms and rapid French, assuming the age and the condition of the car would make me a French citizen.

After a few minutes' talk, he bids us farewell and jumps back into his truck, and as I am getting ready to go I see two gendarmes approaching. I had seen them taking their coffee break earlier, chatting to the staff with apparently not a care in the world of crime today. I guess that's partly because we are in a rural part of the country – they probably live nearby and perhaps the village shop isn't open on a Sunday, who knows.

Of course, I wonder if there is a problem and as they get closer to us, I check my documents and the location of my high vis jacket just in case but it is all OK, they are just being nosey. My initial observation of them being somewhat relaxed in demeanour was correct. They don't even say much, just a "*c'est bon*" and a smile and a nod. I wait for the inspection of Clancy but it doesn't come, yes – they are just bored and passing the time of day.

With policemen, clean toilets and friendly Frenchman behind us and a smile on my face, Clancy, Lola and I start on the next leg of our trip. I have phoned Al Fresco and they have said we can come a day early, which is great as it gives me a whole day of rest tomorrow. Lola's birthday is on Tuesday and my plan is to take her to Disneyland. I am not going to drive, and I'm hoping that the campsite has room on the coach it takes once a week at this time of year. I found out before we came that they do the Disney trip on a Tuesday in the autumn (it runs more frequently in the high season) and it has worked out beautifully as Lola is four this week. She will actually get her fourth birthday in Disneyland, and it's something we have saved five pounds per week for more than a year for in her money box and I set aside the money from my overall trip budget. Lesson to all, consistency and discipline will eventually get you to your goal!

So now, as we roll onto the straight, empty road ahead of us, I feel my shoulders drop ever so slightly; the tension is leaving a little and I have to now make the most of the last few days. I no longer feel the isolation which has been hanging over me during the trip and want to be present with Lola. Clancy purrs along, seemingly feeling the same sense of being on the homeward straight. Is it my imagination or is he running better than ever?

Reims is within touching distance but I don't want to get tangled up in the town so I decide to leave the motorway and head off across country. A brief look at my map shows me that the sign I need to look for is Épernay or Château Thierry and it will be an exit somewhere near Châlons-en-Champagne. We've made good time today and I've had enough of boring roads, so it's time to get back out on the back roads.

What a great decision. After finding the exit easily thanks to the efficient road signs, we find ourselves in Champagne country. The vines sprawl as far as you can see, looking like a lush green carpet. In the south of the country, the vines appeared a lighter shade of green, maybe because of the light that is cast on them rather than the variety, but probably both. Here, it is wetter, darker and lush.

Everywhere we pass through is silent – the residents, I guess, enjoying their Sunday with friends and family at lunchtime. I have no desire to stop here but I am pleased to have seen it and to be able to compare it to other wine growing areas. Now all that is left is to make the final few miles to our last campsite and take a little break. I have yet to research the area surrounding there, as this final part of the trip has always been the one which was left unplanned to a degree.

When I left the UK three weeks ago, I was going to be coming in from Switzerland and visiting the Peugeot museum but of course that has all changed. Knowing what I do now, I understand why the chaps at Peugeot earlier this year looked at each other strangely when I told them my plan to travel deep into Spain and Italy in my given time. It was my determination and spirit along with a little naivety that got me to where I am now, but the memory of how I felt two weeks ago is still in my mind. Scared, exhausted and isolated. The hurdles we have overcome are a reminder that this trip was always intended as a challenge, and a testament to perseverance. It is the same spirit that until recently has allowed my father to live a full life despite living with the unpredictable daily demands that MS throws in your path.

25

And...Relax

Today I have a day free. We managed the drive from Provence in two days rather than the three I had estimated, so I am able to take stock a little today. There is a swimming pool here and a splash area for the children, so it will be nice to relax and stay local.

It's foggy once again when we wake but today the view is different; gone are the mountains and the endless light, yet the perfectly manicured grounds here at La Croix du Vieux Pont still offer a calming sight. There are fishing lakes and a man-made swimming lake here, which are fringed by pretty trees, and in the grey shimmer of the morning mist we can see the outline of the trees, dark silhouettes against silver skies. The silence is broken by a rather loud "QUAAAACK" and we realise that the ducks are awake. We have a cabin next to the water so have very quickly become accustomed to the noise of the locals.

We had a nap yesterday and were woken by the same duck. Wide awake in seconds, Lola soon headed off in her wellies and swimming costume, the attire she loves so much, in search of the duck and his friends. She has bread and is calling –

"Flocky, where are yoooooou?"

Yes, this duck has a name. He is called Flocky The Noisy Duck and he is likely to be the star of Lola's first book, I am told. She found him along with a flock of followers including a swan, and I chuckle to myself – she looks like the Pied Piper of Hamlin leading her crew. The ducks soon lose interest when the bread is gone and Lola wanders back, ready for a swim now.

We walk along the roads of the campsite, a mixing pot of colour surrounding us from the lawns and flowerbeds. I have to say this is probably the best maintained of all the sites we have been on. Everywhere we look there are clouds of red, yellow and orange with a sprinkling of purple thrown in for good measure. Almost at our destination, I can smell the chlorine of the pools, which I've never much liked but I guess it is a necessary evil – salt water pools are popular in Australia, and that seemed a little less offensive to my nose.

"I can see Paris, Mummy."

No, you can't, Lola, it's miles away – I keep my thoughts to myself and turn to look. She has spotted a pink diamante-studded Eiffel Tower in the window of the gift shop. Fortunately, the shop is closed until three o'clock, which reminds me once again of the work ethic that I find quite appealing – long lunches and enjoyment of life.

"Mummy – there's a postcard with it on it too!"

"OK, well how about we come back later and have a proper look."

I have to admit that I can see the tower and the postcard in Lola's room, a reminder of our trip in her own space. I think it will be nice.

"YAAAAY – let's go swimming!"

We continue the short walk to the pools and perform the obligatory foot washing ceremony before climbing the stairs to the complex. Once again this site excels on this front – for adults there are slides and a spa pool but what is the most impressive is the children's area. This is the first time on the trip I've been able to let Lola go into the pool on her own. It is a decent sized pool but deeper than the standard toddlers' pool, and there is also a set of three child-sized slides with a shower over the top – for once I can sit, take photos and watch Lola from the side. In addition, there is a splash zone where water cannons galore shoot randomly at the children as they run through. I have to say, this site is probably the most family-centric we have been to, and it's a shame it's not a bit further south but the proximity to the ports, Paris and Disney probably outweigh the negative.

An hour passes before –

"Um… Mummy, do you think the shop is open yet?"

Perfect timing, I'm getting hungry.

Dried and fed, we venture out to look in the gift shop. Once there, Lola gets her pink tower and a handful of postcards as well as an ice cream, not a bad day's work on all accounts.

Large wooden cabins come into view and one which has been adapted with a ramp catches my eye, and my heart skips a little as I think about the completely flat roads on this site. This would be perfect for a mobility scooter, and dad would love it. I try to ignore the fact that I am kidding myself but after a couple of minutes the elation of seeing a possibility for him to share with us a trip to France turns into a reality check. The problem is not being here, it is getting here – he just isn't well enough. That little pang of sadness rears its head once again.

It is still warm, so out onto the narrow lane we step. A pony sticks his head over the fence, a rusty old cart lying next to him.

"Do you think he still drives it, mummy?"

"Well, ponies don't really drive, Lola, but they do pull the carts. In fact, Grampy's daddy used to have horses and carts when mummy was little."

She asks to know more so I tell her about my Grandfather's horse – Dolly.

"Do you know, when I was at school, sometimes my Grampy would come to get me on the horse. All the other children used to go on the minibus and mummy used to get on a great big cowboy saddle which was carved and stitched in golden leather and ride home."

"Wow."

"You know, another time I was in the cart with my Grampy and he decided to take the pony and trap down the dual carriageway – he

141

wouldn't move for anyone! We had a little dog called Buzz sitting next to us and I remember that when all the cars were getting annoyed he said, 'I'm not moving! I was here first!'"

"That sounds like MY Grampy too, mummy."

I chuckle because yes, it does. I continue to tell her about the day Dolly pulled over the slide in our garden and pulled it around like a cart – she's still amused and then…

"PEUGEOT!"

I look for a car but there are none in sight. We have walked just a little way before coming back into the site, and she is jumping up and down and pointing at another shop. I am confused (doesn't take much) until I realise that the bike hire shop is full of miniature Peugeot bikes – she is beside herself with excitement.

"Mummy, we need to buy one for Gramps."

I explain that they are rentals so she accepts that perhaps it would be OK to buy one when we get home instead, one for her, one for me and one for everyone else. Hmm – I may need some cash for this little project, Lola.

The sun is now losing its warmth so we must go to find jumpers – we do this before taking one more walk around in search of Flocky with leftover bread. He is nowhere to be found so with a reminder given to Lola that she needs an early night because it is her birthday tomorrow, we retire. We have a big day ahead.

26

Skipping With Mickey

Six o'clock and we're up. Lola is four today and is incredibly excited at the prospect of going to Disneyland.

"Mummy mummy mummy – is it today?"

She jumps up and down in the relative peace that surrounds us, with even Flocky still asleep.

It was a promise I made to her a year ago, "We will go to Disney one day."

At the time, I didn't know whether I would be able to manage it but I have put my spare change in a tin named "Disney Fund" ever since. When I opened it in August, I was pleased to find that there was enough in there to pay for our tickets and a little spending money for her. As we are passing back up towards the English Channel on our return, it would be silly to miss the opportunity.

Of course, she has been in the car for three weeks too, so a day of excitement will be a well-deserved treat for her.

Lola insists on two pigtails, which she feels is reminiscent of Minnie Mouse. I take a moment to tie her long hair and hold back a tear – I think it's of relief and pride that we made it this far and she is going to have a birthday to remember.

Now that we are back in the north of France, the mornings are foggy and chilly yet later it is likely to be warm and sunny. We have to take a backpack today, since we'll start off with coats and trousers but may end up in summer clothes later.

We walk down the well-maintained roads of the campsite under the cover of night. The sun won't be up for another hour. The coach is waiting, engine started, heaters on and ready to deliver us to our destination for the day. I can actually sit and talk to Lola properly, enjoy the countryside of this beautiful green area and not worry about which road to take. This is a huge treat for me.

The trip from the campsite takes us across towards Pierrefonds through dense woodland. I am pleased I am not driving as the fog is thick and the road is very twisty. As we emerge from the greenery, we see the reality ahead – rush hour on a motorway outside Paris. It's nice to be sitting up here in a coach looking down on commuters, and I notice that there are many cars with two people in – I guess that means they are car sharing, which is sensible. We don't do enough of that in the UK.

After watching countless ladies applying their makeup while stuck in traffic, we finally turn off and make our way to Lola's dream come true. Disney.

The car park is empty and we are dropped just in time to wander down to the gates. Now, here I should say that I am not going to go into the detail of our day but I will share the highlights.

As we step under the covered walkway, we hear familiar Disney music and I have to say I am extremely emotional. Seeing Lola so happy yet nervous and overwhelmed is quite literally taking my breath away. I inhale a few times and give her a hug before giving in to the urge to skip – yes, I said skip. How can you not when you have happy music playing and your little girl only wants you to have fun with her.

After a long walk, we finally reach the gates and show our tickets. We are here.

We are approached by a huge Winnie the Pooh and Lola almost bursts into tears. I don't think she's ready for oversized stuffed animals yet – it's all far too much for her.

Rather than socialising with Winnie and his friends, Lola and I start walking and she says she'd like to go in a shop. She knows she has her own spending money so I agree and this is where the enormity of the Disney retail machine becomes apparent. It's madness.

Lola chooses a pink dress and a small Pluto which doesn't break the bank, I can cope with that. We leave the shop and head off in search of a toilet. It's already warming up and it's only ten o'clock – this is going to be a long day.

During the course of the day, we spend three-quarters of the time in a queue, but it is worth it. Lola managed to meet Ariel (two hour wait) and Mickey (she wouldn't go near him after a one hour wait) and had a few rides but mostly we just wandered and enjoyed where we were. I would have to say that if I go again on my own with Lola, I would buy one of the fast track tickets. While we were in the queues, there were people also waiting who were able to keep their place in the queue in shifts, one parent relieving the other, taking the children on another ride, that sort of thing. For Lola and me, there was no option but to wait together, and once again she proved herself as an incredibly patient and good girl as she didn't complain once. Amazing, really.

We finally leave at seven o'clock after the parade and return to our campsite. Lola manages to stay awake until the last minute and I inevitably end up carrying her the ten minute walk back to our cabin along with our backpack and all of the goodies she's acquired during the course of the day. I've been on my feet for nine hours today and am ready to drop when we finally open the door and relax. Lola falls asleep, and I am not far behind her, feeling exhausted but content. My little girl is four years old today and I am an incredibly proud mum.

27

Pierrefonds. Home of Princesses and Fairy Tales

Have you seen the "oh so famous" image of the Disney Princess Castle? The one which is on all of the Disney marketing and of course the castles found at the Disney sites around the world? Pierrefonds is home to what is believed to have been the inspiration for the castle and today Lola and I are going for a visit.

Once again, we are shrouded in early morning mist but Lola is excited so we say good morning to Clancy and are ready to leave. We drive through the mist, down winding roads and through deep, dark woodland and eventually we come down a narrow hill to the pretty town of Pierrefonds. Although famous for the castle, the entire place is picture perfect – a small town set on a lake with a lovely market square, and it has to be said that just wandering around you are treated with architecture to look at.

We park in a little gravel car park on the outskirts of the town next to the lake and walk towards the silhouette of the castle. It sits on the horizon, shrouded in mist, giving it a sense of mystery. Yes, it would have been lovely to see the castle in sunshine but I'm not disappointed to see it like this. We are alone as we wander the perimeter of this stunning building – once again we've beaten the residents of the town as well as the tourists. I haven't even found a coffee yet! The château doesn't open the doors to the public until later so I happily take photos of the conical outlines of the roof from many angles. Lola once again is off into her world of Princesses, imagining they are inside, no – they might be at work – or perhaps they are having breakfast. It's a good thing we can't get in really, isn't it – it would spoil the dream she has created if she entered the building.

"Mummy, do you think they are at work?"

"Maybe, or perhaps they are still asleep."

"No, don't be silly, mummy– they won't be able to get to Disney in time if they are still asleep."

"Do you think they drive a Peugeot, mummy?"

I smile, at the simplicity and wonder in abundance – this is what it's all about.

By the time we walk back to the market square, I am spoilt for choice by the locals selling their wonderful wares. This is more like it – cheese, meat, fruit and bread, and I imagine dad would love it here. He would buy too much cheese (not good for the cholesterol!) and, much like me, would be satisfied sitting in the car with a chunk of it on a piece of fresh bread. It would be a shame not to honour him while we're here so I buy a little to taste – just a little, of course. Lola chooses to buy a bag of plums, as sweet as I have ever tasted, for two euros, and we wander on, content to nibble as we do.

Walking back to Clancy, I am struck by a building which is for sale – it is stunning, and it even has a large turquoise gem placed front and centre in a tall spire that reaches up to the sky. I think it is just an exquisite town house, not anything of historical note but wow, wouldn't it be wonderful to live there with a view of the château and the lake.

Finally, a little café on the edge of the lake is open. Lola and I take a seat on the metal chairs, a little cold on the bottom but the view makes up for it. The trees over the courtyard form an arch and through it I can see the château – a dark outline against the grey sky – and in the mist it looks beautiful, framed perfectly by nature's arch, so I take a photo.

My espresso comes, and Lola has hot chocolate and we sit in the misty glory of Pierrefonds, simply enjoying the peace and quiet of the French countryside.

28

Calais

We leave Al Fresco and La Croix du Vieux Port today, and at eleven o'clock we drop our keys off and start the drive up to Calais. The traffic is light and the scenery depicts an agriculture area, vast flat plains interspersed with rolling hills. We don't stop – this is the first leg of the journey home and I just want to get on with it.

My plan had been to drive to Calais in the early hours tomorrow to get the ferry with P&O at lunchtime but I decided yesterday to drive up a day early and stay in a hotel near the port. I've even been able to change my ferry to the eight o'clock one, which means I may be back in Bath by lunchtime. If you find yourself in similar circumstances and are travelling with P&O, they are very accommodating. They are considerably cheaper than Brittany but it is a completely different experience, offering a short crossing with just enough on board to get by, as opposed to the cruise style approach that Brittany take.

We arrive here mid-afternoon and decide to walk into Calais. On reflection, this was a bad idea as we are staying possibly on the wrong side of the town and Lola's legs were not prepared for an expedition. To be honest, it's the first time in France that I've felt uneasy, so after finding a bakery and buying a cake each we return to the hotel. I had hoped to give people a reason to stay in Calais to explore but I'm not in a position to do that. I'm sure there is a nicer part of town but we'll leave that to someone else to write about, since for me Calais is a no go in the future. I love the ports further along the coast and could happily go over as a foot passenger on the ferry for a day, but not here.

So rather than spending time in Calais, I decide to book Lola and me in for dinner in the hotel restaurant. We have had a month on the road and this is our first real meal out; I'm safe in the notion that I have euros to pay for it, and the anxiety of running out of money is all but behind us.

Here's the funny thing, as I wait for my steak to arrive and sip a seldom enjoyed glass of red wine, I notice Lola getting the glazed eyes of dreamland. Our food is delivered and Lola's trance becomes akin to a boat swaying on the waves as she struggles to stay awake. I have taken three bites of my steak as she finally starts to fall forward, and like magic – she never goes without a fight! – she is asleep. The kind staff offer for my food to be taken up to the room and I carry Lola up to bed. That'll teach me for wanting to treat myself!

So now, all that is left of our time in France is for me to sleep and wake up in the morning for an early breakfast before we head to the ferry which is five minutes away. I can't believe that tomorrow we will be back in the UK: two weeks ago I was praying for this to end but now my mind is creeping towards the fact that I have to work on Monday. Straight into a new job, it will be a wrench for both Lola and me; she will have to be in day care all day, and the thought of it makes me feel sick but life is about trial and error and we all must pay our bills. I'm not ready for this, and it feels that my original vision of our trip has been snatched from me. It's all a blur and I haven't been able to do it justice or visit the places I had planned. I guess it's time for me to accept that Italy and southern Spain will have to wait. I'll plan one trip per year and at least next time I'll know what to expect. I was green at the start of this journey and as I think about my nonchalance at the outset I hear dad's words.

"France is a big country."

At the time, I thought what a strange thing to say but now as I sit here with a moment to reflect, I think, yes, I get it. I have learned a lot on this journey – not least, parents can, on occasion, be right!

29

Plain Sailing

I can't believe today has arrived. After being so exhausted and wishing the trip would end after one week on the road, we are now here, in Calais, getting ready to drive to the port which is just five minutes away. This is the first time I've used this crossing, and although it's the shortest, it will take me several hours across the south of England to get to Timsbury. I did the numbers, compared the mileage and fuel costs and although it would not usually be worth the drive, on this occasion as we were north-west of Paris, it made sense.

We are crossing with P&O, which is cheap and fast, with frequent crossings. I'm not sure what to expect, to be honest.

The kitchen opens at half-past-six, so I'm going to take our bags down to Clancy, grab some breakfast, and then head down to the port, and hopefully it won't be too busy.

Arriving at the port is a surprise for me – there is nothing around! I'm not sure how it will be later but certainly now there are no other cars in sights. I am first here, which is kind of eerie. The border crossing operates differently here – the UK Immigration staff deal with your passport on this side so that you can drive straight off on the other side, and compared to the rigmarole of Roscoff where they search every car, it's quite odd. I can see why – they have a handful of crossings in Brittany so they can pay attention to every car, whereas here in Calais we're waved through in the most efficient manner but it feels very weird. This is where they should be paying more attention, surely! Perhaps it's just the time of day.

So we are parked up in the dark, front of the queue, waiting for our boat. Lola is wrapped up in her blanket in the back, and I'm wondering why there's nobody else around but soon a few more cars start to appear. The sun is rising, I can see our ferry, and we should be back on British soil by nine o'clock.

We board the ferry, which is tiny in comparison to what we're used to but it'll get the job done. Lola and I leave Clancy for the last time on this trip and head up to the deck to see what we can find. I won't go into too much detail here but instead tell you what Lola said.

"It's all rusty, mummy."

The basics are here – a shop and café and a place to sit and relax – but that is about it. We're only on here for ninety minutes and I'm quite pleased.

We arrive to Dover as expected at nine. If I'm lucky we'll be back at dad's by two this afternoon, so it all seems to be going remarkably well. As we disembark my first thought is –

"My god, it's bumpy!"

In France you are spoiled by smooth, well-maintained road surfaces, yet here I am definitely reminded that I back in England with potholes galore to contend with. The road ahead appears like a patchwork quilt, a mismatch of patches of tarmac done as a quick solution rather than fixing the road properly. What a huge difference!

Nevertheless, I am relieved to know that this last leg of the journey is underway.

Thirty minutes in and we are on the M25, a road I avoid at all costs usually. I'm hoping that it won't be too bad today, although it is a Saturday morning so I'm not counting on free flow, to be honest.

So far so good, we are making good time and the "Road To Hell" is actually flowing freely……

And then…it stops.

I couldn't have written it better if I'd predicted it – there is no traffic approaching on the other side of the motorway and we are at a standstill. The M25 is closed. The frustrating thing is, much like in Lyon, I know there is a junction about a mile ahead but the road is closed before the exit. This will be an interesting morning.

Well, we've been sitting here for thirty minutes so far and I can see that gradually people are starting to get out of their cars. I think it's time to phone dad and let him know we're OK, since if he sees this on the news he will be worried sick.

And then…. my phone dies.

Do you remember the hot chocolate incident in Provence, the one where I thought I'd got away with flying hot chocolate delicately decorating my phone? Well, it appears that it has come to bite me firmly on the bottom. My phone won't charge, it won't switch on and I am stuck on the M25 for who knows how long.

It is time for us to get out and ask for help.

We get out of the car and I'm surprised to find what turns out to be almost a party-like atmosphere – almost, I said. People who have returned from shopping trips over the channel are opening their boots and offering drinks and food. Hopefully one of them will be so kind as to offer me their phone.

Lola and I start to chat to the people in the cars ahead of us and I manage to borrow a phone but of course – Sod's law, I can't get through to dad. My phone is dead along with my contacts so I don't have access to mobile numbers (note to self, write it down on a piece of paper next time). I can remember landline numbers but nobody is home this morning, so I'll just have to keep trying.

As the hours pass (yes, I said hours) there is a steady flow of people trying to climb the embankment to get to a toilet, but Lola and I, well trained in bladder holding from our experiences in France, manage to stay put and chat to the people in the cars in front of us. The chap in front donates ten pounds to our cause, which is nice, having asked why I have a huge orange sticker on my car. The other man has lost his wife, who left forty-five minutes ago in search of a toilet and is nowhere to be seen; he is getting somewhat anxious and has two young children in the car. Things are not so bad for me, and Lola as usual is going with the flow; however, my concern is that I haven't told dad we're held up yet, and it really is playing on my mind.

After another fifteen minutes, I finally manage to get through and tell dad the situation ,that it's going to be early evening not two o'clock. The plain sailing which had laid the foundation for the day –

a smooth transition into Calais and across to the UK – has been foiled by the M25.

I am definitely back in England.

Eventually, at one o'clock we start to move. The road isn't cleared yet and we are directed over the top of the junction at the next exit, and I hope I can get back on further up the road! We can still see multiple cars on the crash site on both sides of the carriageway, which does not escape Lola.

"Mummy, that car is on its roof!"

I guess we are lucky that Clancy ticks along at 50 mph – any faster and we could have been in that mess.

Finally we are back on the M25 and the next choice is M4 versus A303, and of course I choose the latter, which means I am heading back to my preferred back roads. My experience on the road to Lyon and the M25 cement even further that motorways are not for me. Just as well, really – the whole challenge was about being off the beaten track! This last incident on the M25 is a timely ending perhaps because I can say –

"I told you so!"

We stop at the services to use the toilet and get a drink but I keep it brief, since this is turning into a long day! After rolling along the English countryside, I finally arrive at dad's at five o' clock. I hadn't been able to call since this morning and the relief on their faces when we pull up is apparent.

Lola walks in, plonks herself on Grampy's lap and takes control of their house as if we've never been away. I'm sure I saw a tear in dad's eye as she starts to tell him stories of our trip and show him her toys from Disney. She is not one bit fazed by what we've just achieved.

She is asking where we are going next already.

Thank You

Before you continue to the following reference pages may I take a moment to thank you for reading *Clancy Goes To France*, as every little helps in my continuing fund raising efforts on behalf of the MS Society.

I hope you have enjoyed the book and would like to extend an invite to you.

I am currently working on two new books, "A Weekend In Brittany" as well as the photo journal to accompany this one. If you would like to be notified when they are published please visit www.livinglavidalola.com , sign up for the newsletter and I'll let you know as soon as they are ready. I will also be offering a number of free copies as launch gifts.

In addition to these two books the Loire Valley is on my radar for next year which I am really excited about; there is so much to see, do and write about!

The aim is to inspire you to follow in our footsteps or, if you are unable to travel like my father, to enjoy the journeys with us from the comfort of your armchair.

Please feel free to email me at emma@livinglavidalola.com if you have any questions or comments – I love to hear from happy readers as well as answer anything I possibly can.

There is one more thing.

Reviews go a long way in the world of books so if you could take a moment to leave one online (for example, Amazon) I would be extremely grateful. Good reviews (where warranted) will lead to more sales and in turn more donations to the MS Society.

Once again thank you for your readership, and I look forward to bringing you our stories as Travels With Lola takes us to new places and great experiences.

Routes and Statistics

In this section you will find a brief summary of the routes we took and some facts and figures from the entire trip. Please note, I have listed the main places along the way so that you can either plug them into your SatNav or look them up on your "real" map to see more clearly where we went – I have not included every tiny road. In addition to this, there are interactive maps on our website for your ease of reference.

Facts and Figures

Average MPG	43 mpg	(6.6 ltr/100km)
Distance travelled	2,677 miles	(4,308 km)
Fuel Price (euros)	*Low* 1.29/ltr *High* 1.55/ltr	
Worst Day On The Road	The motorway to Lyon! Should have stuck to my guns!	
Best Day On The Road	D117 from Saint Gaudens to Perpignan through the Pyrenees. Simply stunning!	
Most Concentration Needed	Coastal route to Spain, 90km in 3 hours, half of it negotiating hair pins and trying not to look at the beautiful view!	
Cliché Moment	Getting stuck on the M25 for 4 hours on arrival back in the UK.	
Regrets	Rushing the first few days and not looking after myself.	
Lessons learned	You were right, dad, France is a big country! Now I understand what seemed to be an obvious statement prior to the trip.	

Main Routes

Our travelling time is given first followed in brackets by the approximate time with no breaks and at a higher speed.

Timsbury to Portsmouth
Key towns and road numbers

Miles: 83.3   *KM:* 134   *Time:* 2.5 hours (2)

A36 – Frome and Salisbury
M27 - Portsmouth

St Malo to Onzain

Miles: 210   *KM:* 335   *Time:* 8 hours (4.5)

D137 to Rennes
D41 to Janzé
Changes to D94 then
D775 to Angers
Use ringroad E60 (no tolls) exit J13
D323 to Seiches
D766 to Herbault
D107 (right) to Onzain

Onzain to Parentis-en-Born

Miles: 293   *KM:* 221   *Time:* 8 hours (6.5)

D952 follow signs to Amboise, Vouvray and Tours
D910 to Poitiers
N10 to Angoulême/Bordeaux
Bordeaux ring road – leave at exit 1 (Spain, Biccarosse - E5)
A660 right fork to Mios
D216/D46 south to Parentis-en-Born (Biccarrosse)

Parentis-en-Born to Saint Gaudens

Miles: 162   *KM:* 261   *Time:* 6 hours (4)

> D626 to Sabres/Roquefort
> N524/N124 to Vic-Fezensac/Saint-Jean-Poutge
> D939 to Trie-sur-Baïse/ Lannemezan
> D817 to Saint-Gaudens

Saint Gaudens to Canet Plage

Miles: 147   *KM:* 237   *Time:* 8 hours (3.5)

> D117 taking in Foix/Quillan/Perpignan
> D82/D617 to Canet Plage

Canet Plage to Fontvieille

Miles: 150   *KM:* 241   *Time:* 4 hours (2.5)

> A9 to Montpellier/Arles
> Merge to N113
> D570 (exit 7 Fontvieille)
> D17 to Fontvieille

Fontvieille to Bourg-en-Bresse

Miles: 206   *KM:* 331   *Time:* 9 hours (5)

> D33 to Beaucaire
> D986L to Remoulins/Pont du Gard
> D6086/N86 Bagnols-sur-Cèze
> A7 – The Road From Hell/Montélimar/Lyon
> D1075 – Bourg-en-Bresse

Bourg-en-Bresse to Vic-sur-Aisne

Miles: 331   *KM:* 533   *Time:* 7.5 hours (5)

> A31/A31/A5
> Exit 17 to Épernay D3
> D1 to Soissons
> N31 to Vic-sur-Aisne

Vic-sur-Aisne to Calais

Miles: 144   *KM:* 231   *Time:* 4.5 hours (2.5)

> A1/A26

Calais/Dover to Timsbury (home)

Miles: 192   *KM:* 309   *Time:* 8 hours (3.5)

> M25/M3/A303
> A36 from Salisbury
> A362 from Frome

Places To Visit

I'm going to take a moment to share with you the places we visited while we were in each region, and the routes we took. This is just to give you an idea but the maps and more information are available on our website www.livinglavidalola.com

Loire Valley (Loir-et-Cher), Centre

We stayed at *Siblu, Domaine de Dugny*

Onzain is a pretty town but just a short drive will find you with much to see. Head west towards Blois, east to Tours or simply enjoy the wonderful Château de Chaumont which is five minutes away.

In the area you also have Zooparc de Beauval and the Parc des Mini-Châteaux at Amboise which would be great for children – we didn't make these two places but next time I will be including them in our itinerary.

Les Landes, Aquitaine

We stayed at *Siblu, La Reserve*

Dune de Pilat

From Parentis-en-Born take the D46 north-west towards Bicarrosse then join the D652, follow the road and you will find this huge natural monument.

If you are a lover of oysters you could very easily continue to Arcachon and sample the local speciality while you're there. You are also within easy reach of Bordeaux and the thermal Spa town of Dax -in all honesty there is so much to see in this region that it needs a return visit and another book!

159

Pyrenees-Orientales, Languedoc Roussillon

We stayed at *Al Fresco Holidays, Mar Estang*

Ceret

A wonderful drive up to the mountains brings you to Ceret, which you will know is one of my favourite places from the entire trip. Take the D914 from Argelès and head inland on the D618 past Le Boulou before joining the D115 up to Ceret where you will be greeted with stunning scenery and a town with a wonderful ambience. Spend the day here or continue exploring the other small towns nearby and meander your way back to the coast. If you continue driving on the D115 you will eventually end up crossing to Spain high up in the Pyrenees – sounds like heaven to me!

Collioure

Head south on the D81 coast road towards Argelès then take the D914 and D114 and you will be rewarded with Collioure in all of its glory. There is parking in the town but I recommend that those able to walk well should park at the top and take in the views before wandering down to the town.

Argelès-sur-Mer / Argelès Plage

Two towns south of Canet is Argelès Plage. A modern harbour and plenty of apartments will greet you in this busy seaside town and whilst there is a gearing for tourism the restaurants around the water do offer wonderful views. In contrast, Argelès-sur-Mer displays more of the authentic France and is a short drive inland. There is certainly plenty to do here for both adults and children.

Spain

If you are a lover of scenic coastal drives this one is hard to beat. Take the road to Collioure and continue along the coast to Banyuls-sur-Mer, stay on the D914 until it switches to the N160 when you reach Spain and enjoy the beauty of the Catalonian coast and lunch in one of the small towns along the way. Stunning – that's all I have to say!

Bouches-de-Rhone, Provence

We stayed with *Pierre!*

Saintes-Marie-de-la-Mer

Beautiful, well-kept beaches await you here but beware the thieves. The main part of this little town is smart and cosmopolitan, and you have lovely walks to enjoy along the salt marshes where you can see flamingos.

From Fontvieille you will head south towards Arles on the D17 before joining the D570. As you approach the N113 on the outskirts of Arles, take the exit to Nimes/Saint-Marie-de-la-Mer and after a couple of minutes take exit 4 to continue on the D570 which will deliver you safely to the town.

Aigues-Mortes

Well worth the drive through the Camargue is this quaint town with its stunning medieval walled centre. It isn't cheap here by any means but you don't have to spend any money apart from the car park which is a couple of euros – bring a picnic and watch the world go buy or treat yourself to an ice cream, I can recommend it!

Follow the D570 as described above before you turn right to the D38C then the D58 into Aigues-Mortes.

Coustellet (Musée de la Lavande)

Heading out to the east of Cavaillon you will find Coustellet, home to the lavender museum but if you go even further and you get the timing right you will be spoiled by the fields of the farm at the source of it.

The D33 takes you north of Fontvielle before you join the D99 to Cavaillon. From here take the D15 then the D900 which is the road that will take you to Coustellet and further east to the lavender fields of Provence if you get your timing right.

Pont du Gard

There is little I can say about this World Heritage Site apart from "go there". If you are able to get there early and miss the crowds it is worth the effort – I have some wonderful pictures including one on the front cover of this book from here and I know that if there had been swarms of people there my photos would be much less appealing.

Approaching from the west and Remoulins, you will be given the option to go the main visitor centre which is signposted *rive gauche* or remain on the D6086 and head over to the other side of the river, *rive droit*. We went to the main car park but I think if I return it would be better to park on the other side, perhaps there would be fewer coachloads of tourists! When we were standing on top of the bridge, I could see the road running parallel to the quieter side and I would have loved to have been there driving along it, far from mass tourism.

Aisne, Picardy

We stayed with *Al Fresco Holidays, La Croix du Vieux Pont.*

Pierrefonds

If you are in Picardie or Champagne it is worth the trip to Pierrefonds. Aside from the beautiful château the village feels as though you are stepping back in time and is blessed with an abundance of beautiful buildings. Sit by the lake, buy some fresh produce at the market or just wander around, you won't be disappointed.

From Vic-sur-Aisne we travelled south-east on the D81 and D94 before heading north-east on the D973. The drive is calming and green and the moment you come over the hill into Pierrefonds you will be in no doubt that you have arrived when you see the stunning château overlooking the village.

Resources

These are the resources we used for our trip. Links to these together with reviews and pictures are also available on our website.

Places To Stay

Siblu Holidays

UK tel: 0871 911 22 88
Email: webenquiries@siblu.com

Domaine de Dugny, Onzain – Loire Valley
La Reserve, Gastes – Aquitaine

Hotel Ibis – St Gaudens Pyrenees
Budget Ibis – Bourg-en-Bresse

http://www.ibis.com (+33)892700389

Al Fresco Holidays

UK bookings: 0844 774 1515
Overseas: 0044 161 332 8900
Email: enquiries@alfresco-holidays.com

Mar Estang, Canet Plage – Pyrenees Orientales
La Croix du Vieux Pont – Vic-sur-Aisne, Picardie.

Transport

Brittany Ferries: 0871 244 0744
Email: reservations@brittanyferries.com

P&O Ferries: 0800 130 0030
Email: customer.services@poferries.com

Recommended Tools

SANEF tolling: https://www.saneftolling.co.uk
(For automated tolls payments)

Via Michelin: http://www.viamichelin.co.uk
(My preference over Google Maps)

Michelin Eye Spy On The Road books will keep your kids entertained and you can learn together with them. They are also great to help you with road signs along the way!

Checklist For Driving In France

Minimum age of driving licence	18
Home Country Driving Licence	YES
International Driving Permit	NO
Vehicle Registration Papers	YES
Insurance documents	YES
GB Sticker Or Plates	Compulsory
Emergency Warning Triangle	Compulsory
Reflective Jacket or Waistcoat	Compulsory
Spare Headlight bulbs	Recommended
Headlight adjustment (taped up or stickers)	Compulsory
Front and back seatbelts	Compulsory
Breathalysers	Compulsory *
Age of child allowed in front seat	10
Acceptance of credit cards for fuel	YES
Autoroute / Motorway Toll Booths	YES
Motorway Speed Limit	130kph/ 81mph
On The Spot Speeding Fines	YES

Speed Limits

Road Type	Dry conditions	Wet conditions
Toll Autoroutes	130kmh/ 80mph	110kmh/ 68mph
Dual Carriageway	110kmh/ 68mph	100kmh/ 62mph
D and N Roads	90kmh/ 56mph	80kmh/ 50mph
Built-up Areas	50kmh/ 31mph	50kmh/ 31mph

*Breathalysers – there is a law passed however the French are yet to enforce on the spot fines if you don't carry one. With that said, they cost a couple of pounds so I recommend getting one.

Final Words

That's it!

If you have any questions or feedback, please drop me a line at emma@livinglavidalola.com. We hope you've enjoyed sharing our journey and look forward to hearing from you.

Emma Kate and Lola

Printed in Great Britain
by Amazon